Harris, William
Hamilton, 1944-

Keeping the faith

BLACKS IN THE NEW WORLD
August Meier, Series Editor

BOOKS IN THE SERIES:

Before the Ghetto: Black Detroit in the Nineteenth Century
David M. Katzman

Black Business in the New South: A Social History of the North Carolina Mutual Life Insurance Company
Walter B. Weare

The Search for a Black Nationality: Black Colonization and Emigration, 1787-1863
Floyd J. Miller

Black Americans and the White Man's Burden, 1898-1903
Willard B. Gatewood, Jr.

Slavery and the Numbers Game: A Critique of *Time on the Cross*
Herbert G. Gutman

A Ghetto Takes Shape: Black Cleveland, 1870-1930
Kenneth L. Kusmer

Freedmen, Philanthropy, and Fraud: A History of the Freedman's Savings Bank
Carl R. Osthaus

The Democratic Party and the Negro: Northern and National Politics, 1868-92
Lawrence Grossman

Black Ohio and the Color Line, 1860-1915
David A. Gerber

Along the Color Line: Explorations in the Black Experience
August Meier and Elliott Rudwick

Black over White: Negro Political Leadership in South Carolina during Reconstruction
Thomas Holt

Abolitionism: The Brazilian Antislavery Struggle
Joaquim Nabuco, translated and edited by Robert Conrad

Black Georgia in the Progressive Era, 1900-1920
John Dittmer

Keeping the Faith: A. Philip Randolph, Milton P. Webster, and the Brotherhood of Sleeping Car Porters, 1925-37
William H. Harris

Keeping the Faith

Race workers are the backbone of the Race, and upon their welfare and the advancement of labor depends the progress of all phases of our life, whether religious, social, fraternal, civic or commercial. Hence the problems of the workers are of vital importance to all elements of the group and merit their cooperation and assistance in the efforts toward solution.

— Milton P. Webster, Chicago *Defender*, Dec. 21, 1929

Keeping the Faith

A. Philip Randolph, Milton P. Webster,
and the Brotherhood of Sleeping Car Porters,
1925-37

WILLIAM H. HARRIS

UNIVERSITY OF ILLINOIS PRESS
Urbana Chicago London

LIBRARY OF CONGRESS CATALOGING IN PUBLICATION DATA

Harris, William Hamilton, 1944-
Keeping the faith.

(Blacks in the New World)
Bibliography: p.
Includes index.
1. Brotherhood of Sleeping Car Porters.
2. Randolph, Asa Philip, 1889 - 3. Webster,
Milton P., 1887-1965. I. Title. II. Series.
HD6515.R36H37 331.88'11'385220973 77-8389
ISBN 0-252-00453-1

to wanda
who with cindy and bill
made
the faith worth keeping

Contents

Abbreviations

APR	. A. Philip Randolph
BSCP	. Brotherhood of Sleeping Car Porters
BSCP ChiPa	. Brotherhood of Sleeping Car Porters Chicago Division Papers, Chicago Historical Society
BSCP Oakland Pas . . .	. Brotherhood of Sleeping Car Porters Oakland Division Papers, Bancroft Library, Berkeley, California
BSCP v. *PC*, NA	. United States Mediation Board Case C107, *BSCP* v. *The Pullman Company*, National Archives, Washington
GCB	. William Green's Copy Books, AFL-CIO Headquarters, Washington
JWJ	. James Weldon Johnson
MPW	. Milton Price Webster
NAACP Pas, LC	. National Association for the Advancement of Colored People Papers, Library of Congress
NLCRG Pas	. Negro Labor Committee Record Group Papers, Schomburg Collection, New York Public Library
NUL Pas	. National Urban League Papers, Library of Congress
PC Pas	. Pullman Company Papers, Pullman Company, Chicago

Preface

For more than a decade following 1925, one of the most widely discussed and debated issues in the black press was the Brotherhood of Sleeping Car Porters (BSCP) and its efforts to gain recognition from the Pullman Company as bargaining agent for porters and maids. Indeed, the BSCP commanded attention out of all proportion to the relative importance of the 12,000 service employees at Pullman compared to the total black work force, especially when at one time the union had fewer than 700 members. Thus, this is not a book about the sleeping car porters as such, but a book about their union that focuses upon leadership. The charismatic A. Philip Randolph, articulating the porters' grievances and working in close relationship with his lieutenants (who organized the porters while he appealed for support among the public), was the central figure in the BSCP. Through effective use of propaganda, Randolph transformed the weak Brotherhood into a major movement for advancement of black people. But the study also shows how heavily Randolph relied upon his associates, individuals who by and large have remained in obscurity, but without whom the BSCP could not have succeeded. In this sense, a subsidiary theme is the limits of charismatic leadership.

The BSCP's first problem with Pullman was to oust the well-entrenched company union, the Employee Representation Plan (ERP) — a difficult task, because numerous porters still believed in the company's benevolence and still accepted the view that jobs belonged to employers and that those who held them should be grateful for the right to work. Moreover, Pullman management was adamant in its opposition to unions. Porters knew that they would lose their jobs if they publicly associated with the BSCP. The Brotherhood thus kept its membership lists secret and functioned among the porters in the most clandestine ways. Even at public BSCP meetings, members were forbidden to speak.

The BSCP's challenge to Pullman required the strong publicity campaign which Randolph waged. The largest single employer of blacks in the United States, the Pullman Company exercised wide influence among some prominent Afro-Americans. Moreover, Pullman was not averse to spreading money around to buy support in the black press and pulpit, both shapers of opinion among blacks. Thus Randolph and his associates encountered strong opposition from newspaper editors and other highly placed blacks, opposition well suited for exploitation by Randolph's style of leadership.

The BSCP's conflict with Pullman involved the union with the general labor movement. Randolph believed that black and white workers faced essentially the same problems and that their interests were identical. For more than a decade he maintained that the BSCP represented all organized labor in its fight against company unionism, and he demanded that the American Federation of Labor (AFL) grant his union an international charter. He also insisted in Federation conventions that the AFL reverse a tradition of almost a half-century and adopt strong measures to organize the masses of black workers. Though he failed to persuade the AFL to make an unequivocal stand against racial discrimination, by 1935 he had formed a working relationship with white labor leaders and had gained a place for the BSCP in the House of Labor.

The BSCP finally succeeded in its long struggle against Pullman with help provided by the New Deal. The Roosevelt Administration's insistence on protecting the rights of organized labor, which resulted in legislation outlawing company unions, led directly to Pullman's recognition of the BSCP as bargaining agent for porters and maids. Randolph's activities assured that porters would benefit from the era of reform, but in the end his union actually shared the gains of the general labor movement.

Despite eventual success, the BSCP's struggle for recognition and its two-year negotiations on a contract constitute a story of frustration and dedication. The union suffered repeated setbacks and at one time came close to collapse. But through it all, Randolph and his colleagues persevered. It was a journey of faith, faith in their leader and faith in their cause. And as such, the BSCP's period of trial provided training in leadership for Brotherhood officials, particularly Randolph, who developed his tactics and philosophy of later life through a combination of compromise, initiative, and daring. They kept the faith, and they won.

Though writing this book was at times frustrating and painfully difficult, it was always a labor of love, mainly because of two men: A. Philip Randolph, the central focus of my study and a man whose career has intrigued me for years; and the late Professor Chase C. Mooney. Chase Mooney gave me the courage in the early years of my graduate career that enabled me to endure the throes of graduate study and to master the painstaking rigor which goes into writing history. His commitment to my work was so unstinting that he continued until the eve of his death to offer substantial criticism and encouragement even while seriously ill. He never knew the depth of my gratitude.

My friend and teacher George I. Juergens subjected my work to the most thoroughgoing criticism. Aside from numerous suggestions on prose, he always questioned my conclusions and pressed me to consider points I had overlooked. Two other colleagues at Indiana, Maurice Baxter and William Cohen, read several drafts of the manuscript and offered "general reader" queries and suggestions. Maurice Baxter was particularly helpful in his comments on the final version of the book. James T. Patterson, Charles H. Wesley, Richard Kirkendall, and Alex Rabinowitch all read portions of the manuscript and contributed the benefits of their wider experience. I owe one of my larger debts to August Meier, whose patient and close scrutiny of my work helped me to understand the difference between a dissertation and a book. These and others of my colleagues must share the credit for whatever merits this book might have. The blame for all its shortcomings is mine alone.

My search for sources on the Brotherhood of Sleeping Car Porters led me to numerous libraries and archival collections; as is the case with most scholars, I left a trail of debts around the country as I went from place to place to use manuscript collections. Archie Motley in the Manuscripts Division at the Chicago Historical Society provided valuable assistance when I worked there, as did Jean Hutson and her staff at the Schomburg Collection of the New York Public Library. The main branch of the New York Public Library kindly permitted me to use the papers of the Garland Fund. Lawrence W. Towner, director of the Newberry Library, sympathized with my inability to make sense out of the masses of unorganized Pullman papers at the Library and provided an introduction to officials at the Pullman Company who allowed me to use their limited sources on the subject. The staffs in the Manuscripts Divisions of both the Library of Congress and the National Archives were always cheerful in filling my numerous requests, as was Logan Kimmel at the headquarters of the American Federation of Labor/ Congress of Industrial Organizations, where I used President William Green's copy books.

A. Philip Randolph consented to a long conversation with me, from which I gained new insights into his work with the porters. It was for me an exceedingly pleasant experience to sit and listen as he recounted his memories of those exciting days with the BSCP. His successor as president of the Brotherhood, C. L. Dellums, corresponded with me on his recollection of some of the early years of the union and helped me further through long telephone conversations. Percival L. Prattis, formerly associate publisher of the Pittsburgh *Courier*, also shared with me his memories of the 1920s and 1930s. His recollections helped me to understand why some people so vociferously opposed the BSCP and provided a wider perspective in which to evaluate the relationship between the *Courier* and the Brotherhood.

Generous support from the Indiana University Office of Research and Development supported much of my travel. In addition, I am most thankful to Herman Hudson, Dean for Afro-American Affairs at Indiana University, for financial support which he provided in the final stages of the preparation of this book.

I am grateful to Debra Chase for the care with which she typed my manuscript. And I saved a special thanks for my mother, who in her own way has helped me complete this project. The sacrifices she and my late father made so that I could pursue the early years of my education are known only to them.

W. H. H.

CHAPTER I

An Uncertain Tradition: Blacks and Unions, 1865-1925

Where does the American Negro stand, and where should he stand in the battle between capital and labor? His position is anomalous. Race prejudice violates every canon of logic, and causes its victims to do likewise. Logic aligns the Negro with labor, but good sense arrays him on the side of capital.

— Kelly Miller, *American Mercury,* VII (Nov., 1925)

In the years immediately following the Civil War, as some men moved to complete the transcontinental railway and speed the transfer of commodities from one place to another, others emphasized the movement of people. They envisioned great rewards in catering to the comforts of railroad travelers. One such individual was George M. Pullman, who visualized a railway system that would move passengers across the country in optimum comfort. Pullman had experimented unsuccessfully with sleeping cars before the Civil War and was now determined to make good on his conviction that long-distance rail travel did not have to be miserable.[1] Pullman's service would provide personal servants, a luxury many passengers did not have at home, and the finest equipment. In 1867 he founded the Pullman Palace Car Company and his dream became reality.[2]

The service that Pullman initiated made it possible for passengers to board one of his cars and forget the small worries that often trouble people traveling great distances. Company employees, whom Pullman chose to call porters, stowed the passengers' baggage and thereafter ministered to all of their needs and wants, including even the shining of their shoes. The porters' mission was to insure that passengers arrived at their destinations in the best physical and mental condition. This goal of supreme comfort made it imperative that men who became porters be

[1] Almont Lindsey, *The Pullman Strike: The Story of a Unique Experiment and of a Great Labor Upheaval* (Chicago: University of Chicago Press, 1942), 21-22.

[2] Joseph Husband, *The Story of the Pullman Car* (Chicago: A. C. McClure, 1917), 47.

well versed in the art of making others comfortable, often at sacrifice of themselves. Pullman's combination of attentive servants and the utmost in modern machinery captured the fancy of the American traveling public, and through the years the Pullman Company became a giant among the nation's corporations.

The porters whom Pullman hired during the first years of his company were all black men, many of them recently freed from slavery. The practice of hiring blacks continued until by the turn of the century the word porter had become synonymous with black.[3] Among the reasons Pullman decided to hire only black men as porters, three stand out: the feeling of "elegance" whites were said to experience in having black servants; the fact that blacks were cheap labor; and the accepted social distance between the races.[4] Pullman officials were aware that blacks had been traditionally assigned service roles, and that it was a mark of status among whites to be waited on by them. At the same time, porters necessarily lived in close proximity with passengers, even performing such functions as preparing beds for thousands of white women and girls during the course of a year. Porters also constantly witnessed the indiscretions that occurred on long trips. The company realized that, since white passengers would encounter black porters in no other social situation, the travelers felt secure and content — and Pullman desired above all else the contentment of his clientele. By the beginning of World War I the Pullman Company employed approximately 12,000 porters, most of whom lived in northern urban areas. Thinking that southern blacks would make better servants, Pullman recruited its porters in the South and transferred them to areas where they were needed. Most porters came north alone and eventually sent for their families, often including relatives other than wives and children.

Though Pullman became the largest single employer of blacks in the United States and held numerous outstanding credits among Afro-Americans, at least a few blacks resented company practices. They believed, for example, that the company hired blacks as porters to continue the servant-master relationship that had existed during slavery. A. Philip Randolph, who later led in organizing the Brotherhood of Sleeping Car Porters (BSCP), often expressed this view during the

[3] Sterling D. Spero and Abram L. Harris, *The Black Worker: The Negro and the Labor Movement* (New York: Columbia University Press, 1931), 430.

[4] Brailsford R. Brazeal, *The Brotherhood of Sleeping Car Porters* (New York: Harper and Brothers, 1946), 6, makes the point about social distance.

1920s when he spoke of early Pullman service. Writing in 1928, he accused the Pullman Company of having conspired to keep porters shrouded in slavery-imposed ignorance of their rights as workers. He saw little difference between the company's attitude and that of southern landowners who took advantage of the freedmen through tenantry and enforcement of vagrancy laws:

> Burdened with the heritage of slave psychology, fearing lest they be plunged back into the sinister system of chattel slavery, they were easily induced to accept any wage system, however small and miserable, expecting to solicit gratitude from a sympathetic traveling public. In the year of the beginning of Pullman, 1867 — Negroes were not only incapable of thinking in terms of collective bargaining . . . but they were uncertain of their freedom. In such a state of civil, political, and economic uncertainty, why wouldn't Pullman seek to get them to work on a semi-feudalistic basis?[5]

Since blacks formed an easily identifiable group, it is likely that Pullman managers consciously considered their ex-slave status when deciding to use only black men to provide personal services on sleeping cars. Though the company's position was that it hired blacks out of concern for their welfare, the fact is that Pullman hired very few of them in its repair and erection shops; in addition, management explicitly excluded blacks from service as conductors.

George Pullman's success enabled him to underline his strong commitment to precision and orderly society, a commitment that extended to include some of his employees. To provide what he considered to be the environment in which people should live and work, he built the community of Pullman, Illinois, for his shop employees. The company included in its town everything the founder thought working-class people needed, even libraries and museums to enhance their cultural development. Pullman wanted his employees to consider themselves members of a large, happy family. The benevolent father, who tolerated no outside interference, would fill all of their needs.[6] If Pullman considered blacks members of the family at all, he thought of them as stepchildren at best, or perhaps even distant cousins. He did not invite them to live in Pullman.

[5] Chicago *Defender*, Dec. 29, 1928.

[6] Stanley Buder, *Pullman: An Experiment in Industrial Order and Social Planning, 1880-1930* (New York: Oxford University Press, 1967), discusses the orderliness of the town in great detail.

Pullman expected the same orderliness that existed in his town to prevail on the job and in relations between company and employees. Personal audiences of employees before the boss should settle all disputes, and labor organizations had no place in company affairs. This attitude was typical in American industrial relations at the time, but few companies had a policy as intransigent as Pullman's. The company's reaction to employees' activities during the great railroad strike of 1894 established the point.[7] The major importance of the strike to Pullman was that it disrupted the order that existed in the Pullman Company and marked the beginning of a new era in its labor-management relations. No longer could the company claim that harmony and goodwill prevailed.

The Pullman Strike had far greater impact than just the changes it fostered in the Pullman Company. After Eugene V. Debs and his followers entered the strife, it came to embrace the major railways with termini in Chicago and stands as a major juncture in the development of labor-management relations in the railroad industry. Moreover, the strike marked a defeat for efforts to improve relations between black and white workers and dashed the hopes of those who longed for a breakup of the craft organizations in favor of more broadly based unions. Debs, who had resigned his post as secretary of the Brotherhood of Locomotive Firemen — one of the major craft unions of operating railroad employees — the preceding year in order to organize the American Railway Union (ARU), an industrial union that sought to obliterate craft lines, had failed in his effort to convince ARU members to include black railroaders in the movement. Thus, few if any blacks participated in the strike of 1894.

Debs's inability to convince his associates in the ARU to make common cause with black railroaders by organizing them in the union was not unusual. Indeed, the major unions of operating railroad employees — the Brotherhood of Locomotive Engineers, the Order of Railway Conductors, the Brotherhood of Locomotive Firemen, and the Brotherhood of Railway Trainmen — prohibited black membership by their constitutions.[8] Considering themselves the aristocracy of American workers and employed in the nation's major industry of the time,

[7] Lindsey, *Pullman Strike*, 94-96.

[8] F. E. Wolfe, *Admission to American Trade Unions* (Baltimore: Johns Hopkins University Press, 1912), 119-20; W. E. B. Du Bois, ed., *The Negro Artisan* (Atlanta: Atlanta University Publications, 1902), 167-68.

operating employees on the railroads even remained aloof from the general labor movement, refusing formal association with either the Knights of Labor or the more recently organized American Federation of Labor (AFL). Largely because of the skills required for their jobs, the railroad unions were able to restrict entrance to their ranks through strict apprenticeship and generally eschewed strikes and militant unionism, preferring to improve wages and working conditions of members through quiet negotiations with management. In fact, during the strike of 1894, the "Big Four" actually cooperated with the General Managers' Association in thwarting what they saw as a maverick movement that threatened their favored position. It is ironic that while Debs's failure in 1894 solidified the federal government's use of court injunctions to ward off future railroad strikes and led to rapid decline of ARU, the Big Four came through the whole affair as strong as before.[9]

If most white unionists in other occupations were not so blatant as to write constitutional restrictions against black membership, they did little to encourage participation of Afro-Americans in the general trade union movement. The fact is that from the end of the Civil War, when unionism got a fresh start, white unionists showed a strong bias against blacks. Leaders of the first national federation of unions in the postwar era, the National Labor Union, voiced statements about laborers' need to forget race if they would succeed in their struggles with management, but their words never became more than idle gestures, because the rank and file were hostile toward blacks.

Beginning in 1869 a new federation of unions, the Knights of Labor, soon surpassed the National Labor Union as the leader in the American labor movement. Unlike its predecessor, which contented itself with talk, the Knights actively recruited black workers. These activities represented a ray of hope and encouraged some national black leaders, such as Frederick Douglass and T. Thomas Fortune, to endorse their efforts.[10] Many original Knights were disgruntled trade unionists who had tired of the narrow craft orientation of their former organizations.

[9] Gerald E. Eggert, *Railroad Labor Disputes: The Beginnings of Federal Strike Policy* (Ann Arbor: University of Michigan Press, 1967), is the best study of the development of federal labor-management policy in the railroad industry. For activities of the Big Four in the Pullman Strike of 1894, see ch. 7.

[10] Emma Lou Thornbrough, *T. Thomas Fortune: Militant Journalist* (Chicago: University of Chicago Press, 1972), 81-82, writes of Fortune's flirtation with the Knights of Labor, but emphasizes that economics remained for him secondary to the question of racial justice. August Meier, *Negro Thought in America, 1880-1915* (Ann

Operating in secret local assemblies and employing as their motto the slogan "an injury to one is the concern of all," the Knights of Labor sought to create solidarity among all classes of workers, regardless of race and, eventually, sex. The Knights worked among blacks partly because of the racial sensibilities of their two principal leaders, Uriah Stevens and Terence Powderly; but the union also had selfish motives. The leaders realized the potential danger that unorganized blacks posed to the organized labor movement. Thus the Knights made particularly strong efforts to organize Afro-American workers, notably in occupations which employed large numbers of blacks. It sent organizers, both black and white, into the South to recruit members, and insisted that the rank and file extend brotherhood across racial lines. By its peak year, 1886, between 60,000 and 90,000 Afro-Americans belonged to the Knights of Labor out of a total membership estimated at 700,000.[11]

The craft unions of skilled workers never accepted the principles or the leadership of the Knights of Labor, and in 1881 they came together at Pittsburgh to form their own union movement. This group, the American Federation of Labor, soon became the dominant force in organized labor. Although organized along craft lines, and thus placing a premium on skilled labor that marked the Federation as exclusive and discriminatory, during its first years the AFL did not define clearly its attitude toward black workers. Thus its original constitution did not mention blacks, and the minutes of its first meeting of 1881 reveal that officials proclaimed the right of every worker to be protected by union membership. The issue was present, however: indeed, Jeremiah Grandison, a black delegate at this session who represented Knights of Labor Local Assembly #1665 in Pittsburgh, warned his colleagues that it would be folly to exclude blacks from the organization because such action would encourage employers to use blacks as strikebreakers: "Our object is, as I understand it, to federate the whole laboring element of America. I speak more particularly with a knowledge of my people, and declare to you that it would be dangerous to skilled mechanics to exclude from this organization the common laborers, who might, in an

Arbor: University of Michigan Press, 1963), 46-48, has a good discussion of Fortune's economic philosophy. See also T. Thomas Fortune, *Black and White* (1884), *passim*, for Fortune's own statement of his views. For Douglass's views on the Knights, see Philip S. Foner, *The Life and Writings of Frederick Douglass* (New York: International, 1943), IV, 342.

[11] Sidney H. Kessler, "The Organization of Negroes in the Knights of Labor," *Journal of Negro History*, XXXVII (July, 1952), 248-76.

emergency, be employed in positions they could readily qualify themselves to fill."[12]

Grandison voiced a well-recognized threat to the success of organized labor when he spoke of the use of black workers as strikebreakers. Afro-American workers had stepped in to replace white strikers as early as the Civil War, and just the year before he spoke, mine operators in the Tuscarawas Valley of Pennsylvania had brought in blacks to crush a miners' strike.[13] Though unemployed whites did as much scabbing as blacks, the visibility of black strikebreakers heightened racial hostilities among white unionists and justified in their minds the myth that blacks were not organizable.[14] The irony is that black scab activity also emphasized to union leaders the reality that unorganized Afro-Americans could undercut union workers. They must be organized so they could be controlled.

Most studies of trade union policies toward admission of Afro-American workers point out the difficulty which these conflicting elements — racial hostility on the one hand, and the desirability of workers' unity on the other — caused for leaders of organized labor. Member unions of the AFL controlled their own membership, and even then final decisions on whether to admit an applicant rested with the local to which he applied. Under such conditions, personal bias could play a much larger part in determining a union's makeup than if members were recruited at the national level. National leaders could continue to emphasize the need for labor solidarity and write constitutions that extended membership privileges to both black and white workers, while locals continued to exclude Afro-Americans.[15]

Though leaders of the American Federation of Labor could act only as a moral force on the question of admission of blacks into unions, their

[12] *Report of the First Annual Session of the Federation of Organized Trade and Labor Unions of the United States and Canada*, Pittsburgh (Sept. 15-18, 1881), 16. This report now appears as Vol. I of the *Report of the Proceedings* of the annual conventions of the AFL. Unfortunately, the *Report* does not identify Grandison by trade.

[13] Charles H. Wesley, *Negro Labor in the United States, 1850-1925* (New York: Vanguard, 1927), 261.

[14] Kessler, "The Organization of Negroes in the Knights of Labor," 251, points out that whites did as much scabbing as blacks.

[15] Wolfe, *Admission to American Trade Unions*, ch. 6, discusses procedures used by unions to discriminate against black workers. See ch. 1 for his discussion of general requirements for admission of workers into national unions. See also Du Bois, ed., *The Negro Artisan*, 171, for discussion of importance of local unions in determining union membership.

views did create the general atmosphere in which the trade union movement developed. The dominant figure in the AFL was Samuel Gompers, president of the Cigar Makers' Union when he took part in founding the Federation in 1881. Chosen president of the new organization, Gompers was to serve in that capacity every year except one until his death in 1924. Though initially encouraging racial cooperation, the AFL by 1900 had become a bastion in the development and maintenance of racism in the United States.

One of Gompers's biographers, Bernard Mandel, maintains that during the 1890s Gompers underwent an evolution in his attitudes toward blacks and their participation in the labor movement. Mandel writes that, during the Federation's early years, the AFL leader actually insisted upon organizing blacks and argued with southern unionists that organization of Afro-American workers was not a matter of "recognizing social equality, but a question of absolute necessity."[16] Through the 1880s and into the 1890s, Gompers maintained that blacks served as strikebreakers and shunned organized labor mainly because white unionists refused to join in common cause with them. After 1896 the leader changed his view on this issue and assigned responsibility directly to blacks themselves for their failure to hold union membership. Gompers's interest in retaining his position in the AFL and in upholding the craft nature of the Federation was partly responsible for his shift. He feared the challenge of the large industrial unions of unskilled workers —unions that would benefit most from an expanded membership—and he had not forgotten that his only loss of an election to the presidency of the Federation had been at the hands of John McBride of the United Mine Workers, the largest AFL affiliate.[17]

Gompers explained that he could not accept black workers into the AFL and could not insist that affiliated unions grant them equal rights, because southern whites would not tolerate blacks as equals.[18] Still, it was Gompers who proposed at the convention of 1900 that the AFL

[16] Bernard Mandel, "Samuel Gompers and the Negro Workers, 1886-1914," *Journal of Negro History*, XL (Jan., 1955), 34-60. Quote from p. 40.

[17] Bernard Mandel, *Samuel Gompers: A Biography* (Yellow Springs, Ohio: Antioch Press, 1963), 140.

[18] Arthur Mann, "Gompers and the Irony of Racism," *Antioch Review*, XIII (Summer, 1953), 207. A. Philip Randolph, commenting at the time of Gompers's death, makes much the same point. He writes that Gompers was "silent" on the issue of black workers, and supports Gompers's decision not to challenge the obstinance of Southerners. See *Messenger*, VII (Feb., 1925), 89.

support segregation and create "federal" unions for black workers, a proposal the delegates passed.[19] Gompers claimed that he recommended this new procedure in order to organize blacks who could not join regular unions, but this was only a subterfuge. Implementation of this policy would lead only to results unfavorable to Afro-Americans. Segregation into impotent unions, under the direct supervision of the nearest white local of a particular craft, denied blacks job protection. They had no representation at international meetings, nor did they have direct input in decisions on wages and working conditions. Furthermore, white locals controlled admission to apprenticeship in trades, a lever they used eventually to eliminate blacks from certain crafts.

Strangely, at the very time that the AFL hardened its lines against blacks, one AFL affiliate was in the process of proving how effective leadership could organize black and white workers into the same union, even in the South, particularly when blacks constituted a considerable proportion of the work force. Such efforts were especially effective in mass industries in which employees were largely unskilled. If the activities of the Knights of Labor during the 1880s had not been proof enough that the goal could be accomplished, AFL leaders could hardly overlook the organizing successes of the United Mine Workers of America (UMW). Founded in 1890, the UMW made concentrated efforts to organize miners, regardless of race or locality, and sent both black and white organizers into the most hostile territory. The historian Herbert Gutman has discussed at length the activities of one of these black organizers, Richard L. Davis, a dedicated union man who worked tirelessly for the miners' union. Partly through Davis's efforts, and partly also because of the general attitude of the union's national leaders on organizing blacks, more than 20,000 black miners belonged to the UMW in 1900.[20] In fact, black miners joined the union in greater percentage than did whites. In the bituminous fields, where the majority of black miners were concentrated, approximately 30 percent of all miners joined the union. Among blacks the figure ranged from 36 to 50

[19] AFL Convention, *Report of the Proceedings* (Oct., 1900), 12-13.

[20] Herbert G. Gutman, "The Negro and the United Mine Workers of America: The Career and Letters of Richard L. Davis and Something of Their Meaning, 1890-1900," in Julius Jacobson, ed., *The Negro and the American Labor Movement* (Garden City, N.Y.: Doubleday, 1968), 49-127, is a superb discussion of the union's organizing activities among blacks, and especially of the work of Davis. Gutman points out, however, that even Davis did not receive adequate respect from white UMW officials, despite his dedication to the union.

percent, and Afro-Americans made up a full 24 percent of total UMW membership.[21] Nonetheless, the AFL continued on its path of maintaining its craft orientation and refusing to organize blacks. Gompers sacrificed his principles and yielded to the racist views of other Federation leaders, a concession that was representative of the AFL's "gradual surrender all along the line to the demands and views of big business."[22]

The problems of labor organizations and black workers had long perplexed black spokesmen. If some recognized the necessity that blacks gain employment under any circumstances, many others had come to believe that organized labor should be respected. Even after the AFL convention of 1900 gave official sanction to segregated locals for blacks, some black leaders had continued to push for membership of Afro-Americans in craft unions, while others urged cooperation between black workers and white capitalists. The Niagara Movement, a loose organization of black radicals under the leadership of W. E. B. Du Bois, discussed economic conditions of blacks at its meeting in Boston in 1907 and resolved that the interests of black and white workers were identical. The Movement reportedly assured Afro-Americans that "the cause of labor is the cause of black men, and the black man's cause is labor's own."[23] At the same time others took an opposite view. The Tuskegee Idea, and the personal influence of Booker T. Washington, weighed heavily upon black thought. Washington had convinced a whole generation of blacks that their best interest and hope for advancement lay in hard work and amassing capital. The Tuskegee philosophy had no place in its teachings for organized labor, and Washington and his followers advised blacks to line up with the great captains of industry.[24]

[21] *Ibid.*, 111; Ira DeA. Reid and Charles S. Johnson, *Negro Membership in American Labor Unions* (New York: Alexander Press, 1930), 68, confirms these figures.

[22] Mandel, "Samuel Gompers," 36, 40.

[23] Quoted in Abram L. Harris, "Should the BSCP Join the AFL" (unpublished manuscript in National Association for the Advancement of Colored People Papers, Library of Congress), 14. Hereafter cited NAACP Pas. It should be pointed out that trade unionism was not a major concern of the Niagaraites. Some of their statements fail to mention black workers at all, emphasizing instead improvements in education and civil rights.

[24] Spero and Harris, *Black Worker*, 50. On occasion Washington went beyond merely cautioning blacks against labor unions and warning them of the necessity of remaining loyal to their employers. He advised blacks to become strikebreakers if doing so would enable them to gain employment. But, as on so many other issues in his career, Washington was inconsistent. In an article in *Atlantic Monthly*, CXI (June, 1913),

Though northern whites had long been hostile toward black workers, the relatively few blacks in that region during the nineteenth and early twentieth centuries had not made the organization of Afro-Americans a major issue there. But around 1910 blacks began to trickle north in ever-increasing numbers, both to escape hardships in the South and to gain employment in the allegedly plentiful jobs available in the North. By the time of American entry in World War I, the trickle had become a flood, and northern white unionists became alarmed over increasing competition from blacks. Delegates to the AFL conventions of 1916 and 1917 alerted the leadership to the increasing number of blacks in jobs previously held only by whites, suggesting that the Federation take steps to organize the newly arrived blacks in order to thwart what the unionists saw as efforts on the part of management to import Afro-Americans to obstruct the work of organized labor. The delegates passed such resolutions in both years, though Gompers and the Executive Council refused to implement them.[25] Delegates at AFL conventions might pass such resolutions, but for blacks the East St. Louis race riot of July, 1917, brought realities sharply into focus. This riot, in which organized workers were conspicuous, ended in death for numerous blacks, while many more were injured. It served to widen the gap between organized whites and unorganized Afro-American workers.[26]

If arrival of blacks into northern urban regions raised a new sense of urgency among white labor leaders, black leaders also showed a heightened interest in economic matters and the relationship between Afro-Americans and organized labor. The ambivalence and uncertainty of previous decades remained, and different groups continued to offer various and sometimes contradictory remedies to the plight of urban blacks. Some, like the National Urban League (NUL), which had been founded in 1911 specifically to ease the transition of blacks from rural to urban life, at first counseled a close relationship between blacks and employers. The League's view was that the immediate economic need of newly urbanized Afro-Americans was to find jobs. The National Association for the Advancement of Colored People (NAACP) shared the view that blacks needed work to survive, but some leaders of the

656-67, he allowed the possibility that white labor unionists were changing their attitudes toward blacks and proposed a qualified support of trade union efforts.

[25] AFL Convention, *Report of the Proceedings* (Nov., 1916), 148; (Nov., 1917), 182.

[26] Elliott Rudwick, *Race Riot at East St. Louis, Illinois, July 2, 1917* (Carbondale: Southern Illinois University Press, 1964), esp. chs. 3-5.

Association also recognized the right of workers to organize and bargain collectively.[27] There was still another view of how best to improve conditions for blacks. Some spokesmen called on blacks to oppose the AFL, to form labor unions of their own, and to affiliate with the Industrial Workers of the World. Thus the World War I period saw some influential blacks calling for membership in the AFL and others emphasizing independent black unions, while still others advocated a radical change in the American economic and social order.

The Urban League–NAACP group endeavored during World War I to improve relations between black workers and organized labor, and at the same time to enhance the position of Afro-Americans with the federal government. Their most successful effort came in 1918 when the two organizations, with assistance from other representative black leaders, secured from the U.S. Department of Labor a special Division of Negro Economics. Under the directorship of Dr. George Edmund Haynes, the first executive director of the National Urban League and a professor of sociology at Fisk University, the Division of Negro Economics was intended to keep the secretary of labor informed on conditions among Afro-American workers and to devise methods to end difficulties caused by racial discrimination, while enlarging participation of blacks in war industries. As it turned out, this was an idle hope. Haynes spent most of his time trying to set up state and local affiliates of his agency, causing the Division of Negro Economics to serve mainly as an ombudsman between the government and black leaders. It busied itself with conducting surveys of working conditions among Afro-Americans and seeking to improve race relations between black and white workers.[28]

If black laborers gained little from organization of the Division of Negro Economics, they profited even less from efforts of black leaders

[27] Nancy J. Weiss, *The National Urban League, 1910-1940* (New York: Oxford University Press, 1974), 89-91, 100-101, 123-28; Charles Flint Kellogg, *The NAACP: A History of the National Association for the Advancement of Colored People, 1909-20* (Baltimore: Johns Hopkins University Press, 1967), I, 34-35, 266-71.

[28] U.S. Department of Labor, Division of Negro Economics, *The Negro at Work During the World War and Reconstruction* (Washington: Government Printing Office, 1921), 12, describes from Haynes's point of view the conditions under which the Division was created. Kellogg, *NAACP*, I, 267, and Weiss, *National Urban League*, 133-34, discuss the role of those respective organizations in the origins of the Division of Negro Economics. John Finney, Jr., "A Study of Negro Labor during and after World War I" (Ph. D. dissertation, Georgetown University, 1967), ch. 3, points out that establishment of the Division was more complicated than other sources maintain.

to bring about improved conditions for Afro-Americans within the AFL. After securing minor concessions from the Department of Labor, black leaders met twice with representatives of the AFL. The most important meeting came in April, 1918. At that conference Gompers reaffirmed the Federation's published wish to have all workers organized within the AFL, promised to use his prestige to help break down racial prejudice among whites, and called upon black spokesmen to use their "influence to show Negro workingmen the advantages of collective bargaining and the value of affiliation with the AFL."[29] Unwilling to settle for high-sounding rhetoric, NAACP and NUL leaders offered specific proposals that would improve the position of black workers within the AFL. They encouraged Gompers to publish his views on bringing blacks into the organized labor movement, called on Federation leaders to hold periodic meetings with representative Afro-Americans, suggested that Gompers push a resolution through the next AFL convention confirming his wish that blacks be organized, and recommended that the Federation hire black organizers.[30] The AFL convention endorsed the principle of these proposals in 1918, but made clear that in so doing "no fault is or can be found with work done in the past" with regard to blacks.[31]

Black leaders did not give up on the organized labor movement after passage of the meaningless resolution at the convention of 1918. Both the NAACP and the Urban League devoted much time to economic problems at their 1919 conventions. This marked the first time the NAACP discussed labor problems in convention.[32] The NUL did more than simply discuss working conditions among blacks and problems they faced with organized labor. It advised blacks that they should seek membership in unions, but when that was "not possible, they should

[29] Quoted in Reid, *Negro Membership*, 27. See also Kellogg, *NAACP*, I, 68; Weiss, *National Urban League*, 208-9; Finney, "Negro Labor during and after World War I," 283-93; and NAACP *Annual Report* (1917-18), 69-70.

[30] Reid, *Negro Membership*, 27-29.

[31] Quoted *ibid.*, 29. Though the NAACP took part in the negotiations that led to this dubious concession, it is still questionable how concerned the Association was with organized labor and the economic conditions of blacks. In its *Annual Report* (1918), 76, the NAACP listed its "Program for 1919." The right of blacks to earn a living came eighth on a list of nine items, after "equal rights to parks, libraries, etc.," and just before "an end to color hyphenation."

[32] *Crisis*, XVIII (June, 1919), 89. NAACP founders considered making trade unionism the topic of their first meeting in 1910, but decided against it on the advice of William English Walling and Du Bois, both of whom thought political and social matters more important. See Kellogg, *NAACP*, I, 34-36.

band together to bargain with employers and organized labor alike."[33] In 1924 the NAACP called upon "white unions to stop bluffing [on admitting blacks] and for black laborers to stop cutting off their noses to spite their faces" by joining with management in labor disputes. The Association solemnly warned white labor leaders that unless steps were soon taken to ease discrimination, "the position gained by organized labor in this country is threatened with irreparable loss."[34]

While leaders of the NAACP and the NUL argued for cooperation between blacks and organized labor, other Afro-Americans, particularly during the late years of World War I, began experimenting with independent all-black unions. Ira DeA. Reid found in his study of trade unionism that at least nineteen independent black unions with a minimum membership of 12,585 had developed during the war period. The most successful such activity among blacks came in the railroad industry, which operated under federal direction during the war. The government's positive endorsement of railroad union activity encouraged this development. Two unions, the Brotherhood of Dining Car Employees under the leadership of Reinzi B. Lemus, and Robert L. Mays's Railway Men's International Benevolent Industrial Association, achieved meaningful benefits for their members and helped increase trade union awareness among black employees. The Railway Men's Association intended to serve as a conglomerate organization of all classes of black railroaders denied membership in the unions of their craft. Lemus's dining car employees' union restricted coverage to that particular class.[35]

Among black employees who benefited from the interest in independent unionism were the Pullman porters. Intelligent men, the porters did not remain untouched by the debate that raged about them. Conflicting pressures tossed them about as they assessed their own confused situation. Some porters believed that workers had the right to organize to protect their interests; others thought jobs belonged to the employers and that employees worked at the owners' sufferance. Only in later years would the depth of the schism between the two groups become apparent. For the moment they worked quietly with Mays's organization, ac-

[33] Quoted in Wesley, *Negro Labor*, 278.

[34] NAACP *Annual Report* (1924), 48-49.

[35] Reid, *Negro Membership*, 118-27, discusses independent black union activities during the war period. See p. 123 for membership figures. See also Spero and Harris, *Black Worker*, 116-27, and Finney, "Negro Labor during and after World War I," 341-51.

cepted small increases in pay while the government controlled Pullman, and generally concealed their differences in an atmosphere of soul-searching and quiet talk.[36]

To the general public, the porters appeared a united and harmonious group. Most people assumed that the Pullman Company paid them well, and that they enjoyed favorable working conditions.[37] Statements by porters such as John Ford of New York, who told a Dartmouth College audience that "the Pullman Company takes the best of my race," encouraged the myth that porters were essentially contented with their lot. Most people did not stop to think that Ford's "best of my race" comment, rather than signifying Pullman benevolence, was a sad commentary on the position of blacks in the American economic system during the 1920s. The irony of the situation was highlighted by the case of a porter who died in a train wreck in 1923. Authorities used his Phi Beta Kappa key to identify the body as that of Theodore Seldon, Dartmouth, Class of 1922.[38] Further, porters enjoyed an envied life-style. Many people looked upon them as cosmopolites and believed that their constant travels made them somehow important figures. Porters went daily to places that most blacks merely heard of, and their conversations about these "exotic" spots stirred the imaginations of those not fortunate enough to be on the road. In a sense, porters were folk heroes in the black community, as well as pillars of black society.[39]

From superficial appearances, porters seemed most fortunate. Though there is no way to determine precisely the number of black professionals who had seen service with Pullman during the early twentieth century, a large number of ex-porters undoubtedly had done well. As Ford had told his Dartmouth audience, the Pullman Company made it possible for numerous professional men to acquire their educations by providing them with employment through the summer months. Some of these men, including Perry Howard, Republican national committeeman from Mississippi, Melvin Chisum of the National Negro Press Association, and the Grand Exalted Ruler of the Elks, J. Finley

[36] Reid, *Negro Membership*, 123-25.

[37] Spero and Harris, *Black Worker*, 431; Murray Kempton, *Part of Our Time: Some Ruins and Monuments of the Thirties* (New York: Simon and Schuster, 1955), 242.

[38] Spero and Harris, *Black Worker*, 431. Ford's invitation to speak at Dartmouth suggests the interest the American public had in porters and their activities. Information on the Phi Beta Kappa porter is from George E. Brooks, Sr., classmate of Seldon's at Dartmouth, and teammate of his on the Dartmouth debating team.

[39] Kempton, *Part of Our Time*, 242.

Wilson, felt deep loyalty to the company. But such isolated success stories obscured the fact that porters received lower than average wages and put in more time on the job than did others similarly employed. None of the company loyalists told the public that porters had worked for no wages at all during early Pullman years, but instead had depended upon tips for their livelihood.[40]

Many active porters, as well as former ones, encouraged the belief that they were happy with their situation. Indeed, as Perry Howard put it, they considered Pullman service a "badge of honor among the Race and the Pullman porter coming into contact with 35,000,000 passengers [was] a missionary for his people."[41] Both the company and numerous black spokesmen put pressure on porters to conduct themselves in a manner which would reflect favorably upon Pullman and black people generally. Some porters were unduly impressed with the dubious prestige that came from serving important whites, often bragging to other porters and friends that one or another noted person had been in their cars. Given the prevailing attitudes among blacks at the time, it is understandable that many porters would begin to identify with the people they served. This identification with and emulation of upper- and upper-middle-class values would prove an obstacle to labor organizers, for "even a vicarious captain of industry makes poor trade union material."[42]

Although a number of porters expressed satisfaction with their jobs, and the white press and portions of the black press promoted the idea of contentment, some porters were unhappy with conditions at Pullman. They had sporadically expressed their grievances to the company during the early years of the twentieth century, and had even given some thought to forming a union.[43] Lack of leadership, however, as well as the company's adamant opposition to unionism, made any such attempt dangerous as well as futile.

[40] Chicago *Defender*, May 8, 1926. This comment by a veteran porter describes how in the early days of Pullman service porters earned the title "candy butchers" because they sold candy, apples, newspapers, and sundry other items to earn enough money to stay in the service.

[41] *Ibid.*, Oct. 31, 1925.

[42] Spero and Harris, *Black Worker*, 431.

[43] An article in *Messenger*, VIII (Sept., 1926), 284-85, discusses early attempts to organize porters into unions. Frank Boyd, author of the piece, was a representative of the BSCP, and so one might question the seriousness of some of the grievances he listed and the impact of these organizational efforts on porters. Brazeal, *The Brotherhood*, 6-14,

Benjamin E. Mays, president emeritus of Morehouse College and one of the black professionals who financed his education by working for Pullman, recalled the company policies in his autobiography. Mays described Pullman's firing of him in 1920 because he joined a group of Boston porters who objected to being held on call without pay. Although all the men agreed to accept collective responsibility for the formal letter of protest which they sent to company headquarters, Pullman singled out Mays as the ringleader because he was the only one in the group who had a college degree.[44]

As in most labor-management disputes in the 1920s, wages comprised the porters' major grievance.[45] In 1926, for example, at a time when the government estimated that to maintain an adequate standard of living the average family residing in urban America needed an annual income of $2,088, a porter's base pay totaled $810 per year.[46] In addition, porters received tips which, according to a survey conducted by the Labor Bureau, Inc., of New York for the Brotherhood of Sleeping Car Porters, amounted to an average of about $600 annually. From this income the company required porters to buy their own uniforms during the first ten years in the service. Uniforms and other job-related expenses — such as maintenance of themselves while away from home and including the cost of shoe polish for their clients — amounted to approximately $33 per month. For their $67.50 monthly wage, Pullman expected porters to provide about four hundred hours of service, not including time spent preparing cars for passengers or readying them for storage after runs.[47]

Shortly after the war, the porters attempted to improve their position through collective bargaining. The most serious attempt came in 1920, when several porters formed the Pullman Porters and Maids Protective Association (PPMPA). The company responded by seizing the initiative. Giving the appearance of not opposing unions, it presented the porters with an Employees Representation Plan (ERP), an impressive title for what was in fact a company union. In addition, Pullman allowed

also discusses the porters' grievances and their early attempts to solve them through organization.

[44] Benjamin E. Mays, *Born to Rebel* (New York: Scribners, 1971), 61-63.

[45] A. Philip Randolph, "The Case of the Pullman Porters," *Messenger*, VII (July, 1925), 254.

[46] *Messenger*, VIII (Jan., 1926), 10.

[47] Labor Bureau, Inc., "Survey of Wages, Tips and Working Conditions of Pullman Porters" (New York, 1926). Copy in Negro Labor Committee Record Group Papers, Schomburg Branch, New York Public Library. Hereafter cited NLCRG Pas.

the PPMPA to remain intact, though the benevolent association functioned as a powerless fraternal organization with secret passwords and a modest sickness and death benefit scheme.[48] The ERP was typical of the company unions that sprang up around the country to challenge orthodox trade unions for influence among workers.

Establishment of the ERP and the simultaneous defusing of the PPMPA in 1920 silenced some of the dissident voices, but by 1924 the talk had resumed. Several porters presented the company with a petition requesting that porters' monthly wages be raised to $100. Concurrently, Robert Mays's Railway Men's Association made energetic efforts to recruit porters.

Pullman's director of employee relations, F. L. Simmons, believed the porters' petition meant that Mays had met with some success among the service employees. As a counter-measure, he suggested that the president of the company allow the porters to present their petition through the ERP, thus giving the company time to decide upon a plan of action.[49] President Edward F. Carry accepted Simmons's recommendation and offered to negotiate with representatives of porters and maids at a meeting scheduled for March, 1924. For the company the conference would serve the dual purpose of responding to the porters' petition while at the same time staving off Mays's movement by proving to the employees that machinery already existed for handling their grievances. At the conference of 1924, the company offered changes in the porters' working conditions that would have meant a meaningful reduction in the number of hours it expected them to work per month. According to Pullman sources, the porters' representatives found it difficult to understand what the new proposals meant and refused to accept responsibility to explain them to their fellows. As Simmons reported, "they all realized we were trying to give them some benefits through the new mileage-hour plan, but [said] that they would much rather that [we take] whatever additional expense to the company such a plan would entail . . . and add it to their monthly rate of pay and leave the working conditions practically as they are."[50]

The ERP conference of 1924 should have made plain to porters two important points. First, since their representatives could not understand

[48] Untitled and undated statement [1921], Pullman Company Papers, Chicago. Hereafter cited PC Pas. The PPMPA became the Pullman Porters Benefit Association.

[49] F. L. Simmons to E. F. Carry, Jan. 15, 1924, PC Pas.

[50] Simmons to Carry, Mar. 28, 1924, *ibid*.

the proposals the company put forth, especially when two of them were "among the more intelligent of the porters' representatives," they needed professional representation to guarantee that their views would be communicated to the company by men who knew how to negotiate. Second, the conference revealed that porters were concerned primarily with wages, and had little interest in a union that might concentrate on other issues. Such workers made poor candidates for unionization, since they might leave the fold as soon as a raise had been secured.

Pullman wished to bind porters and maids to an agreement in 1924, before Mays and his group could become strong enough to cause trouble for the company. Consequently, it raised the porters' pay by five dollars per month, approximately an 8 percent increase.[51] Carry believed the company had done its service employees a favor by negotiating with them through the ERP. He wrote Simmons about the benevolence of company unions that protected porters and other black workers from the cruelty and avarice of white unionists.[52]

By 1924, then, porters, like most blacks, remained ambivalent about trade unionism and lacked the essential element of leadership needed to change their conditions. The porters obviously recognized that they needed an organization if they were to improve their situation. Still, they were willing to place their hopes in the goodwill of their employer. Pullman officials had good reason to believe that they had succeeded in quieting most of the porters' concern while staving off the intrusion of orthodox unionism.

Like the situation at Pullman, the general picture of the relationship between blacks and organized labor remained confused by the mid-1920s. A majority of the rank-and-file white unionists, of course, still deeply resented blacks, and widely held the view that blacks were poor risks in time of industrial strife. They used black strikebreaking as evidence to justify this point of view. Some black spokesmen, particularly those from the professional classes, agreed that black strikebreakers had been responsible in the past for defeating strikes, but they were by no means apologetic about that fact. Strikebreaking, they argued, had been the only course available when whites had denied blacks access to jobs by excluding them from membership in unions and closing apprenticeship to young blacks. Abram L. Harris, for example, believed that blacks became strikebreakers in an attempt to find "relief

[51] *Ibid.*
[52] Carry to Simmons, Apr. 2, 1924, *ibid.*

from economic slavery."[53] Whatever the merits of the arguments, it was clear that such deep racial animosity could be overcome only by strong leadership from both sides. The challenge was all the greater because influential voices — black and white — continued to advise blacks to maintain their alliance with white capitalists.[54]

Among blacks, such advice came largely from professionals, churchmen, and fraternal organizations. At its annual convention in 1925, the Southwest Missouri Conference of the African Methodist Episcopal Church passed a resolution unequivocally opposing black membership in the AFL. Bishop Archibald J. Carey, a leading figure in political and religious circles in Chicago, guided the resolution through the convention. Carey even instructed AME ministers that they had a responsibility to caution their membership against the pernicious influence of labor leaders.[55] Such a strong statement from a religious leader of Carey's prominence caused obvious problems for black labor leaders.

The Improved and Benevolent Order of Elks of the World compounded the difficulties of labor organizers when it met at Richmond, Virginia, in August, 1925, and unanimously passed a resolution condemning organized labor and calling on blacks to continue to put their trust in the people who had given them work in the past. The resolution urged blacks to "line up with the best element of American citizenship, which in the final analysis all over the country constitute the large employers of labor." The Elks were one of the largest black fraternities; furthermore, the statement handicapped those who were trying to organize black workers, because the resolution went beyond warning blacks against labor unions. The membership instructed leaders to "discredit and discourage all forms of unionism and economic radicalism presented to us by *white labor agitators and their tools*. . . ."[56]

The most prolific and perhaps most influential exponent of this view was Kelly Miller, Dean of the College of Arts and Sciences at Howard

[53] Abram L. Harris, "The Negro Worker," *Labor Age*, XIX (Feb., 1930), 5; George A. Price, "The New Leadership," *Messenger*, VIII (June, 1926), 169.

[54] Kelly Miller, "The Negro as a Working Man," *American Mercury*, VI (Nov., 1925), 310-13. Horace R. Cayton and George S. Mitchell, *Black Workers and the New Unions* (Chapel Hill: University of North Carolina Press, 1939), 378, wrote that this was a widely held view among upper-class blacks. They shared Miller's view that white employers cared more for black workers than did white trade unionists.

[55] St. Louis *Argus*, Oct. 23, 1925.

[56] *Ibid*. Italics mine.

University, a spokesman for the old school which Randolph and others argued had outlived its usefulness and should step aside for the "New Negro." Randolph recognized that Miller had been a "constant fighter in the interest of civil rights," but pointed out that he "fawn[ed] before the altar of big business and glorifie[d] the so called capitalists' benefactions to the race, apparently unmindful of the service black labor is to white capitalists."[57]

In a major statement on blacks and trade unionism in 1925, Miller argued that Afro-Americans would find their most faithful friends among the great employers. He maintained that though a superficial logic aligned black and white workers, existing racial animosities would make such liaisons impossible. Thus blacks should follow the "good sense that array[ed] them on the side of capital." Miller summed up his views in a statement that emphasized his belief in the inability of blacks to function as shapers of their own destinies and stressed the efficacy of paternalism:

> The Negro is as helpless as a leaf in the wind. He is wholly dependent upon the outside controlling forces by which he is directed and controlled, and thus he becomes the ready victim in both its industrial and racial aspects. In such a situation, he must seek not so much an alliance, as protection from one side or the other. To which side shall he turn, to that of labor or that of capital? Every consideration of caution and prudence compels him to seek shelter from those who have rather than from those who have not. The industrial situation may well be likened to a triangle of which the Negro forms the base, with capital and white labor forming the sides. White labor presses upon the black base perpendicularly, while capital slants obliquely, with a less perceptible pressure.

Miller, a practical individual, had faith in the employing class, and suggested still other reasons why he considered it better for black workers to be allied with the capitalists. He was convinced that labor unions wished to destroy the American economic system; from this it followed that for blacks to join unions would be a form of economic suicide. If they had faith in the American system and supported it, their material needs would be supplied.[58]

T. Arnold Hill, who became the first director of the Urban League's new Department of Industrial Relations in 1925, formulated far different

[57] A. Philip Randolph, "Economic Radicalism," *Opportunity*, IV (Feb., 1926), 63.

[58] Discussion based on Miller, "Negro as a Working Man," 310-13. Long quote on p. 311.

views on blacks and labor. Hill had joined the National Urban League in 1914 as assistant to the executive director, Eugene K. Jones, and went to Chicago in 1916 to help establish the League's branch. He became executive secretary of the Chicago Urban League, where he remained until he returned to New York City in 1925.[59] Though the Urban League's main interest in economics still lay in obtaining jobs for blacks through personal conferences between white employers and League officials, Hill clearly understood the importance of opening organized labor to blacks.[60] From his new position Hill chided AFL officials to make good on their pronouncements of non-discrimination, and he joined efforts of other blacks to break down anti-union views among Afro-Americans.

Hill in effect rejected Miller's view that blacks received employment because of the goodwill of employers, and he was particularly exasperated that skilled blacks were likely to be anti-union. Afro-Americans, he said, could not believe that employers hired them on merit; rather, they were convinced that they owed their positions to the employers' benevolence. White racism made it impossible for blacks to think of themselves as part of an oppressed economic class. "White public opinion," he argued, "condones racial separateness and forces the Negro to think first and always of self as a necessary procedure of defense," and "the only regulatory consideration for all Negroes — workers, ministers, educators . . . and all who shape public opinion, — will be first and last which side, union or non-union, will benefit the Negro worker most."[61] Hill and the League were aware of contradictory evidence used by each side in the debate over trade unionism for Afro-Americans: discrimination by labor unions against blacks on the one side, and low wages and poor working conditions on the other. They emphasized that blacks had reached no clear-cut consensus on the matter, and concluded that the answer to the labor problems of blacks might lie in the formation of all-black unions.[62]

[59] *Who's Who in Colored America* (5th ed.), 255. Arvarh E. Strickland, *History of the Chicago Urban League* (Urbana: University of Illinois Press, 1966), has the best discussion of Hill's activities in Chicago.

[60] Weiss, *National Urban League*, ch. 12, discusses League efforts to find jobs for blacks in the white industrial sector. See esp. pp. 181-91 for her comments on the employment efforts of the Department of Industrial Relations.

[61] T. Arnold Hill, "The Negro in Industry," *American Federationist*, XXXXII (Oct., 1925), 912.

[62] T. Arnold Hill, "The Dilemma of Negro Workers," *Opportunity*, IV (Feb., 1926), 39-41.

Hill's comments showed a clearer understanding of American society than Miller's. The NUL depended heavily upon white philanthropy, much of which came from major corporations. Like Miller, Hill saw the personal hostilities which job competition engendered between black and white workers; in contrast to Miller, Hill recognized that this individual competition among blacks and whites was not the essence of racism in American society. Far more important than racial animosity on the personal level was the institutionalization of that hatred. Workers had little power to control or influence major institutions. That power lay in the hands of Miller's "great employers of labor." When Miller called upon blacks to seek the capitalists' "protection," he was appealing to the very group which maintained his people in the lowliest of positions by excluding them from schools, jobs, and participation in government.

Even as Hill was formulating a pro-labor stance for the National Urban League, several other developments were occurring that indicated the strong desire of some Afro-Americans to improve their economic conditions through unionism. Not only did the Urban League create a Department of Industrial Relations, but black Communists established the American Negro Labor Congress, Frank R. Crosswaith founded the Trade Union Committee for Organizing Negro Workers (TUC), and in August porters organized the Brotherhood of Sleeping Car Porters.

Frank Crosswaith, a black New York Socialist, put the finishing touches on the Trade Union Committee for Organizing Negro Workers, a broad-based organization that included such diverse elements as the NAACP and the Socialist unions, early in 1925.[63] The Garland Fund and the American Federation of Labor provided financial support to Crosswaith's group, which was intended to serve as a liaison between blacks and organized labor and to provide requisite leadership to smooth differences between the two groups.[64] TUC called again for the AFL to

[63] Frank R. Crosswaith, "The Trade Union Committee for Organizing Negro Workers," *Messenger*, VII (Aug., 1925), 296. Weiss, *National Urban League*, 211, argues that Hill's activities did not necessarily represent a pro-labor attitude on the part of the League; rather, the League supported efforts to improve relations between blacks and organized labor out of a feeling of necessity.

[64] TUC Report to the Garland Fund, Jan. 1, 1926, NLCRG Pas. The Garland Fund donated a total of $2,435 to TUC during 1925. See Elizabeth G. Flynn to Thomas J. Curtis, May 7, and Flynn to Crosswaith, June 29, 1925, *ibid*. See the next two chapters for further discussion of the Garland Fund.

hire black organizers to recruit black workers. Hill, author of the proposal, expected such appointments to "remove a large portion of the opposition raised by Negro workers to the AFL," an opposition rooted in the AFL's refusal (despite the rhetoric of its national leaders) to admit blacks to equal membership.[65] The Committee expended much effort in trying to improve the image of organized labor for blacks. One way to do this was to encourage the NAACP and the Urban League, the two most visible black organizations in New York, to organize their office staffs. When put on the spot in this way, the two organizations responded differently: the League acquiesced and allowed the Committee's organizers to talk with its employees, while the NAACP refused to permit a similar session with its workers.[66]

Impetus for encouraging union organization among black workers came from still another direction when the American Communist party convened the American Negro Labor Congress in Chicago. The Congress vowed to create independent all-black unions so powerful that the AFL could no longer afford to keep them out.[67] But in reaching this position, the Communist party faced a dilemma. It believed in the solidarity of all workers and on the surface could not support the idea of all-black unions; yet the party recognized that prevailing hostilities between blacks and whites made integrated unions impractical. Expediency dictated that the Communists go on with organization of blacks in whatever manner possible, worrying about solidarity later. In any event, the Congress never reached a substantial portion of the black population.

[65] TUC Report to the Garland Fund, Jan. 1, 1926, NLCRG Pas. This proposal is spelled out in greater detail in a letter to Hugh Frayne, AFL general organizer for New York, from several black trade unionists (including Randolph and Crosswaith), as well as James Weldon Johnson of the NAACP and Hill of the Urban League. National Urban League Papers, Manuscripts Division, Library of Congress. Hereafter cited NUL Pas, LC.

[66] TUC Executive Secretary's Report to the Executive Committee, Sept. 22, 1925, p. 4, NLCRG Pas. The activities of the TUC continued until early 1926; then Crosswaith began to spend most of his time working with the porters. In the original draft of the report, Crosswaith wrote "I am sure" that continued conversations with Johnson would make possible organizational meetings with NAACP office personnel. The final version read "I hope." As it turned out, he was overly optimistic even to hope.

[67] Theodore Draper, *American Communism and Soviet Russia* (New York: Viking, 1960), 331-32, 346; *Time*, VI (Nov. 9, 1925), 8. The magazine quotes Lovett Fort-Whiteman, national organizer of ANLC, as having declared, "The Negro people as a race are of no importance, but as an industrial class they are one of the most important races in the world. The fundamental aim of the American Negro Labor Congress is to mobilize — to organize the industrial strength of the Negro into a fighting weapon."

Most black and white labor leaders rushed to condemn the ANLC. Green considered the Congress detrimental to the interests of organized labor as well as black workers, warning both groups to stay away from it. Leaders of the National Urban League chided Green for having given the ANLC more attention than it deserved, suggesting in *Opportunity* that the Congress had introduced no new grievances and pointing out that blacks "never paid attention to communist arguments."[68] Randolph and his colleagues at the *Messenger* shared the League's distrust of communism. The magazine editorialized against the Congress, warning blacks against being "lured up blind alleys by irresponsible labor talkers." In direct reference to the Communists and ANLC, the *Messenger* argued that no "labor movement in America among white or black workers can solve the problems of American workers, white or black, whose seat of control is outside the country."[69] On this issue, as on others, Du Bois stood almost alone. He saw the Chicago meeting as one of the most significant gatherings in recent black history. As far as he was concerned, progress of black people was more important than the vehicle through which progress was achieved.[70]

If these new organizations of 1925 served only to stimulate debate on the question of blacks and trade unions, and were of only ephemeral duration, they clearly announced that the struggle had begun in earnest. No longer could leaders of the AFL and local unions deny blacks membership without being called upon to explain their stance. Nor would black workers in the future hear only advice that they should maintain personal loyalty to their employers. It would be left to the Brotherhood of Sleeping Car Porters to lead efforts in breaking down barriers of animosity between black and white workers and bring Afro-Americans into the mainstream of trade unionism.

[68] *Opportunity*, III (Dec., 1925), 354.
[69] *Messenger*, VII (July, 1925), 261, 275.
[70] *Crisis*, XXXI (Dec., 1925), 60.

CHAPTER II

Getting It Together

> The fight of the Pullman porters to organize themselves into a genuine trade union is now the most important economic movement before the American people, and it has the undivided attention of every thinking Negro. Labor leaders with years of experience are aghast at the rapid growth and militant spirit of the organization. They see in the success of this movement a complete change taking place affecting the relationship of Negro and white peoples of the United States.
>
> —Pittsburgh *Courier,* May 15, 1926

The Brotherhood of Sleeping Car Porters began unostentatiously. Indeed, the Pullman Company was correct in its expectation that the wage increase of 1924 would end talk of unionism among most of its service employees. Most porters believed the results of the ERP wage conference of 1924 marked an improvement in their status; they continued to do their work as always.[1] Robert L. Mays, whose union had represented the major threat to the ERP and Pullman tranquility, found it expedient to retire quietly from his efforts to organize porters in Chicago. Talk of a union shifted to New York, far from Pullman headquarters, and even there only a small group participated in the conversations.

The New York group contained three of the best known and most respected porters in Pullman service. Pullman officials had considered one of them, Roy Lancaster, the most intelligent porter representative at the wage conference in 1924.[2] The porters themselves respected another member of the group, Ashley L. Totten, more highly than any other in the service. During the elections for representatives to the conference, Totten received more votes than any other candidate, with 7,968 of 9,477 eligible porters voting for him.[3] The third man in the group,

[1] BSCP officials later claimed in the *Messenger* that a widespread dissatisfaction had existed among porters after the agreement in 1924, but there is no evidence to support the allegation.

[2] Simmons to Carry, Mar. 28, 1924, PC Pas.

[3] *Pullman News* (May, 1924), 6. Each porter voted for twenty-four delegates.

William H. Des Verney, had been with the Pullman Company for many years and was nearing retirement. He served as an official of the local New York committee under ERP and knew its weaknesses.

It is not clear whether Totten, Lancaster, and Des Verney thought at the outset in terms of a national organization. They feared company reprisals because of their activities and were unsure of their own abilities. Consequently, they kept their plans secret and quietly sought someone else to provide the leadership they needed. They found their man early in 1925, when Totten invited A. Philip Randolph to address the Pullman Porters' Athletic Association. Randolph accepted, and in a speech on trade unionism he condemned the porters' participation in the ERP and emphasized the need for porters to have their own organization, free from company control. After this speech, which "stirred and aroused the New York porters," Des Verney persuaded Randolph to discuss with his group the matter of organizing the porters.[4]

The second of two sons of an African Methodist Episcopal minister, Randolph was born in Crescent City, Florida, in 1889; soon the family moved to Jacksonville, where he grew up. His mother, Elizabeth, and his brother James had perhaps the greatest influence on Philip during his formative years. The protective older brother made it possible for young Randolph to stand his ground on things he believed in because he knew James would support him.[5] Though Philip sometimes seemed more adept at starting projects than at finishing them, he did learn from his mother the value of fighting for things he believed to be right. His most vivid recollection from early childhood, for example, was of the occasion when his mother sat up all night with a rifle in her hands to protect her children, while his father spent the night standing guard with other black men at the local jail to prevent white townspeople from lynching a black prisoner.[6]

The Randolph boys attended school in Jacksonville and graduated from Cookman Institute, where (next to his brother) Philip was the finest student at the school. But upon graduation from high school, James and Philip realized that the family did not have money enough to send them

[4] *Messenger*, VIII (Feb., 1926), 37. Brailsford R. Brazeal, *The Brotherhood of Sleeping Car Porters* (New York: Harper and Brothers, 1946), 17.

[5] Edwin R. Embree, *13 Against the Odds* (New York: Viking Press, 1944), 214.

[6] Most of the discussion of Randolph's early life is based on an interview with APR, Jan. 19, 1972. Jervis Anderson, *A. Philip Randolph: A Biographical Portrait* (New York: Harcourt Brace Jovanovich, 1972), pts. I-III, contains a good discussion of Randolph's pre-BSCP activities.

to college. Instead, they took odd jobs about town — hauling firewood, working on roads, and (in Philip's case) serving as a messenger for the local telegraph company. James eventually joined the Pullman service as a porter.[7]

Though short of money, the Randolph home did not lack intellectual stimulus. The Reverend James Randolph read regularly and insisted that his boys do likewise. Together the three of them kept up with the debate over the issue of black education and the general direction of Afro-Americans that raged between the followers of Booker T. Washington and those of the emerging school of W. E. B. Du Bois. Philip Randolph tossed from one side to the other. Washington was a demigod among blacks in the South around the turn of the century, and it was difficult to disagree with his opinions. Yet the young Randolph allowed his intellect free range, and in so doing found much to respect in the views which Du Bois espoused.[8]

Randolph made the fateful decision to leave home and family in 1911, when, at age twenty-two, he requested permission from his parents to go to New York City to work for the summer. Although he solemnly promised to return to Jacksonville in the fall, he had no intention of doing so. He had left for the city to make a career in acting, and he had left for good. When Randolph arrived in New York, the mass migration of blacks from the South into northern cities had just begun. There had been approximately 65,000 blacks in the city in 1910; by 1920 the figure would increase to 152,467. Randolph also arrived at just the time when blacks had started to move into the Harlem section of Manhattan (where he himself settled) in such large numbers that they would shortly make that area a black ghetto.[9]

Caught up in this new world, Randolph spent his first few years in New York as a roving bachelor, moving from one address to another and from job to job. It was a period of intellectual growth for him as he pursued his desire to become an actor. Between 1911 and 1917 he attended classes at the City College of New York, and from time to time he even lectured in economics and history of black people at the Rand School of Economics, a New York Socialist institution. While at City College and the Rand School, Randolph entertained himself through

[7] Interview with APR, Jan. 19, 1972.

[8] *Ibid.*

[9] Gilbert Osofsky, *Harlem: The Making of a Ghetto; Negro New York, 1890-1930* (New York: Harper and Row, 1966), 17-34.

theoretical debates and political participation; he became heavily influenced by socialism, especially by the work of Karl Marx.[10]

While engaged in these activities Randolph encountered two people who were to be profoundly influential lifetime associates. In the spring of 1914 he met Lucille Green, a thirty-one-year-old widow who was exactly five years his senior. A socialite of the Madame C. J. Walker group, Green was a former school teacher who now worked as a beauty shop operator, employing the new processes and products which Madame Walker's company manufactured.[11] After a short courtship, Randolph married Lucille Green in the summer of 1914. Shortly after their marriage the Randolphs met Chandler Owen, a student of political science and sociology at Columbia University. Owen, who studied at Columbia as a fellow of the National League on Urban Conditions Among Negroes (which became the National Urban League),[12] would be Randolph's constant companion over the next several years.

Between 1914 and 1917 Randolph and Owen continued their studies, in the process becoming more and more impressed with socialism, and eventually joining the Socialist party. Lucille Randolph provided much of the financial support for both of them as they searched for ways to solve the problems of the world. When World War I broke out, Randolph and Owen supported the international stance of socialists and condemned the war as capitalist in nature. When the United States joined the conflict in 1917, the two men, true to their convictions, refused to support the American war effort. They even joined with other American Socialist antiwar spokesmen in touring the country in 1918 to speak out against United States involvement. In Cleveland, these antiwar activities led to their arrest by federal agents. Local authorities released Randolph and Owen on the stipulation that they return to their homes, cease their opposition to the government, and register for the draft.[13]

[10] Interview with APR, Jan. 19, 1972.

[11] *Ibid*. Madame C. J. Walker was a businesswoman who made a fortune from her business in Indianapolis. She manufactured beauty aids, especially hair treatments for black women, and was the first American woman to become a millionaire through her own efforts. Madame Walker and her daughter became centers of social life in Harlem and attracted a large number of young black women to their soirees.

[12] Charles S. Johnson, "National League on Urban Conditions among Negroes," *Crisis*, VIII (Sept., 1914), 243-46.

[13] Owen was eventually drafted, and Randolph received his induction papers shortly before the close of hostilities. We cannot know what would have happened had

In 1917 Randolph and Owen also set out on what was to be their first successful venture when they launched the *Messenger* magazine. In January the president of the Headwaiters Union in New York, aware of Randolph's and Owen's interest in trade unionism, had invited the two men to edit a monthly magazine for his union. They agreed, and for several months put out *Hotel Messenger*. The *Hotel Messenger* went out of business rather abruptly in October, however, after the editors decided to expose their benefactor and his organization because of the headwaiters' alleged practice of overcharging sidewaiters for uniforms, accepting kickbacks from dealers in return. Within two months after the Headwaiters Union fired Owen and Randolph, the duo came out with their own *Messenger* magazine, an independent journal of radical economic and political thought among black people.

Partly because of Randolph's antiwar speeches, and partly because of his editorials in the *Messenger*, Attorney General A. Mitchell Palmer called him the "most dangerous Negro in America." After World War I both the U.S. Department of Justice and a special committee of the New York state legislature subjected the *Messenger* and its editors to intensive investigations.[14] J. Edgar Hoover, special assistant to the attorney general, conducted the federal probe. The investigations by the Lusk Committee of New York and the Justice Department were in part connected with the wider activities of Palmer and others who, during the immediate post-war years, tried to silence any group or publication that challenged existing conditions within the United States. The *Messenger* was doubly dangerous in this regard. In addition to calling attention to the economic evils of American capitalism, the editors spoke out against lynching and other manifestations of American racism.But they went further than the NAACP, which contented itself for the moment with pointing out the evils and calling on police powers to prevent them. The

---

the war not ended when it did, for Randolph says he had no intention of serving. Interview with APR, Jan. 19, 1972.

[14] J. Edgar Hoover to Ben Matthews, U.S. attorney for the Southern District of New York, Dec. 3, 1919, Department of Justice Mail and Files Division #9-12-725, National Archives. The New York Legislature's Joint Committee Investigating Seditious Activities (the Lusk Committee) in 1920 condemned the *Messenger* as incendiary, too. New York Legislature, Joint Committee Investigating Seditious Activities, *Revolutionary Radicalism: Its History, Purpose and Tactics, with an Exposition and Discussion of the Steps Being Taken and Required to Curb It* (Albany, 1920), II, 1476-1520, contains a chapter on "Radicalism among Negroes," in which Randolph,

Messenger told its readers that it was their right and responsibility to arm themselves for self-protection. Such comments, and the high quality of the publication, convinced Hoover that the *Messenger* was the mouthpiece of a wide conspiracy to overthrow the government. Determined at all cost to destroy the magazine, Palmer and Hoover asked Congress to expand existing anticonspiracy legislation when they found that they could not put the *Messenger* out of business under current laws.[15] Their requests were denied, and the magazine continued publication.

For all his radicalism, Randolph still put great faith in the idea of American justice, a faith that probably came from reading his father's numerous tracts and sermons.[16] As the years passed, this sense that justice would prevail withstood even the harassment and investigations of government agencies.

One of the most difficult things for the *Messenger* editors to determine during the magazine's first few years was the ideal relationship between black workers and organized labor. Much of the difficulty stemmed from their deep commitment to organized labor and the continued failure of the AFL to include black workers in its ranks. Further, they condemned Samuel Gompers for his insistence that a partnership could exist between organized labor and management, and for the AFL's obstinance in maintaining its craft orientation to the exclusion of industrial unions.[17] The AFL could not solve the problems of workers, they argued, as long as it was led by reactionaries like Gompers, "The Chief Strike Breaker" in the United States.[18] While vilifying the Federation and its leader, Owen and Randolph demonstrated their ambivalence. When they organized a union of elevator operators in New York, they proudly announced in the *Messenger* that the union had received a

---

Owen, and the *Messenger* receive more attention than any other individuals or publications.

Theodore Kornweibel, Jr., "The *Messenger* Magazine, 1917-1925" (Ph.D. dissertation, Yale University, 1971), is a full-length study of the *Messenger*. See ch. 2, esp. pp. 49-68, for discussion of the Justice Department and Lusk Committee investigations of the *Messenger*.

[15] Hoover to Matthews, Dec. 3, 1919, Department of Justice Mail and Files Division #9-12-725, National Archives.

[16] Embree, *13 Against the Odds*, 213.

[17] *Messenger*, II (May-June, 1919), 7; Kornweibel, "The *Messenger*," 220-60, discusses the magazine's ambivalence on organized labor and black labor and the evolution of a pro-AFL stance by 1924.

[18] *Messenger*, II (Oct., 1919), 9-10. For a specific reference to Gompers as a reactionary, see *ibid*. (Jan., 1918), 6.

charter from the AFL. This success, they argued, should be proof to "Negro Solon-leaders" that the Federation would accept blacks into the organization.[19]

Deeply concerned about black workers, and convinced that organization was the only method to improve their conditions, Randolph and Owen joined with other Afro-American unionists and white socialists to organize blacks themselves. For a brief while in 1919 the *Messenger* served as the official organ of the National Brotherhood Workers of America, a group founded to federate all black unions and to organize those blacks who did not hold union membership. Randolph and Owen sat on the board of the new union, but their relationship with the National Brotherhood ended abruptly with the editors being charged with using the organization and black workers only to enrich themselves and to enhance sales of the *Messenger*.[20] This unhappy episode did not dampen their interest in involving blacks in unions. Before the year was over they had founded another group, the National Association for the Promotion of Trade Unionism Among Negroes. Owen served as president of this biracial organization, whose board members included numerous white New York Socialists.[21] A more important organization was the Friends of Negro Freedom, founded by Randolph and Owen in 1920. Under Randolph's leadership, the Friends were to be an international group whose major goal was to organize blacks into trade unions. But the Friends of Negro Freedom also espoused tenants' leagues for workers, a cooperative business league, and wide use of the boycott as a form of workers' protest.[22]

Both Randolph and Owen underwent an ideological shift during the early 1920s, a shift indicated by a change in the *Messenger*'s editorial stance. In February, 1920, the *Messenger* ceased being "The Only Radical Negro Magazine in America" and became "A Journal of

[19] *Ibid*. (July, 1918), 34.

[20] Sterling D. Spero and Abram L. Harris, *The Black Worker: The Negro Worker and the Labor Movement* (New York: Columbia University Press, 1931), 117-19, have a good discussion of the National Brotherhood, and on p. 395 they deal with Randolph's and Owen's alleged use of the Brotherhood for personal gain. The charges were never proved.

[21] *Messenger*, II (Aug., 1919), 11. Among white Socialists associated with this group were Charles W. Ervin, editor of the New York *Call*; Julius Gerber, secretary of the New York Socialists Local and member of Metal Workers Union; Morris Hillquit; and Max Prine, organizer of United Hebrew Trades.

[22] *Ibid*. (Apr.-May, 1920), 4-5; Kornweibel, "The *Messenger*," 364-73.

Scientific Radicalism."[23] This move continued, mainly representing Chandler Owen's changing views of the United States and socialism. By 1923 the magazine had moved considerably away from its previous radicalism. Langston Hughes, one of the "New Negroes" of the Harlem Renaissance, described the *Messenger* of the early 1920s as "God Knows What," a magazine that "reflected the policy of whoever paid best at the time." Randolph remained a Socialist, but he too began to pay more attention to the particular plight of blacks in the United States. Both he and Owen joined other black leaders and spokesmen in opposition to Marcus Garvey, for example, whose scheme of "Back to Africa" they vociferously opposed as impractical. Their work against Garvey, the *Messenger*'s moderated tone, and continued work with the Friends of Negro Freedom seemed to make Randolph, who had emerged as the dominant figure in the *Messenger* partnership, more palatable to other black leaders. When NAACP officials led a delegation of black representatives to petition President Calvin Coolidge to pardon black soldiers who had been imprisoned for their part in a riot that occurred at Houston in 1917, they included Randolph in their group.[24]

On balance, then, when the porters chose Randolph as their leader in 1925, they did not select a man of proven leadership skill, or one with practical experience in labor union matters. Indeed, he had had few successes in his life. Had they sought experienced leadership, they might have talked with Reinzi B. Lemus or Robert Mays, two men active in organizing black workers. Instead, they opted for a man whose achievements to date had been academic rather than practical. Nonetheless, at age thirty-six, Randolph was a man of many parts: an outstanding figure among black advocates of economic radicalism, who had at one time opposed the activities of the AFL while supporting those of the Industrial Workers of the World;[25] a tireless fighter for the rights of

[23] *Messenger*, II (Feb., 1920). In the issue for Mar., 1920, the editors explained their change. The *Messenger* was no longer the "Only Radical Negro Magazine in America," for two reasons. "First, because of its education had [*sic*] produced another radical Negro magazine — the *Crusader*; secondly, because its writing was recognized to be so scientific and generally interesting that it appeals to all races, as shown by its more than ten thousand white readers" (p. 11).

[24] NAACP *Annual Report* (1924), 36-43. It is quite probable that NAACP officials invited Randolph in order to present the widest possible front when meeting with the president. For the opposition to Marcus Garvey — especially that of the Friends of Negro Freedom — see Kornweibel, "The *Messenger*," 142-220.

[25] *Messenger* (1917-24), *passim*; Spero and Harris, *Black Worker*, 388-97; Kornweibel, "The *Messenger*," 220-60.

black people to jobs and to just treatment from their employers; a skilled polemicist and editor of a magazine in which he could publicize his views; and a veteran street-corner orator adept at haranguing the Harlem crowds who gathered on evenings to hear the speeches. In addition, Randolph possessed one other important quality from the point of view of the porters: he was not a porter, and thus he was immune from Pullman vengeance.

Even given these qualities, however, and Totten's invitation to Randolph to speak at the Pullman Porters' Athletic Club, it is not clear whether the porters sought Randolph's leadership or he planted the idea of an international union himself. What is certain is that in 1925 Randolph had little of which he could be proud; he seemed a man whose time had passed him by.[26] Even the *Messenger*, his only remotely successful enterprise, was on the verge of disappearing. Heartsick and broken by the death of his brother in 1923, Owen had given up on socialism and New York City. He had moved to Chicago "not to work against [Randolph],"[27] but to become an editorial writer for the Chicago *Bee*. Though his name remained on the masthead, Owen paid little attention to the *Messenger*, and by 1925 Randolph admitted that "the business end of the *Messenger* magazine had been practically neglected."[28] In addition, the magazine could hardly live up to its claim to be THE WORLD'S GREATEST NEGRO MONTHLY, since its circulation as of September stood at approximately 5,000 copies, and even that issue was held up because the publishers lacked the funds to put it out.[29] In August, 1925, Randolph needed a job.

It is not inconceivable, then, that Randolph saw the porters' movement as an avenue through which to rejuvenate the *Messenger*, while at the same time he followed his life-long goal of fostering trade unionism among blacks. By Randolph's own admission, his speech before the Porters' Athletic Association had been a major success and had convinced Totten and others that he was the man to lead in organizing the porters.[30] To this end, he met with the Totten group at Des Verney's

[26] Murray Kempton, *Part of Our Time: Some Ruins and Monuments of the Thirties* (New York: Simon and Schuster, 1955), 244.

[27] Interview with APR, Jan. 19, 1972.

[28] APR to Elizabeth G. Flynn, Dec. 11, 1925, Garland Fund Pas. APR did not make clear in his letter whether Owen previously had been responsible for "the business end" of the *Messenger*, and the magazine's masthead shows no business manager.

[29] APR to Flynn, Sept. 21, 1925, *ibid.*

[30] *Ibid.*

home on the evening of June 25, 1925. At this session Randolph discussed with the porters the conditions under which they worked at Pullman, and he agreed to write about them in the *Messenger*. At that same meeting Totten, Lancaster, and Des Verney agreed that the solution to the porters' problems lay in a trade union, and they established the nucleus of the Brotherhood of Sleeping Car Porters.[31] The name they chose is significant and probably shows Randolph's influence: though most porters worked for the Pullman Company, the union did not become the Brotherhood of Pullman Porters. From the beginning, its leaders decided to form an international union to represent all porters in the United States, Canada, and Mexico.

After the meeting at Des Verney's, Randolph kept his part of the agreement and filled the pages of the *Messenger* with items on porters and their work at Pullman; in his columns he condemned the company and called on its service employees to form a union of their own. Randolph later believed that two of his articles on the subject had been prime factors in crystallizing sentiment for a union among porters.[32] In any event, Totten and his associates called a meeting of New York City porters for August 25, 1925, two months after the gathering at Des Verney's. Meeting at the Elks Hall in Harlem, the group ratified the actions of Totten and associates, accepted Randolph's leadership (under the title general organizer), and agreed that the *Messenger* would be the union's official organ.[33]

Fully aware of the company's anti-union stance and fearful of being exposed, the Totten group had kept their plans totally secret, refusing even to involve leading porters from other districts who came into New York. Before August, 1925, existence of the cell was known only to a small and trusted group. The BSCP continued the tightest rules of secrecy even after the union's public announcement. So great was the concern about company reprisals that the Brotherhood explicitly forbade the membership to speak at public union meetings; such speech, the leaders reasoned, would mark porters as BSCP members and make it possible for Pullman to take action against them.[34] Early BSCP sessions

[31] *Messenger*, VII (Dec., 1925), 403.

[32] *Ibid*. (July, 1925), 254-55; (Aug., 1925), 289-90, 306; APR to Flynn, Sept. 21, 1925, Garland Fund Pas.

[33] *Messenger*, VIII (Jan., 1926), 37; Spero and Harris, *Black Worker*, 434.

[34] BSCP "Bylaws," copy available among items in National Mediation Board Case File #C-107, *Brotherhood of Sleeping Car Porters* v. *Pullman Company*, National Archives.

resembled public mass meetings, or a revival at a country church. Both BSCP and non-member porters attended these affairs, as did a large number of non-porters, all anxious to cheer the speeches that condemned the Pullman Company and to join in stirring renditions of militant songs. One's mere presence at a meeting did not mean membership in the union.

The BSCP began operations under conditions somewhat different from those of other contemporary unions. Instead of depending entirely upon the porters' entrance fees and membership dues, the Brotherhood in 1925-26 received grants from the American Fund for Public Service (AFPS), generally known as the Garland Fund in honor of its donor, Charles Garland, who gave his inheritance of more than a million dollars to establish the Fund.[35] The Garland Fund specialized in supporting radical and unpopular causes. During the 1920s the Fund expended large sums in support of labor colleges and labor-related publications, paying close attention to the needs of some black organizations. The secretary of the NAACP, James Weldon Johnson, had convinced Garland of the importance of the Association and had received some funds. Moreover, at Garland's suggestion, Johnson had become a member of the board of directors of the Fund.[36]

It is significant that in his first correspondence requesting aid from the Garland Fund, Randolph did not ask for money to help in organizing the BSCP. Rather, he pointed out to the Fund's executive secretary, Elizabeth Flynn, that the *Messenger* had been responsible for setting into motion efforts to organize the porters, and in a candid statement of the magazine's financial problems he asked the Garland Fund to provide money to publish the September issue of the *Messenger*.[37] He appealed "in the name of the biggest and most significant movement among Negro workers ever started in America" for funds adequate to "sustain

[35] American Fund for Public Service, *Report of the Last Three Years*, New York, Feb., 1929, p. 10. The report shows that the Fund gave the Brotherhood $11,200 during fiscal year 1925-26 for organizational work and to aid in preparation of a survey of working conditions among porters. It does not specify how much the Fund appropriated for each project. *Messenger*, VIII (Sept., 1926), 273, places the initial organizational grant at $10,000.

[36] Walter White, *A Man Called White: The Autobiography of Walter White* (Bloomington: Indiana University Press, 1970), 141.

[37] APR to Flynn, Sept. 21, 1925, Garland Fund Pas. Significantly, when the Fund reported in 1929 on its activities for the past three years, it included its contributions to the BSCP under the heading "Negro Work," rather than under the heading "Trade Unions." See note 35, above, for full citation of Garland Fund *Report*.

the magazine in putting out additional thousands [copies of the *Messenger*] to enable every porter to get a copy for the next six months.''[38] The Fund took the request under advisement. When Randolph received no positive reply by late October, he wrote again, still asking for money for the *Messenger* ''to remove the financial embarrassment of the publication.''[39]

Responding almost immediately to Randolph's second request, the Fund voted the BSCP a grant of $1,200. Though the Garland Fund placed no specific guidelines on how the money should be spent, it made its check payable to the BSCP, not to the *Messenger*.[40] Randolph reported to the Fund in December on the expenditure of the original grant: of $1,000 accounted for in the statement, $500 had been spent on the magazine. Randolph considered expenditure of funds for ''rejuvenating and rebuilding the magazine'' justifiable because ''all porters [accepted the *Messenger*] as their mouthpiece.''[41]

In addition to receiving money from the Garland Fund, the Brotherhood also solicited funds from the general public. In March, 1926, the union announced the beginning of a drive to raise $50,000 for organizational purposes, and it sent out letters to wealthy and influential individuals and organizations requesting financial and moral support.[42] Though there are no records to show how much money the BSCP received from this unusual campaign, letters published in several issues of the *Messenger* suggest a substantial sum. Most labor unions did not appeal for public support, but instead financed their own activities. The BSCP's efforts in this regard were unique and marked it as early as 1926 as an organization that saw itself closely connected with the public

[38] APR to Flynn, Sept. 21, 1925, Garland Fund Pas. In his letter to Flynn, Randolph expressed concern that the *Messenger* must come out, because porters would consider a failure at that time evidence that the magazine and its editor had sold out to the company. The cause might thus be destroyed before it could get going.

[39] APR to Flynn, Oct. 23, 1925, *ibid*.

[40] Flynn to APR, Oct. 29, 1925, *ibid*. The Fund made the check payable to Roy Lancaster, secretary-treasurer of the BSCP, and not to Randolph.

[41] APR to Flynn, Dec. 11, 1925, *ibid*. The BSCP statement does not make clear what *Messenger* expenses were covered by the $500 figure. It would be interesting to know, for example, whether Randolph considered payment of his salary as editor of the magazine among legitimate expenses to come out of BSCP monies.

[42] Lancaster to Herbert Seligman, Mar. 22, 1926, NAACP Pas, C413, LC. Later Randolph wrote that numerous white individuals and organizations contributed to the BSCP. Among the organizations were the *Jewish Daily Forward*, the International Pocketbook Makers, the Amalgamated Clothing Workers Union of America, and the milliners' union. See Chicago *Defender*, Aug. 20, 1927.

interest, while at the same time underlining its leader's faith in the efficacy and importance of sympathetic public opinion.

Meanwhile, from August, 1925, through early 1926, the Brotherhood grappled with the problems of solidifying its position in New York and simultaneously carrying the message of trade unionism to porters in other areas. In New York, leaders found sentiment by no means unanimously favorable to the union. Few porters attended the public meeting at which the BSCP was launched, and Randolph's impolitic statement the following week that there were "too many Toms" among the porters did not ease the leaders' task.[43]

Randolph believed that, as general organizer, he should function as a high moral force who could teach trade unionism to the nation at large. Since he planned to leave the matter of recruiting individual porters to his lieutenants, he needed experienced aides in New York. He persuaded the executive secretary of the Trade Union Committee for Organizing Negro Workers, Frank R. Crosswaith, to join the BSCP as a special assistant. An old-line union organizer with the needle trades, Crosswaith agreed with Randolph that he could better further the cause of unionism among blacks by joining the BSCP than by staying with TUC. After September, 1925, he spent most of his time with the Brotherhood, and in June, 1926, he came to work full-time with the BSCP, becoming its first professional organizer. After joining the union on a part-time basis, Crosswaith actually ran the New York office from September to December, 1925, while Randolph was away on an organizational trip. Crosswaith informed the Garland Fund that during this period "every press release written, every mass meeting arranged, every circular letter sent out, have been done by me."[44] Crosswaith showed his loyalty to the union in June. When TUC went out of business, he tried to carry with him to the BSCP the money that remained in the committee's budget. The Garland Fund, which had given the money to TUC, would not approve the transfer, since (as Flynn told Crosswaith) the AFPS supported the Brotherhood under a separate grant.[45]

As it turned out, the problems in New York were mild compared to those faced by the union in trying to organize porters elsewhere. Most of

[43] Quoted in *Time*, VI (Aug. 31, 1925), 5.

[44] Report of the Executive Secretary of TUC to the American Fund for Public Service, Jan., 1926, NLCRG Pas.

[45] Flynn to Crosswaith, July 8, 1926, *ibid*.

the responsibility for carrying the union's message to those who would organize other porters fell to Randolph. When the Pullman Company fired Totten during the union's first month, he joined Randolph on the organizational tour with the title of special organizer. His presence on the platform gave credence to the BSCP's claim that the union was a porter-initiated movement. Their first task was to find someone to carry on the union's work in various cities after the initial organizing contact. In most cases, national leaders preferred "local" porters to head recruiting efforts; this would enable the union to counter charges that the Brotherhood was an outside organization imposed on porters by radicals, and at the same time undo some of the damage caused by New Yorkers holding all the national offices. Porters, skeptical in the past of trade unions, would be more likely to place their trust in local leadership.

Randolph and Totten experienced considerable difficulty in finding men willing to work publicly for the union. Most porters believed that the company would fire them if they engaged in such activity. During the autumn of 1925, when the company initiated a policy of placing Filipinos on club cars,[46] black porters took this action as a warning. They were not alone in this interpretation. The Pittsburgh *Courier* agreed that the move was an attempt to frighten the porters away from the union, adding that the company had also stepped up its policy of importing blacks from the South in a further effort to intimidate the porters.[47] Porters persisted in this view despite Randolph's argument that the actions, which so blatantly disregarded seniority regulations under the ERP, demonstrated all the more clearly why the porters needed an independent union. Their reluctance to accept leadership positions compelled Randolph and Totten to look to men outside the reach of Pullman officials. In most cases, they eventually convinced highly competent men to work for the BSCP. Quite aside from what these men contributed to the union, their work often had an enormous effect upon them personally, catapulting them almost overnight from obscurity to national prominence.

The most notable district organizer was Milton Price Webster. With help from Totten's friend John C. Mills, a highly respected porter from Chicago, Randolph persuaded Webster to accept responsibility for that city, the most important division of the Pullman network. Company

[46] *Pullman News* (Nov., 1925), 221.
[47] Pittsburgh *Courier*, Jan. 2, 1926.

headquarters were there, and more porters worked out of that district than any other. Little is known of Webster before he joined the Brotherhood.[48] Two years older than Randolph, he had been born in Clarksville, Tennessee, in 1887 and had come to Chicago as a young man to work as a Pullman porter. By 1925 he exercised some influence in Chicago Republican circles, serving as a ward leader among black members of the party; he also worked as a bailiff in Cook County Court.[49] His early letters are those of an apparently intelligent man who found it difficult to communicate ideas in writing. Webster wrote so poorly that Randolph often composed circulars in the former's name to be sent to porters in the Chicago division.[50] But by the end of 1926, Webster had acquired justifiable confidence in his ability to communicate both orally and in writing. As the Brotherhood's fortunes rose, his horizons expanded to meet the added responsibilities thrust upon him.

From the beginning Chicago porters showed great respect for Webster and his abilities. Having been a porter as a younger man, he fully understood what such employment entailed; he also had personal friends among working porters. Both of these factors allowed him entry into circles where Randolph would have been unwelcome. His position in Chicago politics gave him access to some people whose friendship could be valuable to the new union, including the leading black politician in Chicago at that time, Oscar De Priest. It was through Webster, for example, that his friend Robert L. Mays became involved with the BSCP's efforts to organize porters in Chicago. Partly because of the sensitive position he held at Chicago, and partly because of his abilities, Webster quickly became the second most important man in the Brotherhood.

The union eventually found organizers for other cities also. E. J. Bradley at St. Louis and Benjamin (Bennie) Smith at Detroit and Pittsburgh, both ex-porters, provided excellent leadership. Of all the local leaders, the individual who made the greatest sacrifice, and who in many ways best symbolized the spirit of the new union, was Morris Moore at Oakland, California, whom BSCP leaders always called Dad. A retired porter, Dad Moore jeopardized both the odd jobs which

[48] Webster's papers are at the Chicago Historical Society, but they begin with the BSCP days.

[49] Robert L. Mays implied in a letter to the Chicago *Defender*, Mar. 6, 1926, that Webster had studied law, but it is highly unlikely that this had been formal study.

[50] APR to MPW, Mar. 5, 1926, BSCP ChiPa.

Pullman made available for him around the yards and his meager pension when he made a public declaration in favor of the union. His selfless action stimulated reluctant younger porters.[51] In 1928 C. L. Dellums joined him in the Oakland area, bringing youth and vitality and helping the West to remain one of the Brotherhood's strongest areas.

In addition to the BSCP's difficulties in finding suitable organizers, and those stemming from apathy, skepticism, and fear among the porters themselves, the union faced stiff opposition from important segments of the national black leadership. In later years Randolph claimed that in the beginning most people paid no attention to the new union,[52] observing that those who wrote or spoke about the BSCP at all "greeted it with indifference or derisive laughter."[53] He pointed out, however, that such an attitude was to be expected because of the position which blacks traditionally had taken on labor questions, and because most people, whatever their race, considered it unthinkable that black porters would form their own union.[54] But this public attitude did not daunt the union's leaders as they continued to crisscross the country, lining up porters to join their ranks.

The creation of the BSCP evoked a major debate among blacks on the question of trade unionism. The organization was so prominently discussed that it moved one spokesman to remark that "too much attention for [the porters'] good . . . attended the attempts to organize the Pullman porters."[55] Debate over the Brotherhood was so brisk, other commentators wrote, that it was "impossible for a leader to remain neutral toward the union"; the position one took became a "fundamental test" of his right to lead.[56] The fact is that the Brotherhood brought unionism into a new focus and forced black spokesmen to discuss the potentialities of economic radicalism.

When most black newspapers began to write of the BSCP late in 1925, they described the union as Randolph's "proposed movement,"[57] and the tone of their comments was generally hostile. Perhaps the most openly anti-Brotherhood paper in the early months was the St.

[51] Various letters; e.g., Morris (Dad) Moore to MPW, MPW to Moore, *ibid*. Also Brazeal, *The Brotherhood*, 29.

[52] Chicago *Defender*, Jan. 5, 1929.

[53] Pittsburgh *Courier*, Jan. 26, 1927.

[54] Chicago *Defender*, Jan. 5, 1929.

[55] Lemus to Hill, Jan. 29, 1926, NAACP Pas, C413, LC.

[56] Spero and Harris, *Black Worker*, 436.

[57] Chicago *Defender* and Pittsburgh *Courier*, both Sept. 26, 1925.

Louis *Argus*, which was not only anti-BSCP, but irrevocably set against trade unionism. It prominently displayed a half-page statement for a St. Louis group named the Allied Economic Alliance, which warned its readers that the "voice of labor union is the voice of danger, betrayal and destruction."[58]

During the Brotherhood's organizational campaign in the Midwest, the *Argus* ran several stories about those activities: Randolph and his associates allegedly lied about the number of porters who attended Brotherhood meetings, and instead of the advertised overflow crowds, the paper stated that only fifty or sixty men convened at the sessions held in Chicago.[59] Correspondence among BSCP organizers describing the porters' widespread indifference toward the union corroborated the *Argus* reports.[60] The letters suggested that Chicago porters made no efforts on their own to join the union, although they also said (a point the *Argus* neglected to mention) that the men readily joined when union organizers approached them.[61]

As the union's organizational activities continued in the Midwest, and particularly in St. Louis, the *Argus*'s editorials turned into a veritable crusade against the Brotherhood and its leaders. The paper's attitude was even more extreme than the generally hostile thought toward unions then prevalent among blacks. The *Argus* insisted that black workers should not attempt to compare their wages with those of whites. Instead, they should recognize that blacks and whites had always worked on different pay scales and should not concern themselves about the discrimination. The porters' worry should be whether they earned as much as other blacks. The paper lectured the porters on this issue, pointing out that Pullman paid its service employees more than black messengers in Washington received from the federal government.

The *Argus* did not restrict its opposition to abstract issues. It carried stories questioning the sincerity of BSCP leaders and accusing them of imperiling the racial monopoly which blacks had developed in Pullman service.[62] Emphasizing the widespread distrust among blacks toward trade unionism, the paper warned the porters that a union's first act would be to call a strike. Pointing out that union leaders owned no railroads or other sources of jobs, the *Argus* insisted that "all they [had]

[58] St. Louis *Argus*, Oct. 30, 1925.
[59] *Ibid*.
[60] See, e.g., Price to Lancaster, Dec. 4 and 13, 1925, BSCP ChiPa.
[61] Price to Lancaster, Dec. 4, 1925, *ibid*.
[62] St. Louis *Argus*, Oct. 30, 1925.

to offer the rank and file [was] talk.'' Porters should think for themselves on this important issue, the paper continued; it advised them to laugh at those who would threaten their right to work.[63]

When Randolph and Totten arrived in St. Louis to begin organizing, they accused the *Argus* of betraying black people by its opposition to BSCP and provoked the paper into a caustic response. In a militant speech at a porters' meeting, Randolph accused certain black editors of working for Pullman; he threatened to destroy them. The *Argus* dismissed Randolph's comments as those of a desperate man and again charged him and his associates with misleading the porters in order to get their hand on the large sum of money that porters would pay to the union in initiation fees.[64] The *Argus* then used other items — some libelous — to damage Randolph. It claimed that Randolph had ''always failed'' in everything he tried to do, and that ''his path of failures . . . is said to be bedecked with shady deals.'' Randolph's sole purpose for working with the porters was to take their money and run off to Russia since he was known ''to like the reds.''[65]

Randolph responded in kind, terming the allegation that he intended to steal the porters' money and run off to Russia the ''last refuge of an impotent intellect,'' and describing the *Argus*'s editor as an ''Idiot-or'' and an Uncle Tom.[66] BSCP officials were certain that the paper opposed the union because of ''Pullman Gold.'' They pointed out that most *Argus* items on the BSCP originated in Chicago and claimed that the paper did not control its editorial policy on this question.[67] The *Argus* was susceptible on this point of having sold out to Pullman because it carried a large advertisement for the company. Clearly, appearance of an advertisement in a newspaper is not evidence that the company

[63] *Ibid.*

[64] *Ibid.*, Nov. 6, 1925. The BSCP charged $5.00 joining fees; 12,000 porters would thus pay $60,000.

[65] *Ibid.*, Nov. 20, 1925.

[66] *Messenger*, VII (Dec., 1925), 384.

[67] The BSCP's claim that Pullman paid for support from black newspapers was probably right. Though no evidence exists in what sparse Pullman papers are available to make definite ties between the company and major black papers that opposed the BSCP, a letter among the papers of Claude Barnett, founder of the Associated Negro Press (ANP) and co-founder with Percival Prattis of the *Light and Heebie Jeebies*, a local anti-BSCP news magazine in Chicago, shows conclusively that Pullman management used black newspapers and the ANP to disseminate its propaganda, and that the company paid for the space. See Claude Barnett to James Keeley, Asst. to the President of Pullman, Apr. 26, 1926. See also unsigned and undated [1926] ''Memo to Mr. K,'' Claude Barnett Papers, Manuscripts Division, Chicago Historical Society.

controls the paper's editorial policy, but this particular advertisement was indeed strange: black people rarely rode sleeping cars, and whites who did ride them did not read the *Argus*.[68] Moreover, it is probably more than a coincidence that the Pullman Company placed its first advertisement in the *Argus* at the very time when the paper launched its opposition to the BSCP.

In Chicago, the seat of Pullman operations, the BSCP also experienced opposition from the black press. Events there lend credence to the union's allegation that Pullman used its influence and money to buy press support. In Chicago both the *Defender* and the *Whip* took the company's side, leaving the Chicago *Bee* — for which Randolph's old friend Chandler Owen wrote — as the lone black paper to support the Brotherhood. The *Whip*'s opposition, and the response it elicited from BSCP spokesmen, raised interesting questions about attempts on the part of influential whites to control segments of the black press. The *Whip*, edited by two young graduates of Yale Law School, Joseph D. Bibb and Arthur Clement MacNeal, had a strong reputation in Chicago as a militant newspaper. During the early 1920s it had been the leader of the "New Negro" element in Chicago; one historian has compared favorably the *Whip*'s views on economics and societal development with those of Randolph and Owen in the *Messenger*.[69] The paper was a strong advocate of unionism among blacks, and as recently as 1923 it had called on porters in Chicago to organize in order to improve their leverage with Pullman.[70]

The *Whip*'s objections to the BSCP, and the union's responses, paralleled the arguments that had developed between the Brotherhood and the *Argus*. The *Whip* cautioned the porters to be wary of organized labor, emphasizing that many members of the AFL belonged to the Ku Klux Klan. As railroad workers, porters should be particularly careful;

[68] *Messenger*, VII (Dec., 1925), 383. Much has been made of this advertisement. Spero and Harris, *Black Worker*, 437n, cite two occasions on which the advertisement appeared, Oct. 30 and Nov. 2, 1925. But the *Argus* was a weekly, and unless a special edition appeared for the latter date (none has been located) the authors are in error on this point. The advertisement does appear in the Oct. 30 edition.

[69] Allan H. Spear, *Black Chicago: The Making of a Negro Ghetto, 1890-1920* (Chicago: University of Chicago Press, 1967), ch. 10, contains a good discussion of the *Whip* and its relationship to blacks on Chicago's South Side, and with the larger city, as well as biographical data on the editors of the newspaper. Citations for MacNeal in *Who's Who in Colored America* (3rd and 6th eds.) do not mention that he received a law degree from Yale University, though it is clear that he did study there.

[70] Spear, *Black Chicago*, 197-99; *Messenger*, VII (Dec., 1925), 378.

they could expect no help from the standard railway brotherhoods, which were notorious for their anti-black stance.[71] Randolph charged the *Whip* with accepting money from Pullman in payment for its stories against the BSCP. He cited as evidence (among other things) the fact that the *Whip*, like the *Argus*, now carried an ad for the company, and that Pullman bought large stacks of both sheets and made them available to the porters. While admitting that there undoubtedly were Klansmen in the organized labor movement, Randolph asserted that members of the Klan could also be found in almost every other branch of American society. If blacks wished to be rid of that crowd, they "had better get out of the country."[72] On the matter of the white brotherhoods withholding support from the porters, Randolph wrote that it was spineless to advise that blacks not attempt to do something simply because whites might not support the effort. Such advice was that of the "*typical Sambo Negro with the inferiority complex.*"[73]

Early in 1926 Chandler Owen joined the argument on the Brotherhood's side, raising pointed questions about the character of the *Whip*'s editors and about financial relations between the newspaper and the Pullman Company. From January through April he wrote a series of articles for the *Messenger* called "The Neglected Truth," which constituted an "exposé" of the *Whip*'s editorial policies and in which he accused its editors of the shadiest deeds, including the practice of resorting to blackmail to attract advertising.[74] The attempts at shakedown extended even to the Pullman Company. Owen wrote that soon after Randolph's original *Messenger* articles on the necessity of organizing the porters, Joseph Bibb called Owen into the *Whip* office and told him that Pullman would pay the magazine a large sum if the articles would cease. Bibb even offered to act as agent in securing an agreement between the *Messenger* and the company.[75]

Of much greater importance was Owen's allegation that certain whites in Chicago owned controlling interests in the *Whip*. The paper's location would provide ample opportunity for Pullman to exercise informal influence over it on the question of the BSCP, but Owen

[71] Copies of the *Whip* for this period were unavailable. This discussion is based on quotations from the *Whip*'s story that APR used in his response to the paper's opposition. See *Messenger*, VII (Dec., 1925), 378-79.

[72] *Ibid.*, 378.

[73] *Ibid.*

[74] *Ibid.*, VIII (Jan., 1926), 5-6, 31.

[75] *Ibid.* (Feb., 1926), 48-49.

claimed that an attorney for the Pullman Company and Chicago utilities interests, Daniel J. Schuyler, held controlling stock in the paper. He quoted Oscar De Priest, Chicago's first black alderman and later a congressman from Illinois, as saying he was an eyewitness to the transfer to Schuyler of 55 percent of the *Whip*'s stock. Horace R. Cayton and George S. Mitchell support Owen's charges in their study of relationships between blacks and trade unions. They cite an interview with an anonymous source, apparently associated with the *Whip*, confirming the allegation that the newspaper had opposed the BSCP because of financial ties with Pullman. The informant termed Owen's exposé "only half the truth," and added that the *Messenger* editor "never did know the whole story."[76] In any event, Owen's articles silenced the *Whip* as an effective opposition paper. Rather than reply in print, the journal sued Owen and Randolph for criminal libel.[77]

Opposition from the *Argus* and the *Whip* troubled union leaders and hindered the cause, but the attitude of the Chicago *Defender* was a source of much more concern. The *Defender*, after all, was not a local paper. It had a national reputation as a leading fighter for the advancement of black people and was one of the most widely circulated black newspapers in the country.[78] The problem with the *Defender* during the Brotherhood's first two months, as far as union officials were concerned, was not so much that it criticized the BSCP as that it printed pro-Pullman material and failed to give space to the Brotherhood's point of view. Yet by January, 1926, Randolph wrote that no other paper in the country had taken such a "palpably unfair position" on the porters' movement.[79]

[76] *Ibid*. (Mar., 1926), 83. Horace R. Cayton and George S. Mitchell, *Black Workers and the New Unions* (Chapel Hill: University of North Carolina Press, 1939), 396, quote their source as follows: "Yes, after 1925 there was a change in the policy of the *Whip*. It came about this way. To save the stockholders who had invested in the *Whip* we made a deal with Insull. In this deal Insull took over $22,000 worth of stock. Then this necessitated the changing of our policy. Later, when Insull's lawyer became the lawyer for the Pullman Company we had to change our policy toward the Pullman Porters' union. Before, we had been favoring it and we just had to pick out something and fight it. There was an exposé in the *Messenger*, but it was only half the truth. They never did know the whole story."

[77] See the next chapter for a full discussion of the libel suit.

[78] Roi Ottley, *The Lonely Warrior: The Life and Times of Robert S. Abbott* (Chicago: Regnery Press, 1955), puts the *Defender*'s circulation for 1925 at 200,000 copies weekly.

[79] *Messenger*, VIII (Jan., 1926), 17.

When the *Defender* criticized the BSCP early in November, 1925, it did so on grounds different from those of the *Argus*. Instead of arguing that the union was detrimental to the porters' cause, and therefore to all blacks, because it threatened to destroy the racial monopoly in Pullman porter service, the *Defender* maintained that the union had as one of its aims the perpetuation of that condition. The paper claimed that such a monopoly could cause "great dangers, not only to the Pullman porters themselves, but to laborers in other branches of American industry," though it did not make clear why it opposed a reservoir of jobs for blacks.[80]

Despite their need for the *Defender's* support, or at least its neutrality, Randolph and his colleagues could not resist attacking the paper in print. On this occasion they stopped short of an outright accusation that the *Defender*'s editor-publisher, Robert S. Abbott, accepted money from the Pullman Company in exchange for its support. Writing that the union's leaders believed "Brother Abbott's heart is all right," Randolph explained Abbott's stance by saying that either "his head is wrong or his hands are tied." The clear implication was that if the company did not pay Abbott directly, it did exercise some financial control over his actions. Abbott was a director of the Binga State Bank in Chicago, a black-owned bank in which the Pullman Porters Benefit Association (PPBA) had a deposit of at least $10,000. Randolph alleged that the company controlled PPBA funds and that Abbott supported Pullman to preserve the account.[81] The truth is difficult to know, since one cannot say with certainty just how important that account was to the bank. The BSCP enlarged on its allegation that money was indirectly responsible for the *Defender's* support of Pullman by asserting in the *Messenger* that the company bought numerous copies of the *Defender,* along with the *Argus* and other pro-company papers, and placed them at the porters' disposal. Yet even here a different moral can be found. That the company took every opportunity to spread its point of view is not in itself evidence that Pullman paid for the favorable comments.

The *Defender*'s case was special and, indeed, odd, as later events would show. Though union leaders never proved that there were any financial dealings between Abbott and Pullman management, some incidents do cast suspicion on the paper's early position. The most important occurrence came in March, 1926, the month when Chicago

[80] Chicago *Defender*, Nov. 7, 1925.
[81] *Messenger*, VIII (Jan., 1926), 17.

waiters formed a union. Applauding the action, the *Defender* emphasized the strength of numbers, "especially if the numbers are organized and made to function as a unit," and forecast many benefits which the union would bring to its members. Such a response is hard to square with the paper's silence about the founding of the BSCP, though the waiters' union did not intend to create a racial monopoly (the *Defender*'s chief criticism against the Brotherhood).[82]

One black newspaper of national circulation and influence did come to the BSCP's aid during the formative months. The Pittsburgh *Courier* first commented on the Brotherhood in rebuking Perry Howard, a black politician from Mississippi, for his opposition to the union. Comparing him to a Judas Goat leading porters to the slaughter, it enthusiastically endorsed the BSCP.[83] The *Courier* advised readers to discount allegations that Communists were behind efforts to organize the porters, insisting that such comments were cowardly. The paper also depicted A. Philip Randolph in favorable terms and did much to create a favorable national image for him. It conceded that he was a Socialist, but added that he was known to be a "staunch supporter of the Negro and his rights, regardless of politics." Describing Randolph as brilliant, honest, and able, a man who knew economics and the history of his people, the *Courier* wrote that he could hold his own with anyone the Pullman Company could produce, black or white. Porters should support Randolph because he would persevere in the battle for their rights.[84]

So forthright was the *Courier*'s stance that BSCP leaders probably sometimes wondered if they could afford the kind of support it gave. While writing favorably of the union, the newspaper showed a disrespect for the porters that bordered on contempt, referring to them as a cowardly, unintelligent group, so ignorant that they had to look outside their ranks for leadership. Once the leadership was forthcoming, they viewed it with jealousy and suspicion.[85] The *Courier* went further, attributing the porters' characteristics to blacks as a whole. When the company placed Filipinos on its cars, a step many interpreted as a warning to the porters that they could be replaced, the *Courier* argued that the threat should be ignored. The Filipinos were not menials, it said,

[82] Chicago *Defender*, Mar. 31, 1926. See the fifth chapter for further discussion of the *Defender*'s position.

[83] Pittsburgh *Courier*, Oct. 24, 1925.

[84] *Ibid.*, Oct. 31, 1925.

[85] *Ibid.*

and would not become such. The editors recognized that it would be good to see others working as menials for a change, but suggested that only blacks would "stoop to dust the traveling public."[86] Although agreeing with the *Defender* that a racial monopoly was not a good thing for black workers, they still endorsed the porters' movement as the opening wedge for blacks to use in moving into other unions and jobs.[87]

The problems of misguided support and unconcealed hostility continued to bedevil the organizational efforts of the porters and their leadership. From the perspective provided by a half-century, it is still fascinating to observe the slow upward movement of the union during the 1920s. To gain the support of whites seemed, in that benighted decade, almost impossible; to gain support even from blacks seemed equally difficult.

Though in the past Randolph had condemned the economic stance of leaders of the National Association for the Advancement of Colored People, the largest and most influential black advancement organization in the country, he now sought and received that body's support.[88] NAACP officials recognized the importance of efforts to organize the porters and extended both financial and moral support. From the Brotherhood's beginning, NAACP Secretary James Weldon Johnson responded to BSCP requests and joined the union's leadership in their efforts, often speaking to porters under BSCP auspices, and even allowing the *Messenger* to publish letters of endorsement which he wrote to union officials.[89] In a *Crisis* editorial Du Bois wrote that the Pullman Company had conspired with every element in American society in its attempt to block the porters' union, and that it threatened to fire porters who listened to Brotherhood leaders. He declared that it would be better for porters to have no jobs than to work under such conditions. In poetic prose, he maintained that if being good porters meant being "driven

[86] *Ibid.*, Nov. 28, 1925.

[87] *Ibid.*, Nov. 7, 1925. See the fifth chapter for further discussion of the *Courier*'s position.

[88] The organization had among its leadership black men who wielded wide influence among both blacks and whites. Among those were James Weldon Johnson, W. E. B. Du Bois, and Walter White. For examples of APR's condemnations of NAACP officials, see *Messenger* (1917-24), *passim*.

[89] APR to Johnson, Jan. 19, 1926, NAACP Pas, C413, LC; Pittsburgh *Courier*, Sept. 26, 1925. In his letter to Johnson, APR requested the NAACP leader to send a letter to the BSCP that the union could publish in the *Messenger* to prove that it had Johnson's endorsement. Johnson complied, resubmitting a letter of Nov. 20, 1925, which he had sent to Lancaster.

slaves and alms-taking servants, then God haste the day we outgrow *that* job.''[90] Aside from the influence of the NAACP as an organization, it is noteworthy to point out that Du Bois's prominence as an individual made his personal support even more valuable to the union.

In June, 1926, Randolph asked Johnson to use his influence at the annual NAACP convention to secure passage of a resolution endorsing the Brotherhood's program. Randolph believed such a resolution would demonstrate to the Pullman Company the degree of solidarity among blacks on the porters' fight, while actually helping to remove some of the opposition of other black organizations — especially ''those encrusted in conservatism.''[91] After the Association passed the desired resolution, Randolph rejoiced that the most powerful organization among black people had endorsed the BSCP.[92] Interestingly, the NAACP's assistant secretary, Walter White, informed Randolph that the union owed the Association no thanks: the work Randolph was doing was so valuable that the NAACP would have been derelict in its duty had it failed to offer support.The Association even seriously considered awarding Randolph its Springarn Medal (given in recognition of the most outstanding contribution to the cause of blacks) in 1926 because of his work with the porters.[93]

Although the BSCP enjoyed the valuable support of the NAACP, it still encountered considerable opposition from other highly placed blacks. The National Urban League did not share the NAACP's early enthusiasm for Randolph and his union. Its executive secretary, Eugene K. Jones, was himself a former porter; he extended personal congratulations and endorsed the union, but there is no mention of the national office taking any action on the BSCP during its first months.[94] From Chicago it was reported that the local Urban League expressed grave reservations about supporting the union.[95]

The BSCP's standard charge that its critics were paid by Pullman to

[90] *Crisis*, XXXII (Apr., 1926), 271.

[91] APR to Johnson, June 22, 1926, NAACP Pas, C413, LC.

[92] *Messenger*, VIII (Aug., 1926), 248.

[93] White to APR, July 6, 1926, and Robert Bagnall to Crosswaith, Apr. 15, 1926, NAACP Pas, C413, LC. It is not clear whether APR knew of the nomination, for he never mentioned it.

[94] *Messenger*, VIII (Feb., 1926), 56.

[95] MPW to A. L. Foster, executive secretary of the Chicago Urban League, Apr. 21, 1926, BSCP ChiPa. The Urban League depended to a large extent upon gifts of corporations for its operating funds. Neither Arvarh E. Strickland, *History of the Chicago Urban League* (Urbana: University of Illinois Press, 1966), nor Nancy J.

oppose the union was not universally true.[96] Some respectable black men opposed the Brotherhood either because they did not believe the new union was in the porters' best interest or because they did not fully understand the issues involved. For example, the distinguished AME minister, Reverdy C. Ransom, who had just attained a bishopric in 1924, wondered if the BSCP might be a plot on the part of white labor leaders to get porters to go out on strike so the Pullman Company could dismiss them and whites could take over the jobs of porters.[97]

Though some opposition of blacks to the BSCP was free, the company did use its funds to buy support. The most notable example of an individual who admitted working for pay on behalf of Pullman was Perry Howard. An ex-porter, he had risen through Mississippi politics to become the state's perennial Republican national committeeman. By 1925 he was so prominent in party politics that the administration made him a special assistant to the attorney general. When the porters began airing their grievances, Howard wrote the Pullman Company and offered his services to oppose the movement; soon he became a paid consultant, working to devise ways to thwart the Brotherhood.[98]

Howard claimed that he opposed the Brotherhood because it represented the first of a series of Communist attacks against American capitalism. He argued that Moscow backed the BSCP and that the union intended to involve black workingmen in the meshes of communism and socialism to the detriment of their happiness and prosperity. The union movement against the Pullman Company represented the beginning of a nationwide conspiracy, and he volunteered to help in "awakening and in pointing out to the race the conditions that confronted them."[99] On a less ideological level, Howard accused the Brotherhood of threatening to destroy existing "amicable relations" between porters and Pullman.

Weiss, *The National Urban League, 1910-1940* (New York: Oxford University Press, 1974), mentions early Urban League views of the BSCP.

[96] *Messenger*, VII and VIII (1925-26), contains numerous editorials and comments. It also carries several cartoons which depict its black opponents as broken-down Uncle Toms who bowed and scraped as they took the Pullman Company's money.

[97] Reverdy C. Ransom to APR, printed in *Messenger*, VIII (Mar., 1926), 93. For biographical data on Ransom, see *Who's Who in Colored America* (6th ed.), p. 426.

[98] Pittsburgh *Courier*, Oct. 24, 1925. Howard was so adept as a politician that during an election in Mississippi the Ku Klux Klan burned a cross on the lawn of his white opponent. See Claude A. Barnett, "Fly Out of Darkness" (unfinished and unpublished autobiography), ch. 2, p. 5. The manuscript is available among Claude A. Barnett Papers, Manuscripts Division, Chicago Historical Society.

[99] Quoted in Pittsburgh *Courier,* Oct. 24, 1925.

Bragging that "the door to the office of the president is always open" to porters, Howard insisted they were free to bargain individually and collectively with the company.[100]

Howard's activities caused grave concerns for the Brotherhood, especially his use of the terms socialism and communism (which he considered identical) to characterize the union and its leaders. Defending its position, Randolph categorically denied that the BSCP had ties with either communism or socialism, any more than it had with any of the American political parties. It was an organization of, for, and by the porters, who represented numerous political groups.[101] Though Randolph was a Socialist, Crosswaith was the only other BSCP leader who entertained "foreign" notions. Webster in Chicago was a Republican, and Lancaster leaned toward the Democrats.

The BSCP then endeavored to bring influence of respected blacks and whites to bear in its efforts to diminish the impact of Howard's attack; this same tactic was to be a hallmark of Randolph's strategy in years to come. NAACP officials and other influential persons joined with the BSCP to destroy Howard's credibility and to undercut whatever official trappings he used to legitimize his opposition to the union, with Du Bois dismissing Howard as just "a silly black lawyer."[102] Reacting to Howard's claim that his anti-BSCP stance resulted from his position as a special federal agent on labor matters,[103] the BSCP, through a so-called Citizen's Committee in Chicago, petitioned President Coolidge to disavow any connection with Howard's opposition to the Brotherhood. The Citizen's Committee not only called on the President to stop Howard's opposition; it urged that the President replace him with a black leader "truly representative of his race."[104] In December Randolph followed this petition with a personal letter to President Coolidge in which he asked that the administration get Howard either "out of the government or out of Pullman."[105] Randolph also secured the services of Represen-

[100] Quoted in Chicago *Defender*, Oct. 31, 1925.

[101] *Messenger*, VII (Dec., 1925), 400, 402.

[102] *Crisis*, XXXI (Dec., 1925), 60. For the Brotherhood's attack on Howard's lack of judgment and his poor character, see *Messenger*, VII (Oct.-Nov., 1925), 352; (Dec., 1925), 400, 402.

[103] Spero and Harris, *Black Worker*, 437.

[104] Pittsburgh *Courier*, Nov. 7, 1925.

[105] Printed *ibid*., Dec. 5, 1925. The union's argument was that Howard's actions constituted a conflict of interest in the government, especially if the BSCP-Pullman dispute reached federal agencies.

tative Victor L. Berger of Wisconsin in his endeavors to be rid of Howard. Berger's socialism rendered his services of dubious value, especially with the conservative Coolidge Administration, but the congressman agreed to investigate Howard's activities to see if they warranted his removal from federal service.[106] The Coolidge Administration disavowed any knowledge of Howard's actions — a denial that convinced neither the Brotherhood nor its supporters.[107] In an editorial in the *Crisis* for January, 1926, Du Bois accused the administration of creating an unhealthy atmosphere in which the BSCP must function. Proof of this, he claimed, was that administration officials allowed Howard to stay in a governmental position while accepting a fee from Pullman.[108] In any event, attacks by union officials and others had ended Howard's effectiveness, and he was no longer a major threat to the BSCP.[109]

While utilizing Howard's services, Pullman also put Melvin Chisum into the battle against the BSCP. Purcival L. Prattis, a Chicago journalist at the time, described Chisum as the smoothest of a large group of underhanded operators in Chicago during the 1920s; he had a long history of secretive and unprincipled missions for pay. Chisum had served as an agent for Booker T. Washington in the Tuskegeean's efforts to disrupt the plans of those whom he considered his enemies.[110] Holding the office of field secretary for the National Negro Press Association in 1925, Chisum had ideal credentials with which to dis-

[106] Berger to APR, printed in *Messenger*, VIII (Feb., 1926), 57. Berger's efforts resulted in no positive value for the BSCP, but his connection with the BSCP is part of APR's pattern of operation: he liked to bring important individuals to his aid, even if nothing resulted immediately from their involvement. Their names gave him and the union a good press, and he believed he needed the publicity.

[107] Spero and Harris, *Black Worker*, 438.

[108] *Crisis*, XXXI (Jan., 1926), 113.

[109] Spero and Harris, *Black Worker*, 438.

[110] Interview with Percival L. Prattis, June 6, 1974; Louis R. Harlan, "The Secret Life of Booker T. Washington," *Journal of Southern History*, XXXVIII (Aug., 1972), 393-416, paints a marvelous picture of Chisum and his activities. Stephen R. Fox, *The Guardian of Boston: William Monroe Trotter* (New York: Atheneum, 1971), 67-68, discusses Chisum's work for Washington in trying to undermine the work of Trotter and others in Boston. Fox describes Chisum as a "good henchman-errand boy for Tuskegee" and quotes Washington's close friend, Charles W. Anderson, as having said in 1906 that Chisum had "made up his mind not to work, and plans to live by borrowing."

During his distinguished career in journalism, Prattis rose to the position of associate editor of the Pittsburgh *Courier*. He became an outstanding civic and civil rights leader.

seminate Pullman propaganda among blacks. Yet the company chose to use his talents in another way. During November, 1925, he hosted a mysterious conference of fifty prominent black men and women in Washington. At a gathering called ostensibly to map ways to decrease racial discrimination, he did not invite representatives of the NAACP—an oversight that made the conference suspect in several quarters from the beginning. President Coolidge's meeting with the group gave it a prestige which it otherwise would have lacked, and assured national publication of the conclave's resolution in opposition to unionization of Pullman service employees.[111] But the resolution did not have the desired effect. Several black newspapers, notably the *Courier*, refused to carry the story and maintained that the Washington conference was not a meeting in the interest of improving the conditions for black people, but a front for the Pullman Company.

Randolph credited the *Courier* with uncovering the company's part in bankrolling the meeting.[112] Although neither Chisum nor Pullman admitted that the company had been involved, there was considerable evidence to support the allegation. Perry Howard's activities on the company's behalf were enough to prove that Pullman was not above paying for opposition to the union. More telling was the fact that Chisum paid transportation, hotel, and food bills for all participants. In answer to the *Courier*'s questions about how he could afford such a substantial sum, Chisum explained that he had earned a large amount of money the previous summer as an "efficiency engineer" and that he wished to show his gratitude to his friends.[113] The most striking comments about the conference, those which most strongly supported allegations that Chisum received outside backing, came from several participants who denied that the group passed resolutions against unions.[114] Reinzi B. Lemus of the Dining Car Waiters' Union, and no friend of the BSCP, emphatically denied that any such action had been taken; others corroborated his testimony.[115] After the meeting Chisum returned to Chicago and founded the National Negro Advertising Agency, a clearing house

[111] Pittsburgh *Courier*, Nov. 21, 1925. In its report on the conferees attending the meeting with President Coolidge, the *Courier* captioned the accompanying picture derisively, "Fooled to Washington," conveying the paper's belief that the men and women had been assembled for something other than the published reason.

[112] APR to Coolidge, in Pittsburgh *Courier*, Dec. 5, 1925.

[113] *Ibid.*, Jan. 9, 1926.

[114] Spero and Harris, *Black Worker*, 439; Brazeal, *The Brotherhood*, 35.

[115] *Messenger*, VII (Dec., 1925), 389.

for placing advertisements of utilities' interests in black newspapers. The agency expected favorable comments about the Pullman Company in return for its services.[116] For all his efforts, Chisum's propaganda caused only temporary problems for the Brotherhood and was soon forgotten.

During the BSCP's early months the company itself maintained an aloof public posture, refusing to indicate any awareness of the union's existence. Publicly, Pullman operated as usual. It announced its Filipino policy as simply the latest in a series of Pullman innovations that would improve customer service. Likewise, the company did not change its attitude toward the porters. It continued to publish accounts of porters' activities, carrying items on porters' baseball teams and quartets, one of the latter of which was dubbed "the president's own"; its official organ ran a monthly column called the "Porters' Honor Roll" to single out porters who had performed above the average during a given month.[117]

This public posture did not represent Pullman's private thoughts on the Brotherhood. Interoffice memoranda show conclusively that company administrators paid close attention to BSCP activities and carefully dissected Brotherhood propaganda in preparing to present their side of the story.[118] Pullman officials took particular exception to Randolph's assertion that blacks had no means of rising in Pullman service to any position higher than that of porter. The official memorandum on this matter pointed out that many black men served as storekeepers of the company's valuable linen and supplies, emphasizing that they were paid well for their supervisory and custodial duties.[119]

For Pullman to have acknowledged the union would have been a form of recognition the company could not afford, especially when Brotherhood leaders and others claimed that Pullman used both subtle and overt acts of intimidation against the porters to keep them from joining the BSCP. Although opponents never proved their allegations, the record is clear that the company did dismiss several porters who were active in the union. For example, it fired Roy Lancaster, the Brotherhood's secretary-treasurer, shortly before the meeting at Des Verney's in June, 1925. Pullman claimed that Lancaster had reported to work intoxicated; the union answered that he was fired because of his efforts to overturn

[116] Ottley, *Lonely Warrior*, 264.
[117] *Pullman News* (Nov., 1925), 221.
[118] See, e.g., Pullman Company memorandum for Aug., 1925, PC Pas.
[119] *Ibid.*

the results of the wage conference of 1924. Available evidence is inconclusive, but Pullman's firing of Totten and some others who worked for the union does suggest that retaliation might have had something to do with Lancaster's dismissal.

Claims and counterclaims of intimidation were rife during the winter of 1925, especially while porters voted on whether to approve the ERP. Porters themselves engaged in intense debate over the relative merits of the BSCP and the company plan, while both the Brotherhood and Pullman jockeyed to gain majority support. The interest became so intense that some allegedly pro-BSCP porters formed the Black Klan, an Omaha-based secret organization apparently bent upon frightening reluctant porters into joining the Brotherhood. To one porter, W. R. Estelle, who worked for the ERP, the Black Klan wrote:

> Mr. Estelle, excuse me I meant Uncle Tom what the matter you have not joined the union?
>
> Now listen old boy we are still here in Omaha and will be here the rest of our lives. You had better join the union and show your receipt in the next meeting of our club; if not we will make you spend more than five dollars by shelling your home if you don't spend the money for one thing you will spend it for another;
>
> Now if you bring any of that PPBA mess up in any of our meetings you will be sorry in days to come The Black Klan[120]

Apparently Estelle neither joined the BSCP nor ceased his opposition, for in a later letter the Black Klan threatened him with death, saying that he would not see another Christmas if he continued to oppose the Brotherhood.[121] The threat was not carried out.

We have no way of knowing how many other porters in the Omaha vicinity received similar abuse, yet it is not clear whether the Black Klan had any relationship to the BSCP. While it is improbable that the union would officially condone acts such as those of the Black Klan, monthly assaults in the *Messenger* on union opponents — and the leadership's penchant for labeling non-union porters as Uncle Toms — could lead misguided members of organizations like the Black Klan to believe they acted in the union's best interest. It is at least equally likely that the organization was a devious group cooked up by the Pullman Company to discredit the BSCP.[122]

[120] Black Klan to W. R. Estelle, n.d. [1925], *ibid*.

[121] Black Klan to Estelle, Dec. 17, 1925, *ibid*.

[122] *Messenger* (1925-28), *passim*. It is significant that nowhere among BSCP papers

Intense debate among porters and in the black press, paid propagandists, and threats of intimidation and violence were all parts of the public atmosphere within which the Brotherhood functioned. However, during late 1925 and early 1926 the BSCP also experienced dynamic internal developments which for the most part remained outside the public view. In addition to trying to present a favorable public image, the union had to face difficult and crucial questions of strategy and policy, and to solve problems of personality clashes and cleavages among its leaders.

The depths of disunity and the existence of varying views on strategy among BSCP leaders burst upon the public consciousness with amazing suddenness in January, 1926. Robert L. Mays published in the *Defender* a letter of resignation which he had written to Randolph just the week before. Mays said in the letter that he could no longer remain a part of the BSCP because of the undue control exercised over the union by the leaders in New York. Mays claimed that the influence of New York, and the failure of the national leaders to move boldly in formulating a public policy on two major issues, had caused the Chicago leadership to consider joining his defection.[123] Differences of opinion between Mays and other BSCP leaders on the value of pending federal railway labor legislation, and the union's equivocal actions during the ERP elections late in 1925, brought him to his final decision.

The first issue of dispute, new railway labor legislation, was important not only for the porters, but for all railroad workers. Late in 1925 Congress had begun debate on a bill that would change the laws that had governed federal involvement in railway labor disputes since the government had restored the lines to private ownership in 1920 after running them under federal control during World War I. The existing law, the Esch-Cummins Act, provided for a Railway Labor Board to hear cases involving workers and employers and to decide grievances that could not be settled in conferences between disputants. The major problem with Esch-Cummins was that the board had no authority to mediate disputes, nor did it have power to enforce its decisions. The theory behind the law was that public opinion by itself would be enough to cause corporations and unions to obey the board's rulings.[124]

is there a reference to the Black Klan. The only mention of the group can be found among Pullman Company papers.

[123] Chicago *Defender*, Jan. 23, 1926.

[124] United States National Mediation Board, *Annual Report* (Washington: Government Printing Office, 1934), 64.

The crisis that caused serious difficulties for the BSCP arose because some black labor leaders opposed changing Esch-Cummins, and they asked that Randolph join them. They argued that the pending Watson-Parker bill would work to the disadvantage of black workers, especially since it did not empower the federal government to force agreement between unions and employers, short of a strike. Nor did it provide for a wage board to order pay increases on its own. Mays, the central figure of the opposition, maintained that the new law would benefit only members of unions large and strong enough to strike and force the president to create emergency boards to impose agreement, as the act would provide.[125] Lemus agreed with Mays, but went further. He believed that the movement to undo Esch-Cummins stemmed directly from "Mr. Randolph's challenge to the gods."[126] Lemus's comment must have been flattering to Brotherhood leaders, for surely they realized that he had granted them more credit than they deserved. But Lemus's statement underlined his view that a major aim of the new legislation was to hinder the advancement of black workers in the railway industry. Nonetheless, Brotherhood leaders would not support efforts to prevent passage of the bill. Unlike Mays and others, Randolph thought the new law would benefit all workers in the trade. His trust that justice would prevail convinced him that federal agencies would treat porters in the same manner as they did members of large white unions.

Debate over Watson-Parker was just part of a wider philosophical disagreement between BSCP leaders and others over the goals of trade unionism. Mays had long urged the Brotherhood to take its case before the Railway Labor Board under Esch-Cummins and demand a wage increase. Randolph had refused, and Mays insisted that with this action he had "bungled" the porters' chances of receiving a pay raise.[127] Spero and Harris write that Randolph and his colleagues did not appeal to the Labor Board because they feared that they could not get a majority of the porters to vote for the BSCP as their representative. These critics contend that had the Brotherhood appealed to the Labor Board in 1925, it would have received a sympathetic hearing.[128]

BSCP officials never spoke to this point, though comments on the union's weakness were accurate. At the end of 1925 the Brotherhood

[125] Mays quoted in Chicago *Defender*, June 19, 1926.
[126] Lemus to Hill, Jan. 29, 1926, NAACP Pas, C413, LC.
[127] Mays to APR, Jan. 15, 1926, in Chicago *Defender*, Jan. 23, 1926.
[128] Spero and Harris, *Black Worker*, 448-49.

could count only 1,904 members. In addition, the union had not yet developed to the point where it could put forth a strong and united front. Rather than dwell on the question of strength, BSCP leaders argued that it would have been folly for a struggling new union to oppose legislation which was supported by the major brotherhoods and railway companies.[129] Randolph later pointed out, for example, that Pullman had an obligation to honor the right of porters to organize under Watson-Parker because, as a member of the Association of Railway Executives, the company had endorsed passage of the act.[130]

There is, however, another important reason why BSCP leaders refused to go before the Railway Labor Board and instead supported passage of Watson-Parker. It centered on the question of union recognition, and marked a major difference between Randolph and his critics over the means and goals of trade unionism. The critics believed wage increases to be the main goal of unions, whereas Brotherhood leaders considered participation of workers in helping to determine working conditions far more important. Thus Mays and others could argue that the porters should go before the Labor Board because the board was empowered to investigate cases and, if conditions warranted, order pay increases. But the board could make no determination on the right of an organization to represent a group of workers, nor did its powers extend to the all-important field of working conditions. Brotherhood leaders insisted that their aims were much higher than mere increases in pay, and that they intended to be part of Pullman for a long time.[131] This was the beginning of a new direction for black labor leaders. After it won the debate with the Mays crowd, the Randolph group could not back away from this commitment to their version of trade unionism, even though they might sacrifice some immediate wage increases.

The second major issue that entered into Mays's decision to quit the union, and to condemn remaining BSCP leaders as failures, centered on the impending ERP conference between the Pullman Company and the porters. In November, 1925, the company announced in *Pullman News* that it expected all porters to vote in the upcoming "election" under the company plan, and it scheduled a wage conference to consider the

[129] APR to JWJ, Feb. 1, 1926, NAACP Pas, C413, LC. Spero and Harris, *Black Worker*, 449-50, 459-60.

[130] *Messenger*, VIII (June, 1926), 186.

[131] Numerous letters from BSCP files support this conclusion. See esp. MPW to APR, Nov. 11, 1927, and APR to MPW, Dec. 1, 1927, BSCP ChiPa, when the two leaders discussed the matter of a pay increase on a later occasion.

porters' grievances and pay requests.[132] The spectre of a new meeting between Pullman and the porters bewildered Brotherhood leaders, because they knew the company intended to use the conference to show the porters that the Plan worked and that they did not need a new union.

The BSCP could not decide how best to deal with a new conference. Leaders divided over whether to tell members to refuse to vote in the election, or to attempt to get BSCP members elected as delegates to the conference and thus control it. Some even considered trying to sabotage the elections. According to Mays, several union organizers and men outside the BSCP who sympathized with its activities advised the leaders that this was the time to take a firm stand and instruct the porters to boycott the election. Any other strategy would work to the union's disadvantage.[133] Brotherhood correspondence refers to a secret plan to undermine the company's meeting, but no program was ever produced. Seemingly confused on how best to respond to this direct challenge, the BSCP ended by doing nothing. It depended instead on a publicity stunt in the hope that it would goad the company into firing John Mills, a known union porter in Chicago, and thus rally the porters to the union's side. The scheme failed when Pullman allowed Mills to go out on his run.[134]

Though the union's apparent inability to act left the leaders open to criticism, the situation was such that the leadership undoubtedly made a sound decision by postponing direct confrontation over this issue. Given the BSCP's meager membership, few porters were likely to heed a direct order that they refuse to vote in the ERP elections, especially when their jobs were on the line. A major porter turnout for the ERP in the face of explicit instructions from the BSCP would have caused irreparable damage to the morale of both Brotherhood leaders and the rank and file. Rather than risk destruction of their entire program, Randolph and others kept quiet on this issue, reserving for a future fight what little strength they had. As had been the case in the past, the porters voted overwhelmingly for the conference.

Criticism of the union's stance was not long in coming. The wait-and-see attitude muddied the already troubled waters between Randolph

[132] *Pullman News* (Nov., 1925), 222.

[133] Mays to APR, Jan. 15, 1926, in Chicago *Defender*, Jan. 23, 1926. In his letter Mays reminds Randolph of the involvement of other BSCP organizers with his defection.

[134] Price to Lancaster, Nov. 27, 1925, BSCP ChiPa.

and Mays, leading directly to Mays's defection. Accusing the New York leaders of "impractical theorizing and vainglorious ambition," Mays placed blame for the union's failure to stop the porters from voting at Randolph's feet "because of his arrogance, ignorance, or possible wrong intention."[135] Commenting further on what he saw as Randolph's faults, Mays accused the union leader of inability to act in time of crisis. He also implied that BSCP men in the Chicago office considered turning against the New York crowd:

> From things I know and have reason to believe about Randolph's action at the moment of crisis from what I am told almost daily by porters who know me and seek my advice I take this occasion to advise and warn porters against this man, who seeks 80 or 90 percent of the porters as members of his proposed brotherhood which seems to be a distributing agency for his personal business and a meal ticket for certain men associated with him who are now ready to "repudiate" any statement of fact, but who a few weeks ago were ready to break up the organization, lock up the Chicago office or take the whole works out of Randolph's hands because he had done that of which they accuse him, namely failed to act at the right time, scooted out of Chicago without giving motive to his fellow workers and remaining quietly in New York while the Employees Representation Plan was being voted on, accepted, and approved by 80 percent of the men directly concerned.[136]

Such strong condemnations from a man of Mays's standing among porters and in labor circles in Chicago — the *Defender* called him "the most active and successful organizer and representative of railroad labor of our group" — and his linking of Webster to his defection, necessitated an all-out campaign of rebuttal. The BSCP attacked Mays so vigorously that he threatened to sue Randolph and the union for libel.[137]

Categorically denying any collusion with Mays to destroy the BSCP, Webster told porters that Mays's intent in releasing the letter and his subsequent comments had not been to help the porters and to warn them against Randolph, but to create confusion among the men and to destroy the union.[138] Joining in this attack (but on another level) Randolph

[135] Mays quoted in Chicago *Defender*, Jan. 23 and Mar. 27, 1926. The debate raged over several months, as both sides issued charges and rebuttals.

[136] *Ibid*., March 27, 1926.

[137] *Ibid*., June 19, 1926. Quote appears in same issue.

[138] MPW, Statement to the Brotherhood Men, Jan. 21, 1926, NAACP Pas, C414, LC. This statement reads like one APR wrote for MPW. It is somewhat strange, too, that a copy of this statement does not appear among BSCP ChiPa.

wrote James Weldon Johnson that Mays had encouraged the BSCP to take the porters' case before the Railway Labor Board within two months after the union had been founded. Randolph explained that to have done so would have been absurd, and he suggested that Mays recommended the step in order to wreck the union before it got off the ground. Randolph further alleged that Mays was operating in the interest of the Pullman Company, and that the company was paying for his services.[139]

Although these accusations were never proven, they had positive results for the Brotherhood, forcing Mays into an extreme position which made him much more vulnerable to the union's attacks. Mays, who had joined with Randolph and others in numerous attacks against Pullman and the ERP, and who just the year before had led an attempt to destroy the company union in order to gain the right to represent the porters through his organization, now found himself arguing the merits of the Plan for the porters.[140] Such an appeal, possibly sincere from one who considered any plan better than having the porters misled by the Brotherhood, called Mays's honesty into question, seeming to justify BSCP accusations that he was working for Pullman. Mays also renewed his claim that Randolph was personally responsible for the union's failure to act. Citing Randolph's ignorance of railroad labor problems and his personal arrogance, Mays charged that Randolph had taken the position of BSCP general organizer primarily in order to make the Brotherhood a distribution agency for the *Messenger*, the profits from which went into his own pockets.[141]

Union officials claimed that Randolph's magazine had been one of the major factors causing New York porters to choose him to lead their movement. Randolph did use members of the Brotherhood to sell the magazine, but the *Messenger* was in financial difficulty all during the time that it served as the BSCP's official organ. On several occasions, the magazine's financial problems compelled Randolph to appeal to the Garland Fund for subsidies and loans to continue publication.[142] Ran-

[139] APR to JWJ, Feb. 1, 1926, NAACP Pas, C413, LC.

[140] Chicago *Defender*, Jan. 23, 1926.

[141] *Ibid*. A point to keep in mind is that personal jealously might have motivated Mays's actions. In 1924 he had tried to organize porters, only to be undercut by an ERP wage conference. He conceivably could have wished to get rid of APR and assume leadership of the organization himself. This could explain his claim that MPW and others in Chicago wanted to "take the whole works out of Randolph's hands."

[142] American Fund for Public Service, *Report of the Last Three Years*, 10.

dolph realized little, if any, profit from the *Messenger*, and he could easily have saved himself the necessity of explaining its relationship to the union had he placed the magazine under BSCP ownership.

Though Brotherhood leaders spent much of their time trying to minimize the effects of the Mays crisis, they did not allow the wage conference to occur without comment. After having decided not to face the company head-on over the conference, the union claimed credit for having forced Pullman to call it. Randolph asked porter representatives to the conference to make several demands of the company; if those demands were not met, they were to refuse to sign the agreement. His terms constituted the first systematic statement of the Brotherhood's program: a 240-hour month, rather than the approximately 400 hours currently in effect; a wage increase from $67.50 to $155 per month; conductors' pay for conductors' work; time-and-a-half pay for overtime; elimination of Filipinos hired in violation of seniority rules; pay for porters who reported for work and were not sent out; and the right of porters and maids to have their own union.[143] Neither Randolph nor other union leaders expected the company to agree to these demands, but the conference provided a forum for the union to publicize its grievances and announce its goals.

The ERP wage conference met during the first week of February, 1926, and came to agreement on work rules and wages. In addition to an increase in pay that brought starting wages from $67.50 to $72.50 per month, the company agreed to make changes in work rules which would result in less work and greater income for many porters. Work rule changes included extra pay for individuals whose trains arrived late at their destinations, and a reduction in the number of runs required of porters without time off.[144] The concessions made important differences in the porters' working conditions; as the BSCP had anticipated, Pullman sought to use the conference to destroy the Brotherhood and gain support among the porters for the ERP. After the parties signed the agreement, the company released a statement with the blaring headline "GRANT PORTERS MILLION RAISE." Several papers, notably the *Defender*, carried the story without comment. At least one writer pointed out that such announcements stood to harm the porters because the

[143] *Messenger*, VIII (Feb., 1926), 45.
[144] *Pullman News* (Mar., 1926), 357.

public, believing the porters were paid good wages, would cut back on tips.[145]

After having claimed credit for forcing the company to call the conference, the BSCP found itself in the position of having to discredit the results of the meeting. The Brotherhood argued that the porters were disgusted with the agreement and that it would serve only to cause more of them to join the union.[146] Furthermore, the agreement was invalid because two porters at the conference refused to sign it.[147] The NAACP supported the BSCP's interpretation of the events and advised Randolph to be satisfied with having caused the company to act.[148] Agreeing that the BSCP had forced the conference, the *Courier* told porters that they should recognize the union's importance and join it, so it could continue to improve their conditions.[149]

The results of the conference had a somewhat mixed reception. James Sexton, chairman of the porters' group at the meeting, wrote that the agreement was the best the porters could expect. He reported that management allowed long and frank discussion on all subjects, and even made its books available to the porters so they might see the company's financial difficulties. Sexton dismissed Randolph's allegation of widespread dissatisfaction among the porter representatives and contended that only two members of the group had been dissatisfied. Their disquiet stemmed from the fact that the pay increase had not been as large as they had hoped.[150] Praising the company for the courtesy with which it had treated the porter representatives, Sexton said, "The impression of your fairness in dealing with us has been such that we will never forget it."[151]

The Brotherhood thus had reached a major plateau by March, 1926. Although it responded indecisively to the ERP and the wage conference, the company had called the meeting to mollify grievances raised by the union. The BSCP had also dealt effectively with much of its black

[145] Chicago *Defender*, Feb. 13, 1926; Ben Stolberg, "Pullman Peons," *The Nation*, CXXII (Apr. 7, 1926), 366.

[146] Price to Lancaster, Feb. 8, 1926, BSCP ChiPa.

[147] The ERP required unanimous consent of porter delegates for an agreement to become effective. Two BSCP men had gotten elected to the conference and refused to sign the compact.

[148] Walter White to APR, Feb. 18, 1926, NAACP Pas, C414, LC; Pittsburgh *Courier*, Feb. 27, 1926.

[149] *Messenger*, VIII (Mar., 1926), 68.

[150] Chicago *Defender*, Feb. 13, 1926.

[151] *Pullman News* (Mar., 1926), 357.

opposition. The resolve and hard work required of the leaders to present a united front against the Howards, Chisums, Mayses, and hostile newspapers — to say nothing of Pullman — had created a bond among them. The Brotherhood had survived the public crises of its turbulent birth and was now ready to grow in size and strength.

CHAPTER III

A Year of Trial

> In all their organizational work the officials of the Porters' Union keep this issue constantly to the fore. It has been claimed that the black man is unorganizable. Again and again unscrupulous corporations have recruited from his ranks the "scab" labor which breaks or tries to break, a strike of white workers. . . . If the porters can organize their industry, hold their ranks, prove their fighting ability in the interest of the working class, it will have a profound effect on the attitude of white organized labor. And it will have a profound effect upon the organizable capacity of Negro workers in other industries. These men who punch our pillows and shine our shoes and stow our bags under the seat bear in their hands no little of the responsibility for the industrial future of their race.
>
> —*The Nation,* CXXII (June 9, 1926)

By the spring of 1926 the BSCP presented itself to the public as an organization that had effectively countered much of the opposition among black spokesmen and apparently was on the way to rapid success. The membership shared the leaders' optimism; they were convinced that their cause was just and that their efforts would result only in victory. This public expression of optimism, the union's militancy, and its developing strength contradicted the American public's stereotype of black porters as obsequious and infinitely good natured. So striking and clear-cut had the new image become in some quarters that the *Courier* called the porters' movement the "most important economic movement" going among black people. This paper, which previously had castigated the porters for their lack of manliness, now noted a change in their countenance and outlook on life. Because of the establishment of the BSCP, the *Courier* said, many porters had begun to see themselves as important human beings who could effectively participate in determining the direction of their lives.[1] By the end of 1926, the union of the guardians of the American traveling public would be strong enough to bring action against the Pullman Company.

Renewed support by the Garland Fund, which resulted in significant

[1] Pittsburgh *Courier*, Jan. 2, May 5, 1926.

improvement in the Brotherhood's financial condition, enhanced the sense of militancy and optimism which the union exhibited in 1926. Early in January of that year Randolph and Lancaster asked the Fund to give the BSCP the substantial sum of $29,000 to help support the union. They wanted $14,000 for organizing, $12,000 for propaganda, and $3,000 for economic research. Appealing in the name of the "most important move to organize Negro workers that has ever been made in this country," Randolph and Lancaster requested that the Fund set aside $3,000 explicitly for the *Messenger*.[2] The Fund responded with remarkable dispatch, and within a few days decided to award the BSCP $10,000. It set aside $3,000 for the survey of working conditions among porters, with the remainder to be given to the union as problems arose.[3]

Union activities had also brought increased stature to BSCP leaders, both among porters and with the general public. At least one porter already considered Randolph the dominant black man in the country, a person at least as important in history as Booker T. Washington. The porter prophesied that the Brotherhood would stand as a monument to Randolph's organizing abilities "to a greater extent than Tuskegee stands to the undisputed genius of Booker T. Washington." History, he said, would surely judge Randolph to be the "biggest man of this half century."[4] The Philadelphia Sesqui-Centennial Commission gave some credence to this estimate of Randolph's importance when it invited him to share the platform with the U.S. secretary of state, among others, at the official opening ceremonies of the Sesqui-Centennial celebration. Under the grandiose title, "Orator of the Day for the Negro Race of the World," Randolph spoke on behalf of all black citizens. Although the press, black and white, took little notice of the occasion — even the *Courier* barely mentioned the event — Randolph himself attached great significance to the invitation. He felt that it represented a new direction as far as understanding between blacks and whites, since the Commission had invited him, "a New Negro," rather than the usual "hidebound conservatives of the Russell-Moton type or the Emmett Scott group."[5]

[2] APR and Roy Lancaster to Flynn, Jan. 6, 1926, Garland Fund Pas.

[3] JWJ to Flynn, Jan. 7, 1926, *ibid*.

[4] George A. Price, "The New Leadership," *Messenger*, VIII (June, 1926), 168; Price to Lancaster, May 29, 1926, BSCP ChiPa. First quote is from *Messenger* article; second, from letter.

[5] APR to MPW, May 26, 1926, BSCP ChiPa.

In fact, this was undoubtedly the first time that a black spokesman before a popular audience had presented a major address on an economic interpretation of the problems besetting blacks, a statement that placed the remedy in the hands of workers themselves. Discarding any idea of black inferiority, Randolph told his audience that "in American social relations, [blacks would in the future] insist upon equality, upon being recognized as the social equals of any man regardless of color."[6] The achievement of peace between labor and capital, and the participation of blacks in the gains of labor, were just as important as peace between races and nations. The "continuance of modern civilization" depended on meeting those challenges. Protesters from the Ku Klux Klan heckled his speech and tried to prevent Randolph from finishing, but he persevered.[7]

Randolph believed that with this speech he had become a national figure. His audience now exceeded the intellectuals around the *Messenger*, extending instead to all levels of American society, black and white. Some people at Pullman apparently shared his opinion. In fact, Randolph's name had become almost synonymous with the BSCP; Pullman officials recognized that if the union would be stopped, Randolph must be totally discredited. The first major attempt to accomplish that end came in the spring of 1926, in the form of a suit for libel and criminal conspiracy brought by the Chicago *Whip*. Charging that Chandler Owen had maliciously misrepresented the paper in "The Neglected Truth," a series of articles the *Messenger* had run in response to *Whip* attacks on the Brotherhood, the *Whip* sought punitive action against both Owen and his partner and co-editor, Randolph.[8] The *Whip*, with aid of Pullman attorneys, secured from a Chicago grand jury an indictment of Owen and Randolph for conspiracy to commit libel.[9] Randolph termed the indictment "Pullman propaganda purely and simply," and claimed that the action against himself merely represented an attack against the union. Discounting the threat of jail and placing the union and its future above himself, the embattled leader exhorted his followers to stand fast

[6] *Messenger*, VIII (July, 1926); Pittsburgh *Courier*, June 12, 1926. For a similar expression of the views Randolph put forth, see Abram L. Harris, "The Negro and Economic Radicalism," *Modern Quarterly*, II (1924-25), 198-208.

[7] Roland Gibson, "The New Negro," *The World Tomorrow*, X (Feb., 1927), 81-82.

[8] It should be borne in mind that Owen maintained only a formal relationship with the *Messenger* after he moved to Chicago in 1923. See the preceding chapter.

[9] Owen and APR to Walter White, Apr. 7, 1926, NAACP Pas, C413, LC.

at this moment of crisis. He reminded them that the Brotherhood could not expect success to come easily, but must be prepared to "sail through bloody seas," and proclaimed that the union would continue to progress even if he were removed.[10]

In their effort to secure legal counsel, Randolph and Owen appealed to the NAACP. Both men realized that the Association would be reluctant to participate in a case between blacks because such participation would set an unpopular and troublesome precedent. Accordingly, they insisted that it was not a case between blacks; the Pullman Company was responsible for the suit and had used the *Whip* as an intermediary only in order to keep itself out of the public eye. The co-editors supported their claims by saying that the Chicago associate state's attorney had informed them that the grand jury brought the indictment only after a Pullman Company attorney appeared before that body and requested that it do so.[11] They did not make clear, however, whether the attorney appeared as representative for the company or for the *Whip*. To them there was no difference; his very presence justified their allegation. Although the NAACP's assistant secretary Walter White initially raised their hopes by requesting that Randolph and Owen supply further information upon which to justify intervention, the BSCP's expectations of NAACP support were quickly dashed.[12] Within three days James Weldon Johnson vetoed White's overture of aid. He informed Owen that the libel case was outside the scope of the Association's work and told him frankly that he could expect no help from that organization.[13]

The NAACP's refusal to support Randolph and Owen deprived them of the publicity which such support would have brought, but they did win their case. When the *Whip* could not substantiate its charges, especially those of conspiracy, the judge dismissed the suit without sending it to the jury. Randolph and his associates counted this a signal victory since the Pullman Company — and not the *Whip* — was their real opponent.[14]

The libel suit raised an interesting but elusive question about expenditure of BSCP funds. After the case had been settled, Owen, who had paid almost all the expense for the defense, appealed to Randolph to

[10] *Messenger*, VIII (Apr., 1926), 114.
[11] Owen and APR to White, Apr. 7, 1926, NAACP Pas, C413, LC.
[12] White to Owen, Apr. 9, 1926, *ibid*.
[13] JWJ to Owen, Apr. 12, 1926, *ibid*.
[14] *Messenger*, VIII (June, 1926), 177.

share some of the financial burden. When Randolph failed to comply, Owen turned to the union's Chicago division for help, maintaining that since Randolph had been brought into the suit solely to damage the union, the BSCP should assume some of the financial responsibility (amounting to $2,000, of which the union had paid only $100).[15] In answer to Owen's pleas for help in meeting his pressing debts, Randolph told him, through John Mills, that the Brotherhood would pay him something from time to time, "as it finds it convenient" to do so, pointing out that the BSCP was short of money and intended to spend what it had conservatively.[16] Strangely, Randolph's letter to Mills, outlining the union's financial straits and refusing to give Owen's request further consideration, came more than a month after the Garland Fund had granted the BSCP permission to use $1,000 of its grant for defense in the *Whip* case.[17] Apparently the money was not spent for the purpose for which it was intended.

While the *Whip* incident unfolded, numerous porters continued to show deep loyalty to the company and ERP, demonstrating an attitude of apathy toward the Brotherhood and satisfaction with the company union. The Brotherhood responded with a two-pronged attack; it undertook overt efforts to discredit the ERP among porters and geared its organizational efforts toward enrolling enough porters to gain support from federal agencies in its bid to gain recognition as the bargaining agent for porters and maids.

[15] Owen to Chicago BSCP, Aug. 10, 1926, BSCP ChiPa.

[16] APR to John Mills, Aug. 12, 1926, *ibid*.

[17] Telegram, JWJ to Flynn, June 29, 1926; Anna Marnitz to H. H. Broach, July 1, 1926; Asst. Treasurer of the Garland Fund to Lancaster, July 14, 1926; all in Garland Fund Pas. Owen's request for aid in meeting expenses for the suit as much as a month later raises numerous questions, and points up the grave difficulty which the papers missing from BSCP Headquarters for the years before 1940 cause for scholars of the Brotherhood. We cannot determine what happened to the $1,000. It might be that there were expenses connected with the case other than those Owen mentioned, and that the BSCP spent its money on the unnamed group. If so, APR did not inform Chicago, or (apparently) Owen, of the existence of other expenses. As a matter of fact, Chicago did not know that the Garland Fund had made the original grant. It is likely that APR decided, after receiving permission to use the $1,000, that the BSCP had other financial responsibilities more pressing than the *Whip* case, and spent the money for other purposes. But we would like to know that, too. The Garland Fund had already noted APR's tendency to make expenditures of monies for purposes other than those for which they originally had been appropriated. To remedy this situation, the Fund established a subcommittee of the board of directors, composed of JWJ and H. H. Broach of the Brotherhood of Electrical Engineers, to pass on expenditure of Garland Fund monies given to the BSCP.

In May, 1926, President Calvin Coolidge signed the Watson-Parker Act that had been the center of the debate between Randolph and Mays during late 1925. Despite the fact that it contained no provisions to force disputing parties to submit to arbitration and did not adequately explain the standing of company unions, BSCP officials, particularly Randolph, saw Watson-Parker as the vehicle through which the Brotherhood would end the system of company unionism at Pullman and establish the BSCP as legal representative of the porters and maids. Displaying his faith in "justice and fair play," Randolph told the porters that passage of the Watson-Parker Act, which Pullman and other railroad companies supported, meant that leaders of both industry and labor recognized the principle of collective bargaining and the right of workers to choose their own organizations. He could see no way by which Pullman could continue to oppose the BSCP when the company had endorsed Watson-Parker. Brotherhood organizers should make every effort to bring in enough porters for the union to qualify for an appeal to the Mediation Board. Randolph told his colleagues and union members that the BSCP would be one of the first unions to go before the new Mediation Board.[18]

The Brotherhood was fortunate that this elementary appraisal was not the union's official policy, but instead represented a combination of Randolph's rhetoric and his desire to maintain interest among the porters. During the BSCP's first few months, Randolph had recruited a battery of technical experts to advise the Brotherhood on legal matters. Mainly on the advice of one of these individuals, Donald R. Richberg, a leading railroad labor attorney and one of the experts who had provided technical assistance to the drafters of Watson-Parker, the BSCP had determined that it was in its best interest to allow one of the larger and more experienced unions to make the first test of the new law. Richberg argued that such a test would provide opportunity for the inexperienced Brotherhood to observe the new board's procedure, and pointed out that one of the established unions would be in a better position to extract favorable precedents from the board. Rather than rush into negotiations with the board and Pullman, Richberg suggested that the BSCP should busy itself with signing up porters and collecting data on wages and working conditions of its members so that, when the time came, its case could be based on solid data rather than on allegations.[19]

[18] *Messenger*, VIII (June, 1926), 186.
[19] *Ibid*. (July, 1926), 217.

Randolph's July announcement in the *Messenger* that he would abide by Richberg's advice did not please many porters who had looked forward to the day when the union would take definite action against the Pullman Company; they saw this as a delaying tactic on the part of the leadership. But the fact is that the BSCP had not intended to take action during the spring. As early as January, 1926, the Brotherhood had asked the Garland Fund for money to finance a survey of porters' working conditions,[20] the very action Richberg later suggested, and Randolph had announced in April that the union was contracting with Labor Bureau, Inc., of New York to conduct the investigation.[21] Apparently BSCP officials announced that the union would move immediately only in order to maintain interest among its members, many of whom longed for the union to take some action. In any event, the labor survey, made public in September, enhanced the BSCP's reputation by providing facts to support its allegations, giving the union an image of responsibility and professionalism. Randolph published the data in a pamphlet, *The Pullman Porter*, which received wide circulation.

The Brotherhood's preparation for an appeal to the Mediation Board, occurring simultaneously with the argument over payment of the *Whip* defense fund, taxed the union's organizational structure. Together they suggest that the public image of optimism and impending success which the union enjoyed did not altogether comport with reality. In fact, the Brotherhood's position was not nearly as strong as it appeared. That the BSCP's internal operations did not run smoothly during its first year was hardly unusual, since any new organization is likely to experience growing pains. The limited experience and inadequate training of BSCP leaders in union matters compounded the normal difficulties. Furthermore, these men, most of whom had just come to know each other, faced fearful handicaps in trying to organize a group of workers as large as the porters, scattered throughout the country and largely unfamiliar with principles of organized labor. The situation did not permit the use of simple organizing techniques. The immediate task was to complete the work of creating a national union so the organizers could present a united front. To accomplish this, leaders had to end the animosity and distrust that existed between New York and district offices, especially Chicago.

General officers at New York caused most of the discontent and difficulty through their efforts to keep control of the organization in their

[20] APR to Flynn, Jan. 6, 1926, Garland Fund Pas.

[21] *Messenger*, VIII (Apr., 1926), 123.

hands. One of the officers, Roy Lancaster, had through his job as secretary-treasurer attained a position of power which he was determined to keep. Lancaster particularly feared the growing importance of the Chicago division. As early as December, 1925, he attempted to insure that Chicago members looked to New York for leadership rather than to Webster and his associates.[22] To carry out his plan, Lancaster withheld from Chicago headquarters the names of porters who had joined the union during Randolph's organizing tour through the Midwest in October, 1925.[23] Lancaster reasoned that if he required new recruits to report directly to New York, he could prevent Webster and others from gaining much influence among them. He presented his scheme in terms of consideration of the welfare of the organization, explaining that he did not send the names to Chicago because he did not want them to fall into Pullman's hands. George Price, secretary-treasurer at Chicago, responded that the names Lancaster held were no more sacred than those of men who had joined the union directly at Chicago, and so far none of those had turned up in the possession of Pullman agents.[24] Under continued pressure, Lancaster eventually agreed to provide Chicago organizers with names of those porters who belonged to their district.

Many people, including some members of the Chicago group, considered Lancaster the second most important BSCP leader during the early days. Price at one time even suggested that Lancaster was more important to the movement's future than Randolph.[25] But this opinion was short-lived, as Lancaster's vanity surfaced in condescending comments to the field organizers; for example, he once assured Webster that he had "the utmost confidence" in him.[26] But the abuse went even further. After reading one of Lancaster's letters, Price exploded that he did not like what he had read "worth a damn," and added that some of

[22] Lancaster to Price, Jan. 20, 1926, BSCP ChiPa.

[23] Price to Lancaster, Jan. 2, 1926, *ibid.*

[24] See numerous letters, Price to Lancaster, Lancaster to Price, Jan.-Apr. 1926, *passim*, *ibid.*

[25] Price to Lancaster, Nov. 9, 1925, *ibid.* Price's comment must be kept in context. He possibly expressed many porters' strong view that Lancaster, an ex-porter, would have greater credibility among the porters than would Randolph. In another letter to Lancaster, in which Price commented on APR's physical condition, he wrote, "I fear that if we lose [Randolph] we lose the cause." This was also the same Price who called Randolph the "biggest man of this half century."

[26] Lancaster to Price, Jan. 20, 1926, *ibid.*

Lancaster's letters were "actually insulting."[27] Such episodes, however petty, were significant partly because of Lancaster's important position in the organization. They also say much about how the New York office treated districts less able to stand up for themselves than Chicago. Under the circumstances, it is not surprising that the Brotherhood experienced difficulties in enrolling members.[28]

The annoyances stirred by Lancaster were symptomatic of a deeper dissension within the union. At the root of the problem was the fact that the small group of men in New York who made decisions for the Brotherhood — Randolph, Des Verney, Lancaster, and Crosswaith — often did so without consulting leaders in the field. Their failure to solicit other points of view on policy and their refusal to keep district leaders informed on financial matters caused those outside the city to see the New York leadership as a self-centered group who assumed a higher knowledge of union affairs, and heightened hostilities already caused by New Yorkers holding all national offices. Two examples will illustrate how little input came from people outside the New York office and how little information headquarters gave out. When the Chicago leaders saw the BSCP constitution and by-laws, the document was already a finished product. They had been given no opportunity to offer suggestions for deletions or changes, and even ratified it by mail.[29] When Chicago leaders prepared to celebrate the BSCP's first anniversary, they had to write to New York to find out what date they should honor.[30]

Some of the major unilateral decisions made by the general officers suggested basic differences between them and others, particularly Milton Webster, over the union's methods. Under Randolph's dominance, the New York leaders believed that the union could attain its goals by indirect means. Placing vast faith in the idea that public pressure and government agencies would cause the Pullman Company to accede to their demands, they spent much time asking groups to offer endorsements or lining up citizens to sign petitions on the union's behalf.

[27] Price to Lancaster, Feb. 27, 1926; Price to Lancaster, Lancaster to Price, Jan.-Apr., 1926, *passim*, *ibid*.

[28] Except for a sprinkling of items from Oakland, there is no correspondence between New York and districts other than Chicago. But Chicago correspondence shows that the New York office treated other districts at least as badly as it did Chicago. Other district organizers often appealed to Webster at Chicago for aid and/or intercession with New York on problems.

[29] MPW to APR, May 15, 1926, BSCP ChiPa.

[30] MPW to APR, Aug. 2, 1926, *ibid*.

Webster, a gruff, practical man, believed the porters' future as an organized body of workers lay in their own efforts. Though he agreed that the young union might need government protection, he insisted that in the end the porters' success would depend upon their ability to force concessions from Pullman in the event legal efforts failed. He wanted his colleagues to spend more time in the streets organizing porters and less on speaking tours organizing the public. For all his practicality, however, Webster agreed with the New York group on one important matter: he, too, saw the future of black people in the United States as intricately tied to the general trade union movement.

Mounting disgruntlement of division leaders, and problems which the union experienced in recruiting members and maintaining itself, were probably instrumental in bringing about a change of attitude on the part of the general officers that came in 1926. The union's Western Branch, centered at Oakland, suffered because of the unpopularity of the local secretary-treasurer and because of organizer Dad Moore's inability to disseminate union propaganda effectively, mainly because of his advanced age.[31] At the same time the union was in danger of losing some of its key men; George Price, at Chicago, threatened to leave unless he received a pay raise.[32] The first evidence of a major change in policy came on August 20, 1926, when the New York office solicited views of the several district leaders on a wage-scale demand which the union would present to the company when it initiated negotiations.[33] The next day Randolph announced the creation of a National Advisory Committee composed of the chairmen of the several district organizing committees, thus extending the involvement of non–New Yorkers in the policy-making procedure.[34] Though the committee never achieved real influence, the important point is that many of the men so ''honored'' believed they would have a voice in determining the union's course. They saw creation of the advisory board as a progressive move and immediately concerned themselves more with the union's future.[35] The

[31] MPW to APR, June 5, 1926, *ibid*.

[32] APR to MPW, Aug. 17, 1926, *ibid*.

[33] APR to John Mills, Aug. 20, 1926, *ibid*.

[34] APR to Mills, Aug. 21, 1926, *ibid*. This was a strange announcement. BSCP bylaws provide for an advisory committee within the union's structure. The problem is that the bylaws are undated; thus we cannot determine if the provision for the advisory committee came before APR's announcement, or if it was added after the committee became part of the organizational structure.

[35] Mills to APR, Sept. 7, 1926, *ibid*.

fact is that the problems of continued exclusion of non–New Yorkers had forced Randolph to extend participation in the union without loosening control over it. Randolph thereby demonstrated effective leadership, because the decision came at a crucial time and probably forestalled many additional problems the infant union could hardly afford.

Randolph's change of stance developed mutual trust and friendship between himself and other BSCP leaders around the country. Most important in this regard was the relationship that developed between Randolph and Webster during mid-1926. Because of Randolph's skills at bringing in outside support and Webster's abilities at organizing porters — especially in the all-important Chicago district — the union's hopes rested largely with these two men. Thus it was imperative that they work together. The two were very different; Randolph was haughty and aloof, whereas Webster was much more down to earth. One contemporary observed of Randolph that he was a man "of no common clay," adding that most Brotherhood leaders did not feel at ease with him.[36] Webster, on the other hand, was an unpretentious, direct, gruff individual who met others easily and was easy to know. But however different their personalities, they did agree on the most fundamental point: the Pullman porters must have a union. They harnessed their energies to improve the conditions of that group of workers, and hoped thereby to set an example others could follow so that all black workers would know the advantages of organization.

That Randolph and Webster, men so unalike — the philosopher and the practical organizer — could find a meeting of minds, or at least of spirits, and agree to disagree, was the single most important development of the union's first year. The movement's two most dynamic leaders were positioned side by side. Randolph could continue to carry the porters' message to the public and to serve as a moral leader for the ranks, while Webster pushed the day-to-day operations of increasing the union's membership in hostile Chicago. Webster actually was a prototype, and throughout the country other BSCP organizers also demonstrated deep loyalty to Randolph and the cause. However, they continued to raise questions about policy and strategy. These developments permitted Randolph to function as a symbolic leader.

Efforts to increase BSCP membership caused the first serious policy debate between Randolph and Webster and underlined the different

[36] Murray Kempton, *Part of Our Time: Some Ruins and Monuments of the Thirties* (New York: Simon and Schuster, 1955), 246-47.

tactics which the two men considered necessary to succeed in their conflict with Pullman. Randolph believed that the union's chances of success depended upon the number of men it could publicly claim as members, whether they paid dues or not, whereas Webster insisted that the BSCP must base its hopes on strong, dedicated members who supported the union by paying dues and assessments. The difference stemmed from the fact that Randolph believed the union needed only to present the Mediation Board with membership lists including the names of a majority of the porters and maids in the employ of Pullman and the board would certify the Brotherhood as the official representative of those classes of workers. Thus, though the union's official policy was that all new members were required to pay back dues to August, 1925, in order to share the financial burden, in May, 1926, Randolph unilaterally decided to exempt from back dues those porters who would join the BSCP during a thirty-day dispensation on dues and initiation fees. Webster objected, arguing that the policy would be an admission of weakness and of inability of the union to enroll porters on a legitimate basis; he further stated that it would be unfair to the porters who had already anted up their money to allow others into the union without an equivalent sacrifice. Moreover, such new men would not be truly dedicated union members and were likely to leave just as quickly and easily as they had come.[37] Overriding Webster's objections, Randolph instituted the dispensation as he had planned, and even extended it for thirty additional days, through both June and July. For additional persuasion, Randolph told the porters that the initiation fee would be ten dollars, instead of five, after the dispensation period expired.[38] Though Webster disagreed with the philosophy behind the dispensation, he showed himself to be a good organization man and supported the policy.

Randolph's dispensation policy apparently caused porters to sign up at a quicker rate, for when the union prepared to go before the Mediation Board in September, Randolph proposed another dispensation. On this occasion he consulted Webster on the matter before the union promulgated it as official policy, attempting to disarm Webster's objections. Randolph pointed out that the action could not be taken as evidence of union weakness, since it would come simultaneously with the institution of litigation against the company. Placing his personal prestige behind this call for a second dispensation of initiation fees and back dues,

[37] APR to MPW, June 1, 1926, BSCP ChiPa.
[38] *Messenger*, VIII (Aug., 1926), 258.

Randolph wrote Webster that "it is my wish that it be carried forward with utmost vigor and efficiency."[39] A second dispensation was more than Webster could accept. He heatedly disagreed with Randolph's reasoning and informed his colleague that the initiation fee was not the only thing keeping porters out of the Brotherhood. Webster suggested that many more men would join if they could see that the union was making some progress toward achieving its goals. He told Randolph that many of the Brotherhood's oldest and most responsible members had informed him that they had no intention of paying any more money to the union until they saw some signs of activity, and maintained that the increased membership that would result from another dispensation would not "offset the damage which would be done to the morale of our present membership which we have had so hard a time bringing up."[40] Although Randolph refused to agree with Webster's objections to the dispensation, he decided to go along with him on this occasion, and the BSCP did not institute a dispensation in September, 1926.[41]

Though the dispensation debate raised important questions about the union's tactics and strategy, the larger importance of the whole affair for the BSCP lay in the fact that this was the first time Webster had his way over Randolph on a major matter of policy and pointed up how much Randolph valued Webster's work in Chicago. From a point of pure constitutional power, Randolph could have promulgated any policy he desired without paying attention to Webster's objections. District organizers fell under Randolph's direct supervision; indeed, Randolph could have fired Webster.[42] But instead, the dispensation dispute ended by placing the two men on a footing of equality which had not formerly existed — and still did not, in constitutional terms — thus making the exchange of ideas between them much easier and smoother.

Though Randolph was determined to maintain a close working relationship with his indispensable colleague in Chicago, he was equally determined to increase BSCP membership. He considered dispensations as the best vehicle for expanding membership lists, and when he decided to call for another one in December, 1926, he accepted no objections, though he discussed it with Webster in advance. Admitting the Brotherhood's current weakness, Randolph argued that the BSCP could not

[39] APR to MPW, Sept. 13, 1926, BSCP ChiPa.
[40] MPW to APR, Sept. 16, 1926, *ibid*.
[41] APR to MPW, Sept. 20, 1926, *ibid*.
[42] BSCP constitution and bylaws, copy *ibid*.

afford to keep any porter out until it gained control of the industry and could require all porters to join the union.[43] Webster, of course, agreed with this analysis, but the two men had different ideas about the meaning of strength. Webster did not believe that a paper organization could ever effect a settlement from Pullman. Showing more concern for the need of dedicated members than did Randolph, Webster asserted that the disadvantages and confusion caused by dispensations outweighed the benefits to be gained from merely adding new names to the rolls. But this time Randolph persisted and instituted the new dispensation for the beginning of 1927. Webster accepted defeat graciously and supported his chief.[44]

While wrestling with problems of strategy, organization, and personality, the BSCP was also busily engaged in its program of trying to convince the porters that the Brotherhood was the proper body to represent them in disputes with Pullman about wages and working conditions. The existence of Pullman's well-entrenched company union made the Brotherhood's task almost impossible. Thus the BSCP's first step was to try to discredit ERP among porters. In their effort to do so, union leaders argued on the one hand that the company did not believe porters would organize because they were black, and on the other hand charged that Pullman had attempted to buy off BSCP leaders.[45] They also alleged that the company's attitude toward the Brotherhood was an example of inbred American racism, since Pullman had allowed its white conductors to form a union independent of company control and had negotiated with that organization.[46] Their aversion to the ERP was not new, of course, but there was a difference in that now the BSCP took the offensive and constantly disputed the company's allegation that the ERP could represent the porters.

A major ploy used by the Brotherhood in trying to lure porters away from the ERP was appealing to them in the name of manhood and self-respect. As early as December, 1925, Randolph had warned porters that such an organization functioned purely in Pullman's interest because the company controlled its machinery. He likened the porters' position under ERP to that of a rat expecting justice from a jury of cats.[47]

[43] APR to MPW, Dec. 22, 1926, *ibid*.

[44] MPW to APR, Dec. 27, 1926, *ibid*.

[45] *Messenger*, VIII (Sept., 1926), 264; MPW to APR, Aug. 17, APR to MPW, Aug. 19, 1926, BSCP ChiPa.

[46] APR to MPW, Aug. 3, 1926, BSCP ChiPa.

[47] *Messenger*, VII (Dec., 1925), 383; VIII (Apr., 1926), 109.

BSCP leaders insisted that porters must be able to take pride in their work, and that such pride could come only when porters actively participated in determining working conditions. They emphasized that the ERP functioned only after grievances had occurred — and even then rarely — and that it had little to say in negotiating working conditions, while the goal of the BSCP was to give porters an equal voice with management in that regard. Should uncommitted porters throw in their lot with the BSCP, they would soon be better able to provide for their families and would have more time to spend at home with them. And the added dignity which came to them in being porters would make them more concerned about the kind of job they did, thus improving their level of efficiency.[48]

The Brotherhood believed that the Pullman Porters Beneficial Association (PPBA), the insurance and fraternal arm of the company union system, represented as great a threat to the success of the union as did the ERP. Randolph considered the two organizations simply "two wings of the same bird": both must be eliminated.[49] The BSCP did not wish to destroy the benefits which the PPBA afforded the porters; it simply wished to make those benefits a part of the union's activities. Realizing the attractiveness to the porters of the fraternal and insurance provisions of PPBA membership, the BSCP attacked the benevolent association on grounds of who controlled it, claiming for example that the PPBA treasurer could withdraw funds from the association's account only with the prior consent of the treasurer of the Pullman Company. According to Randolph and his colleagues, the fact that benevolent association leaders were ex-porters who now held soft jobs in the company as welfare workers or porter instructors (all of whom the Brotherhood classified as stool pigeons) should serve as evidence that the company used the PPBA as an instrument to control porters and keep them in line. The BSCP had some success in stirring up quarrels among PPBA leaders, but none of them joined the union, though some local PPBA men did.[50]

So strong was the hold of the PPBA on its members that even some strong BSCP porters, seeing no contradiction in supporting the union

[48] *Ibid.*, VIII (Apr., 1926), 109. In *ibid.* (July, 1926), 209, APR appealed to the public for support. In the same appeal he suggested that, if the porters raised their standards, Pullman would have less reason to object to the union.

[49] APR to Mills, Aug. 19, 1926, BSCP ChiPa.

[50] MPW to APR, Aug. 4, 1926, *ibid.*

and maintaining their connections with the benevolent association, protested BSCP attacks against the fraternal organization. In August, 1926, on the eve of the Beneficial Association's annual convention, Ashley Totten circulated anti-PPBA propaganda which John C. Mills, Webster's associate in Chicago, thought unwarranted. Mills complained to Randolph and warned the union's chief that actions like Totten's could permanently damage the union's chances of increasing its membership.[51] Appreciating the validity of Mills's warning, Randolph agreed that Totten's attack had gone farther than it should have, and promised that in the future the BSCP would not discuss the merits of the PPBA program but would confine its anti-PPBA propaganda solely to the issue of control. Randolph, recognizing that the Brotherhood could not hope to take over the Beneficial Association, proposed that the BSCP should instead create its own insurance and benevolent program in order to demonstrate to porters that the Brotherhood could provide precisely the same benefits as a company-sponsored plan.[52]

Aware of the company's superior position in the quest for the loyalty of porters, Pullman's management took the offensive to keep employees convinced that the ERP worked. Pullman also paid close attention to BSCP activities in order to be able to counteract any propaganda the union might put out.[53] The company wished to impress upon its employees that the Plan was their union (unlike the BSCP, which was an "outside organization"), and to that end management used every opportunity to discuss with porters the merits of the ERP. Brotherhood leaders anticipated that the company would try to counter BSCP attempts to influence porters to leave the ERP, even to the extent of increasing participation of porters in the company union, which of course Pullman did. Though some of the company's changes did bring positive gains to the porters, it is doubtful that there was any real increase in the porters' control of ERP. Nonetheless Randolph, discussing this matter with Webster, was forced to admit that in isolated cases the ERP did work for the porters, causing difficulties for the BSCP.[54]

Pullman took its most significant step in trying to change the image of

[51] Randolph responded to Mills's views in APR to Mills, Aug. 19, 1926, *ibid.*

[52] *Ibid.* Further development of this point suffers from the unavailability of New York papers. Correspondence between New York and Chicago refers to both a BSCP benefit plan and a credit union, but no details are available among BSCP ChiPa.

[53] MPW to APR, May 28, Sept. 3, 1926, *ibid.*

[54] APR to MPW, Aug. 16, 1926, *ibid.*

its company union when it promoted a porter to the Board of Industrial Relations, the ultimate authority in the ERP, in August, 1926.[55] Deeply disturbed, Brotherhood leaders believed the company's action would further dampen the porters' desire for another union and thus hinder the BSCP's progress. Unable to argue against the merits of the new action, Randolph and his colleagues attacked both the ERP and George Shannon, the man Pullman placed on the board. Charging that the move did not represent a substantive change for the porters, BSCP leaders claimed that this lone porter representative on the Board of Industrial Relations would be powerless, especially since he worked for the Pullman Company and could not be expected to oppose the company's wishes.[56]

Stepping up its initiative, the company did more than make administrative changes to demonstrate the Plan's effectiveness and set out to adjust grievances with porters on a wider and more systematic basis. At about the same time the company announced Shannon's promotion, the porters' ERP representatives from Seattle entered discussions with Pullman industrial relations representatives for the return to the Seattle district of two runs that had been transferred elsewhere; because of the transfer some Seattle men were out of work. The company agreed to return the lines, although BSCP officials maintained that the whole affair had been prearranged to impress the porters with the workability of the Plan.[57] Yet Pullman continued on its way and initiated an important new aspect in its handling of grievances in November, 1926: then, for the first time in the history of the ERP, the Board of Industrial Relations convened to hear porters' grievances. The Brotherhood immediately claimed credit for having forced the board to call the session and, working through John Mills in Chicago, successfully represented some porters in settling their difficulties with Pullman.[58] Despite the BSCP's claim, and its success in a few grievance cases, Pullman's action served only to raise the ERP's standing among the porters.

Brotherhood involvement with ERP grievance procedures placed the union in an uncomfortable position. On the one hand, the union wished to support porters' efforts to get fair hearings from existing mechanisms until it could establish itself as their official bargaining agent; on the

[55] APR to MPW and MPW to APR, both Aug. 2, 1926, *ibid*.; *Messenger*, VIII (Sept., 1926), 263.

[56] APR to MPW, Aug. 3, 11, 1926, BSCP ChiPa.

[57] MPW to APR, Aug. 14, 1926, *ibid*.

[58] MPW to APR, Nov. 10, 1926, *ibid*.

other hand, as Webster pointed out, the BSCP could not continue to oppose the ERP and still work within it.[59] To do so was counterproductive for the Brotherhood. The union might succeed in helping an occasional porter, but each time at the cost of bringing increased prestige to the company and the Plan. Webster recommended that the union instruct all BSCP members who held positions of responsibility in the ERP to resign immediately. Their resignations would decrease the possibility of successfully settling grievances in the porters' favor through the company union, but the Brotherhood would be placed on a higher and sounder moral level.[60]

Randolph agreed with Webster and instructed Brotherhood members to resign ERP positions,[61] suggesting that the BSCP continue to support porters who had grievances against the company, but in a different way. Randolph told his colleagues that on grievance matters the union should, after protesting to the company through letters (which he expected the company would ignore), organize mass demonstrations against Pullman to show public support for the union's position.[62] He recognized that the method might fail, but his recommendation foreshadowed the mass demonstrations which were to attract so much national attention later, and which he threatened to use against the government in 1941 during his March on Washington Movement. His proposal showed again how deeply Randolph believed in the efficacy of moral pressure as a way to force corporations or governments to change their policies when the public interest demanded change.[63]

By late fall and early winter of 1926, Pullman efforts to improve the porters' situation had improved the ERP's standing and had forced the BSCP onto the defensive. Nevertheless, the changes actually had come about largely in response to pressures posed by the union. Thus Pullman continued its efforts to ingratiate itself with the porters and initiated policies with which the union could not disagree. One such policy change came in October, when the company ended the long-standing and widely practiced custom of calling all porters ''George.'' On October 19, 1926, it announced that thereafter all Pullman cars would have

[59] MPW to APR, Oct. 19, 1926, *ibid*.
[60] MPW to APR, Nov. 10, 1926, *ibid*.
[61] APR to MPW, Nov. 12, 1926, *ibid*.
[62] APR to MPW, Nov. 19, 1926, *ibid*.
[63] Interview with APR, Jan.19, 1972.

the active porter's name displayed in a prominent place so that the passengers would know how to address him when he was needed. The company instructed porters that they were to answer only to their own names, and that Pullman would take no disciplinary actions against them for refusing to respond to "George."[64] The BSCP immediately claimed credit for this new departure, too, suggesting that porters should support the union in order to continue to improve their position in the company. It contended further that although company officials had instructed the public in the proper use of porters' names, they did not follow their own rules and continued to refer to porters as "George" or with other racial sobriquets.[65] The company reaped considerable gains from this innovation, even though passengers continued to call porters "Porter" and "George."

While locked in a public debate with Pullman over the merits of the ERP and the right of the Brotherhood of Sleeping Car Porters to represent porters, BSCP officials had also been preparing their case to go before the Mediation Board. The union collected data on wages and working conditions at Pullman, conducted a surreptitious referendum among porters on whether the BSCP should be their official representative in employee-management disputes, and appealed to the public for support. Still mindful of the importance of favorable public opinion, Randolph had his colleagues circulate petitions in several large cities in which citizens — alleged riders of sleeping cars — could note their endorsement of the BSCP. In his instructions Randolph pointed out that union leaders should concentrate on professional people when soliciting signatures, and he defended the petitioning process by saying it was in the union's interest to go to the board with evidence that citizens in every community favored the Brotherhood's "fight for economic justice."[66] Randolph's suggestion that his men should concentrate on getting professional people to sign the petitions raises an important question about his priorities. Some observers have argued that he had an insatiable desire for publicity, any sort of publicity, and could not distinguish between groups and individuals who had power and influ-

[64] Chicago *Defender*, Oct. 25, 1926.

[65] BSCP press release, Oct. 19, 1926, NAACP Pas, C413, LC. By 1933, APR included this change in Pullman's policy among the most important achievements of the BSCP to date. See Chicago *Defender*, Dec. 30, 1933.

[66] APR to MPW, Aug. 26, 31, 1926, BSCP ChiPa.

ence and those who did not.[67] Actually, Randolph recognized that the Mediation Board and Pullman would pay more attention to the views of influential individuals than to those of ordinary citizens. Far from failing to understand existing power relations, on this occasion Randolph astutely saw how outside influence could be used as a weapon to forward the porters' cause. This was an unorthodox tactic for a labor union to employ, but given the BSCP's unique characteristics, unorthodox solutions were more than warranted.

By the end of August this wide-ranging campaign had progressed to the point that Randolph informed his colleagues that the BSCP should be prepared to initiate legal action against Pullman by the middle of September.[68] Porters' response to the BSCP referendum had been heartening for the leaders of the young union: Randolph reported that a majority of the porters, contacted by undercover BSCP members on the cars and in Pullman yards, had endorsed the Brotherhood as their bargaining agent. Randolph decided that conditions were right to ask Pullman for a meeting and informed his district chiefs that he would send his first letter to the company on September 20.[69] He and his colleagues did not expect that the company would grant their request to meet with management on behalf of porters and maids. In all likelihood, the union did not even wish the company to consent to a meeting at that time, since the BSCP stood to gain more from public hearings before a government agency than from private sessions with Pullman officials. BSCP organizers were certain the Mediation Board would determine that, since a majority of the porters endorsed the Brotherhood as their representative, the Pullman Company should meet with the union to settle outstanding disputes; the board would then lend its services as mediator. Thus, the BSCP would correspond with Pullman, not in hopes of attaining a meeting, but simply to comply with the provisions of the Railway Labor Act of 1926 that required a union to seek to meet with the disputant company before it could appeal to the Mediation Board.[70]

On September 20, 1926, the letter went out, and the Brotherhood

[67] Sterling D. Spero and Abram L. Harris, *The Black Worker: The Negro Worker and the Labor Movement* (New York: Columbia University Press, 1931), 459.

[68] APR to MPW, Aug. 10, 30, 1926, BSCP ChiPa.

[69] Circular letter, APR to District Organizers, Sept. 17, 1926, *ibid*. The BSCP employed a variety of methods to conduct its referendum. In addition to direct contacts at work, numerous porters signed forms at district union headquarters. See variety of correspondence in BSCP ChiPa.

[70] Circular letter, APR to District Organizers, Aug. 30, 1926, *ibid*.

officially joined battle with the Pullman Company over the right of porters and maids to organize any union they chose, free of company control. In his letter Randolph emphasized that he wrote on authority granted by a majority of the porters and maids that the BSCP represent them on matters of grievances, wages, and working conditions; he assured President E. F. Carry that the Brotherhood intended to encourage "initiative, intelligence and responsibility to the end of . . . the building up and maintenance of a high standard of service."[71] Official BSCP correspondence claims that this request for a conference created a new wave of enthusiasm among BSCP membership and shocked company officials, who did not believe a group of blacks would take such a step.[72] Shocked or not, the company continued in its refusal to recognize the BSCP and predictably ignored the letter. When a second letter from Randolph to Carry of September 30 received the same fate, union officials determined that they had complied with the law and could now invoke the services of the federal Mediation Board. On October 15, 1926, the union applied to the Mediation Board for help.[73]

The BSCP's application to the Mediation Board stimulated even more porter interest in the union than the letters to Pullman. The Chicago office reported a marked increase in dues payment for the days immediately after announcement of the appeal, and Webster rejoiced that he could now interest a large number of previously indifferent men in the union's activities. Unfortunately, however, during the first year BSCP leaders had placed so much emphasis upon organizing as a collective bargaining unit to appear before the board that, consciously or not, they had led the ranks to believe that the Mediation Board would bring them immediate victory. Some leaders even thought they would win right away. Webster, for one, was confident that the board would recognize the BSCP, and he recommended to Randolph that the BSCP take the company to court the first time it attempted to coerce any porter to stay away from the union.[74]

Ostensibly ignoring the whole affair, the Pullman Company not only refused to submit to the union's request for a conference, but continued its efforts to convince the porters, and whatever government bodies

[71] APR to E. F. Carry, Sept. 20, 1926, in United States Mediation Board Case File #C-107, *Brotherhood of Sleeping Car Porters* v. *Pullman Company*, National Archives. Hereafter cited *BSCP* v. *PC*, NA.

[72] MPW to APR, Sept. 24, 1926, BSCP ChiPa.

[73] APR to U.S. Board of Mediation, Oct. 15, 1926, *BSCP* v. *PC*, NA; APR to MPW, n.d. [mid-Oct., 1926], BSCP ChiPa.

[74] MPW to APR, Oct. 21, 1926, BSCP ChiPa.

might inquire, that the ERP was the porters' official representative by their own choice, further announcing ERP elections for October-November, 1926. The company resumed the policy initiated as early as September, 1925, of putting all its responsible and better-known porters — including George Shannon of the Bureau of Industrial Relations and Perry Parker, chief official of the PPBA — into the field to influence porters to continue their loyalty to their employer.[75]

The BSCP promptly protested the elections and accused the company of using intimidation to force porters to vote for the ERP. After filing their bid to the Mediation Board, BSCP officials told union members and other porters that they could legally refuse to vote; if the company forced them to do so under threat of discharge, they should sign affidavits to that effect and submit them to BSCP headquarters so the union could bring the evidence to the attention of the Mediation Board.[76] In New York, porters took to picket lines at Pullman buildings and rail yards to show uncommitted porters that they had support for their refusal to vote for the company union.[77] All these efforts were ineffective. After the election, the company claimed that 85 percent of the employees had indicated their desire to stay in the ERP. Randolph and other BSCP officials maintained that the Plan had received such an endorsement only because of intimidation, and they dispatched signed affidavits to the Mediation Board so alleging.[78]

Meanwhile, the Mediation Board began its preliminary investigation of the BSCP-Pullman dispute. The board recognized that first it must determine which union represented the porters.[79] In order to examine the union's records, it dispatched board member Edwin P. Morrow, a former governor of Kentucky, to Chicago to consult with Brotherhood and Pullman officials.[80] Morrow, initially unimpressed with what he saw in Chicago, asked the BSCP for further documentation of its claims.[81] Randolph complied and produced additional data from the

[75] MPW to APR, Sept. 1, 1926, *ibid*.

[76] Circular letter, APR to District Organizers, Nov. 1, 1926, *ibid*.

[77] APR to MPW, Nov. 1, 1926, *ibid*.

[78] *Messenger*, VIII (Dec., 1926), 370. *BSCP* v. *PC*, NA, contains numerous statements by porters alleging intimidation and coercion by Pullman officials and others on the company's behalf. W. R. Estelle, who was involved with the Black Klan in Omaha, was particularly energetic in his efforts to line porters up to vote for the ERP in the election.

[79] MPW to APR, Dec. 2, 1926, BSCP ChiPa.

[80] APR to MPW, Nov. 26, 1926, *ibid*.

[81] MPW to APR, Dec. 2, 1926, *ibid*.

New York office.[82] Randolph's evidence convinced Morrow that the board should open a full investigation into the dispute. The BSCP had taken the first step toward gaining recognition as bargaining agent for porters and maids.

[82] APR to MPW, Dec. 2, 1926, *ibid*.

CHAPTER IV

A Quitter Never Wins

> We have every reason to believe that powerful interests other than the Pullman Company are watching the outcome of the porters' case as it involves the serious question of whether or not a Company Union, organized and controlled by the company can be recognized as the true and lawful spokesman of its employees, or whether the principle of self-organization of employees will be recognized and maintained. Fate has chosen the Pullman porters to be the instrument through which this important precedent will be set up.
>
> — Randolph in BSCP news release, Feb. 19, 1927

Instead of ushering in an era of respect and recognition, the BSCP's appeal to the United States Mediation Board in 1926 became the first of a series of major defeats over a two-year period which almost proved fatal to the young union. During those years the Brotherhood used every provision of the Watson-Parker Act in its attempt to gain recognition, even threatening a strike against Pullman. In its efforts to force the company to raise wages, the union also initiated a novel flanking tactic, appealing to the Interstate Commerce Commission to end tipping as a method of pay in Pullman service.

Brotherhood officials took their case before the Mediation Board with utmost seriousness. They believed they stood to help undermine the legality of company unions and that powerful labor interests were observing their action with keen interest.[1] BSCP leaders therefore endeavored to insure that they had substantial membership and sufficient funds with which to press the case. When Governor Edwin Morrow of the Mediation Board informed Randolph on February 14, 1927, that the board would have to make further investigations into the Brotherhood's membership rolls before it could decide whether to hear the case,[2] BSCP leaders were deeply disturbed. The fact is that while the union had registered impressive membership gains during the early months of 1927, most of the new members were not paying dues.

[1] BSCP news release, Feb. 19, 1927, NAACP Pas, C413, LC.

[2] Morrow to APR, Feb. 14, 1927, *ibid*.

Though the BSCP claimed a membership of 5,700, only 30 percent paid dues with regularity, while many others had not so much as paid initiation fees, having enrolled in the union under dispensation terms.[3] Indeed, the dispensation had been so successful from the viewpoint of sheer numbers that in April a new dispensation was initiated — this time at the suggestion of Webster, who had once been a major opponent of the method.[4] Still, Brotherhood leaders feared that the Mediation Board might not recognize as bona fide members those who did not pay dues; and indeed, Morrow suggested that the board did not believe that the BSCP had sufficient members to support its claim to represent the porters. He hinted that the board might find it necessary to administer an election among the porters to determine whether they preferred the Brotherhood or the ERP.[5]

The BSCP definitely did not want an election. For one thing, the union could ill afford the additional expenses which an election would entail.[6] Moreover, the organizers feared that an election would cause the public to question the accuracy of previous Brotherhood statements about its membership and bookkeeping. And there was the question whether the union could hold its members in a head-on fight with Pullman. Webster impressed upon Randolph the necessity of insisting that the union's signed membership forms should be sufficient evidence to show the board that porters preferred the BSCP to the ERP.[7]

BSCP leaders proved correct in wishing to prevent a possible election between the Brotherhood and the Pullman ERP because the company, employing a combination of conciliation and bribery, moved to insure an ERP victory in that eventuality. Pullman quickly complied with Watson-Parker regulations by establishing a labor adjustment board, and it then called a meeting of porters to discuss how the ERP could be made to work more efficiently.[8] To make good on its promise to improve matters for the porters, the company made conciliatory changes

[3] APR to MPW, Dec. 28, 1926, BSCP ChiPa; APR to Baldwin, Jan. 14, 1927, NUL Pas, LC.

[4] MPW to APR, Feb. 23, APR to MPW, Mar. 30, MPW to APR, Apr. 25, 1927. Randolph had ordered an indefinite extension of the dispensation in January. See APR to BSCP organizers, Jan. 21, 1927, all in BSCP ChiPa.

[5] Morrow to APR, Feb. 14, 1927, *ibid*.

[6] MPW to APR, Feb. 25, 1927, *ibid*.

[7] MPW to APR, Feb. 15, 1927, *ibid*.

[8] APR to MPW, Feb. 9, 1927, *ibid*. Unavailability of Pullman Company papers on these activities require that I rely on BSCP sources.

in working conditions — particularly in Chicago, where it eliminated preparatory time from some runs, saving affected porters as much as three hours per trip. The clear indication was that the porters could expect the practice to be extended to other districts if they refused to follow outside agitators. Pullman's generosity even included a promise to supply porters with shoe polish in the future.[9] According to Brotherhood sources, the company also instructed its agents to inform porters that they would receive an eighteen-dollar pay raise during the winter of 1927. Though Pullman agents denied that the BSCP had in any way influenced its decision to grant the raise, Brotherhood officials believed the company had used the offer of a wage increase as a bribe to insure porters' support of ERP.[10] Further, the BSCP accused the company of attempting to trick porters into designating the ERP as their representative, alleging that the company asked porters to sign blank forms which its agents later filled in with statements certifying the ERP as bargaining agent.[11] Finally, Pullman characteristically maintained its policy of having blacks speak to porters in support of the company's position, trotting out George Shannon of the Bureau of Industrial Relations to issue a statement along the company line in March, 1927.[12] Claiming that all this activity was evidence that the BSCP had killed the old ERP, Randolph and other BSCP leaders warned porters to be wary of deception in the company's actions and urged that they not allow Pullman to reinstitute the company union.[13]

Meanwhile, the Brotherhood was struggling to establish procedures by which it could present an effective stance before the Mediation Board. The need for direction became apparent soon after Morrow notified the BSCP of the possibility of an election. Some district organizers, particularly Totten in Kansas City, took his comments to mean that the decision to hold an election had in fact been made. In an apparent effort to prepare his men for the impending conflict, Totten circulated a bulletin advising them that they would soon be asked to vote. Webster, believing that it harmed the union's cause to broadcast such statements before a decision had been reached, was outraged; he demanded that

[9] MPW to APR, Mar. 23, 1927, *ibid.*

[10] MPW to APR, Feb. 15, MPW to APR, Feb. 16, 1927, *ibid.*

[11] MPW to APR, Feb. 18, 1927, *ibid.*

[12] Reprint of article in Chicago *Light and Heebie Jeebies*, Mar. 25, 1927, BSCP ChiPa.

[13] APR to MPW, Feb. 14, 1927, *ibid.*

Randolph recall Totten's circular.[14] Webster then raised a more important matter with Randolph: the Brotherhood could not continue to allow individual district leaders to prepare their own propaganda on such significant matters because erroneous, misleading, and sometimes contradictory statements resulted. He insisted that in the future Randolph maintain central control over publication of all major policy statements.[15] Randolph acquiesced in both Webster's understanding of the board's statement and his appraisal of the problems raised by Totten's circular, and recalled copies of the circular before they became too widely distributed. To Webster's delight, Randolph also agreed to give central direction to future publicity handouts.[16]

Yet the union's problems were not over. Though its leaders exuded confidence in their public statements, privately they feared that they might have trouble even maintaining the membership. There was widespread dissatisfaction and impatience among Brotherhood members over the snail-like pace at which BSCP's case was proceeding before the Mediation Board; a further decline in dues payments resulted. Brotherhood members had been led to believe that the governmental body would work instant magic and force the company to recognize the BSCP as their representative. Accordingly, Randolph was understandably exuberant when Morrow informed him in mid-April that the board would return to the Brotherhood's case the latter part of that month. He used this occasion to put out a circular exhorting porters to remain steadfast.[17] This information stimulated interest among the members and made it possible for the union to hold its own, although there is no evidence that it experienced an increase in membership or improvement in collection of dues.

The mediators finally got to the BSCP's case on May 5, 1927. Morrow, along with a Mediation Board statistician, came to Brotherhood headquarters to investigate the union's membership lists and financial figures in order to determine the merits of its claims. For three days the mediator and his assistant pored over the union's books; then, unable to make an immediate determination, they returned to Washington. Randolph, by now as impatient as the union's members for

[14] MPW to APR, Feb. 19, 1927, *ibid.*
[15] *Ibid.*
[16] Telegram, APR to MPW, Feb. 21, MPW to APR, Feb. 28, 1927, *ibid.*
[17] APR Circular Letter, Apr. 14, 1927, *ibid.*

a decision, followed the officials to Washington in order to lobby and to be on hand when the board reached a decision.[18]

When Randolph talked with board officials during his Washington visit, they refused to discuss the merits of the union's position on company unionism and insisted that their chief interest was in the number of members the BSCP had and the amount of dues porters paid.[19] Such comments disheartened Randolph because they again raised the possibility that the mediators might resubmit the matter to porters in the form of an election. Randolph still feared the result would be to deny the union a chance to have its case heard on its merits; given company activities among porters, the BSCP had little hope of winning an election. Luckily, the board continued the case until June.

During the weeks between the board's investigation and its return to the union's case, Randolph moved to attract public attention to the Mediation Board's involvement in the BSCP's case. On June 4 he addressed a long open letter to the Pullman Company, a copy of which went to the board, in which he attempted to dispel what he considered myths surrounding the Brotherhood, especially that the BSCP was an "outside organization" being imposed on the porters against their will. He emphasized that the Brotherhood had been founded by porters, was controlled by porters, and sought simply to improve conditions for porters, insisting also that the BSCP was neither communist nor socialist. In this partly conciliatory letter, Randolph gave much space to advantages which would accrue to the company through the union in the form of improved relations between porters and management. He affirmed the union's recognition of Pullman's right to demand certain standards of performance from its employees, and suggested that the BSCP would be in a better position than the ERP to guarantee maintenance of such standards. The fact of having their own union would, he averred, create a sense of belonging among porters and cause them to take a new pride in their work.

Although Randolph thus muted some of the BSCP's usual militancy, he could not pass up the opportunity to accuse the company of racism in its attitude toward porters and their efforts to organize independent of

[18] APR to MPW, May 10, 1927, *ibid.*

[19] In an earlier statement, John Marrinan to Henry Hunt, Apr. 6, 1926, *BSCP* v. *PC*, NA, the board had pointed out that the matter of representation was crucial in the BSCP-Pullman case. This did not say, of course, that the board would not recognize the company union should it win in an election among porters.

company control and supervision. He pointed out that white conductors already had such a union with which the company negotiated, and he questioned the consistency in recognizing one union and refusing to deal with another. He also told the company that it was ignorant of the changed mentality and feeling of manhood among porters presently employed in Pullman service. Just as the company's rolling stock had improved over the years, so had the minds of porters. The company needed the Brotherhood to give it a clear picture of the men in its employ because management, being white, could not possibly understand black porters. According to Randolph, blacks to whom Pullman officials turned for information about porters, and about black people in general, gave out only what information they thought their benefactors wanted to hear.[20]

No company official or member of the Board of Directors answered Randolph's letter, though private company memoranda show that they read it. One such memorandum said Randolph was right in his belief that the company recognized a racial difference among its employees, especially on the matter of wages, and that Pullman purposely intended to maintain the differential. The important consideration from the company's point of view was that porters earned more than blacks in many other industries. Repeating the theme developed earlier by the *Argus*, one company official wrote that Randolph understood "no comparison between the wages and working conditions of Negroes in Pullman service and wages and working conditions enjoyed by the race in other industries."[21] He was correct in observing that Randolph gave no importance to such comparisons. Of course Randolph realized that porters earned more than many other blacks doing comparable work, but what mattered to the union leader was the inequity of distinguishing workers by race. Attaining equal pay for equal work was a basic commitment of the porters' union.

The BSCP was fortunate: when the Mediation Board returned to the dispute in June, it ruled that the union's records were sufficient evidence to establish its claim to represent a majority of the porters. The board requested that the Pullman Company recognize the Brotherhood and

[20] APR to Pullman Company, June 4, 1927, BSCP ChiPa.

[21] See, *e.g.*, Memorandum from MJB [unidentified Pullman employee] to Mr. Greenlaw, June 11, 1927, *ibid*. It is impossible to explain how this sensitive internal company memo came into the hands of the BSCP. For a discussion of the *Argus*'s position on this point, see the second chapter, above.

submit the dispute to mediation. But the company replied that no dispute existed between itself and its employees, and that sufficient machinery for settlement of disputes was already in effect when Congress passed the Watson-Parker Act. Further, an agreement between porters and Pullman was presently in force, and the company could not in good faith to its porters negotiate "with such persons mentioned" in the board's letter.[22] Pullman officials still refused to mention the BSCP by name.

News of the Pullman Company's refusal to cooperate with the board and the BSCP leaked to the press. On the basis of that information, articles appeared in several daily newspapers on July 2, 1927, inaccurately reporting that since the Brotherhood had brought no new issues before it, the board had denied the BSCP's plea for mediation. Within a week, black weeklies picked up the story. The *Defender* wrote long articles condemning the BSCP,[23] while newspapers sympathetic to the Brotherhood decried the statement as just another instance of Pullman propaganda trying to destroy the union. The *Courier* went so far as to call it the most daring hoax perpetrated since the announcement of the "false signing of the armistice in 1918."[24]

Appearance of a public statement that the board had dismissed the union's case troubled BSCP leaders. Randolph queried the Mediation Board about the source of the story and requested that it be retracted.[25] Agreeing that the stories harmed the Brotherhood's position, the board denied that it was the source of the articles and agreed to request that newspapers print corrections.[26] The board's efforts caused some retractions and helped to ease anxiety among BSCP leaders. But publication of the rumor had a negative effect on the union, because some papers refused to retract the original story.

For its part, the Mediation Board continued during summer, 1927, in its efforts to bring the company and union together. Morrow went to Chicago to try to persuade general manager Hungerford that Pullman should hear the BSCP's arguments, but his plea failed. On August 9,

[22] L. S. Hungerford to Mediation Board, June 21, 1927, BSCP ChiPa.

[23] Washington *Herald* and Chicago *Evening American*, both July 2, 1927; Chicago *Defender*, July 9, 1927; St. Louis *Argus*, July 8, 1927.

[24] Pittsburgh *Courier*, July 16, 1927.

[25] Telegram, APR to Mediation Board, July 2, APR to Mediation Board, July 6, 1927, *BSCP* v. *PC*, NA.

[26] Telegram, Mediation Board to APR, July 2, Mediation Board to Washington *Herald*, July 6, 1927; Managing editor, Washington *Herald* to Med. Bd., July 12, 1927, *BSCP* v. *PC*, NA.

1927, Morrow announced on behalf of the board that mediation was impossible, and he called upon the parties to submit the case to arbitration, the next step under Watson-Parker.[27] The BSCP immediately accepted the invitation. The Pullman Company, after a short delay, informed Morrow that nothing had changed since its letter of June 21, and that therefore there was no dispute to be arbitrated.[28] The company's refusal to send an immediate rejection suggests that some people at Pullman entertained the idea of meeting with the BSCP. But the rejection was final.

Pullman's decision was a major setback for the BSCP, highlighting a fundamental flaw in the Watson-Parker Act which certain black labor leaders like Mays and Lemus had seen before it became law. The Mediation Board had no power to force arbitration; in the event that one party refused to cooperate, the board's only recourse was to recommend that the president create an emergency board to ward off a strike, should the dispute reach that point. Pullman recognized that if it submitted the case to arbitration and lost, the decision would be binding upon both parties and enforceable through federal courts. It astutely decided not to take that chance and, without violating the law, continued to withhold recognition from the BSCP.

Randolph considered the company's attitude another example of racial discrimination. Citing again Pullman's relationship with the Order of Sleeping Car Conductors, he called upon all blacks to join with the BSCP to force the company to give black people equal respect.[29] He also called upon standard railroad unions to support the Brotherhood's cause, claiming that if Pullman could flout board decisions with regard to porters, the same would be done to them.[30]

Randolph now recognized that Watson-Parker made no provisions for disqualifying company unions. Though the Mediation Board ruled that the BSCP represented a majority of the porters, it had no power to declare the ERP illegal and to force the company to deal with the Brotherhood.[31] In fact, company control of the ERP was never a factor

[27] Morrow to BSCP, Aug. 9, 1927, BSCP ChiPa.

[28] Hungerford to Morrow, Aug. 12, 1927, *ibid.*

[29] APR to BSCP Organizing Committees, Aug. 18, 1927, *ibid.*

[30] APR to William Painter of Rail Road Engineers, Aug. 19, 1927, *ibid.*

[31] BSCP attorneys interpreted the Watson-Parker provision that carriers not interfere in election of employee representatives as an explicit statement against company unions. See Richberg to APR, Dec. 7, 1926, *BSCP* v. *PC*, NA, for example of this counsel.

in the dispute. The issue, as far as the board was concerned, centered on which union Pullman should accept as bargaining agent for the porters. The decision incensed Randolph and his colleagues so much that they mused about calling a strike against Pullman, but they laid no definite plans at that time.[32]

Press reaction to the company's refusal to permit arbitration was swift and predictable. The *Argus* gloated that it had correctly prophesied the union's failure two years earlier. It renewed its accusation that Randolph had taken the porters' money under false pretenses and advised them to demand that he repay all the money they had given him because he had produced nothing to show for it.[33] Agreeing with the *Argus*'s appraisal of the situation, the *Defender* wrote that the BSCP was dead. It exulted that the two years of "petty wrangling" had come to an end and advised porters to spend as much time and energy trying to repair the union's damage to employer-employee relations as they had spent supporting the BSCP. In what amounted to an obituary of the union, the *Defender* offered its own service as mediator, calling upon Pullman to "reinstate those who left the company during the dispute and now seek reinstatement, those especially who were competent." Probably speaking unofficially for the company, the *Defender* added that here was a chance for Pullman to prove its good will toward its service employees, pointedly reminding porters and maids that they now had an opportunity to demonstrate their "loyalty and worth" for positions they wished to hold.[34] But the *Courier* was conspicuous for its denunciation of the company's decision, contending that Pullman, by its actions, placed itself above the law.[35] Accusing the company of racial discrimination in its treatment of the BSCP, the editors implored non-porter blacks to support the union because it represented the kind of organization blacks must have in order to attain equal treatment in all areas of life.[36]

Randolph, as always, attempted to find some consolation in this bitter defeat. He claimed that failure to attain arbitration was a victory for the union: it proved that the rich and powerful company was afraid to sit

[32] BSCP press release, Aug. 12, 1927, BSCP ChiPa.

[33] St. Louis *Argus*, Aug. 19, 1927.

[34] Chicago *Defender*, Aug. 20, 1927.

[35] Pittsburgh *Courier*, Aug. 20, 1927.

[36] *Ibid.*, Aug. 20 and Nov. 5, 1927. The second editorial reads like Randolph's writing. As he is known to have written editorials on the BSCP for the Chicago *Defender* after Nov., 1927, it is likely that he wrote this one, too.

down with BSCP officials to write a contract. It even represented a change in relations between blacks and whites. Formerly, he asserted, whites would have welcomed the opportunity to sit down with a group of black men because they knew from the beginning that they would win. According to Randolph, the Brotherhood had changed all that. The company's refusal to meet the BSCP in arbitration or mediation was proof that the "New Negro" had arrived in the United States, and whites knew it.[37] Whatever rationalizing Randolph might do, however, he could not alter the fact that the company's position represented nothing more than a continuation of existing conditions. Pullman had simply refused to recognize Randolph and his colleagues as equals. Indeed, despite Randolph's protestations, the Mediation Board decision had damaged the union's standing among porters, leaving it even less able to threaten the company with a strike. But Randolph's optimism, and his ability to infuse it in others, largely enabled the union to pick itself up and continue in its endeavor to represent the porters in their dealings with Pullman.

Unable to take on the powerful company in direct battle, the BSCP astounded observers by initiating a novel flanking movement. Rather than threaten a strike and hope for an emergency board settlement at that time, the Brotherhood petitioned the Interstate Commerce Commission to investigate Pullman involvement in the practice of tipping porters, and to outlaw the activity. Abolition of tipping, union officials reasoned, would necessitate a raise in porters' wages: they could not be expected to live on their current regular pay of $72.50 per month. ICC Case #20,007 introduced a new dimension in labor-management relations.

It is not clear who originated the idea of taking the porters' case before the regulatory commission. Randolph sent the petition to the ICC on September 7, 1927, and it was probably at his suggestion that BSCP attorneys (particularly Henry T. Hunt, a white New York labor lawyer and a former member of the now defunct Railway Labor Board) prepared a brief outlining the Commission's authority to undertake the investigation the union desired. Recognition that tipping was an inadequate form of pay for Pullman service employees was hardly new. Randolph and others had long argued that tips placed porters in a position of mendicancy and extended the servant-master relationship

[37] *Messenger*, IX (Dec., 1927), 357.

between those who received the gratuity and those who gave it.[38] Moreover, union leaders had concluded as early as March, 1927, that porters were receiving less in tips than formerly because of changing clientele on sleeping cars — tourists now made up a larger share of the passengers — and changing conventions about how much, if anything, should be offered.[39] The novelty in fall, 1927, was in recognizing that tipping could be used as a way to get at Pullman. Moreover, union leaders believed that abolishing tips would increase BSCP membership, because porters would come to realize that coins tossed at them were at best an uncertain source of income.

The Brotherhood did not stand alone in its anti-tipping campaign. Other service employees and their unions, including teamsters and hotel waiters, voiced support. Outside agreement ranged from acquiescence with the Brotherhood's position on the peculiar condition of porters because they were black, to a total condemnation of the practice as alien to American values.[40]

Though moral support from other workers employed in service-related occupations buoyed the Brotherhood's spirits, frightful financial problems remained to be worked out before the BSCP could hope to succeed in its plea before the Interstate Commerce Commission. Dispensation of initiation fees had caused some increase in the number of porters who called themselves BSCP members, but the union received little income from these newcomers. Furthermore, adverse publicity surrounding the Mediation Board's inability to bring about arbitration diminished the will of old-line BSCP men to continue contributing to the union. Conditions deteriorated so badly that by summer the union found

[38] Labor Bureau, Inc., *Survey of Working Conditions Among Porters*, paid particular attention to tipping, especially to the average amount porters received from that source per month. Other sources likened tipping to slavery. As an article in *America*, IX (Nov., 1927), 338, remarked, "The closest thing to a slave observable in this country is the Pullman porter. He has the same color to begin with, and to conclude, he toils under conditions that are not remarkably dissimilar.

"The ante-bellum slave received no wages, but as a rule was provided with enough food to keep him alive and in fit condition. His modern counterpart, the Pullman porter, manages to extort a money wage, but it is not a living wage. Far from it. But for the generosity of the public, he would starve. About half of his income is doled out by the Pullman Company, a corporation of enormous wealth, and the other half is carelessly tossed to him — or in some cases slowly given with unspeakable groaning of reluctance — by the traveling public."

[39] APR to MPW, Mar. 21, 1927, BSCP ChiPa.

[40] *Collier's Weekly*, July 30, 1927; *Locomotive Engineers' Magazine* (Apr., 1927), 260.

it necessary to make drastic retrenchments in its operations.[41] To remedy its plight, the Brotherhood turned again to the Garland Fund.

Shortly after filing their petition with the ICC, BSCP officials asked the Garland Fund for $10,000 to finance litigation before the Commission and to initiate procedures in federal court to enjoin Pullman from holding elections under the ERP.[42] Without delay the Fund approved the full amount, but, because of past experience with Randolph and the union, this time it informed the BSCP that the money must be spent for no purposes other than those for which it was appropriated. To safeguard this requirement, the Fund set up a subcommittee of James Weldon Johnson and Morris Ernst, whom Norman Thomas soon replaced, to pass on BSCP expenditures.[43] Soon afterward, in November, the Garland Fund refused to approve certain BSCP expenses, insisting that only designated use be made of the appropriation. The secretary wrote that the board did not "care to have the money used for any purpose but the one for which it was originally voted." Since the union had taken no action in its injunction procedures, the Garland Fund impounded money designated for that project and authorized the Johnson-Thomas subcommittee to "release only such amounts as are necessary to finish the legal case before the Interstate Commerce Commission." In February, 1928, the Fund officially withdrew support of the injunction.[44]

Meanwhile, armed with moral support and a replenished war chest, the BSCP had found the ICC favorably disposed to its initial petition. The Commission ruled the complaint sufficiently meritorious to require Pullman to respond, and ordered the company to satisfy the complaint or show cause why not.[45] Pullman answered in a brief requesting that the Commission drop the case for lack of jurisdiction and pointing out that the union simply wished to force the company to raise wages, an action that lay beyond the ICC's authority.[46]

[41] APR to MPW and MPW to APR, both June 9, 1927, BSCP ChiPa. See the next chapter for further discussion.

[42] Lancaster and Crosswaith to Garland Fund, Sept. 27, 1927, Garland Fund Pas.

[43] Garland Fund to BSCP, Sept. 30, 1927. On Oct. 14 Norman Thomas replaced Ernst as member of the committee with JWJ to pass on BSCP expenditures. See Garland Fund to BSCP, Oct. 28, 1927, all *ibid*.

[44] Garland Fund to BSCP, Nov. 28, 1927; Robert W. Dunn to BSCP, Feb. 18, 1928, *ibid*.

[45] ICC to Pullman Company, Sept. 17, 1927, ICC Case #20,007, ICC Files. See also telegram, APR to MPW, Sept. 21, 1927, BSCP ChiPa.

[46] PC Motion to Dismiss Complaint (Oct. 5, 1927), ICC Case #20,007, ICC Files.

The Pullman Company's request for dismissal provided opportunity for the BSCP to present an exhaustive reply outlining porters' duties and responsibilities and the relationship of tipping to those chores. The BSCP argued that the Pullman Company was a public service corporation, and that as such its business was the public's business. Sleeping car companies lay explicitly within the ICC's authority, and matters affecting wages were major considerations in the operation of any business. According to the union, by allowing tipping the company gained from the public approximately $8,640,000 on its wage bill in addition to published charges, an explicit violation of federal regulations that forbade corporations from charging more than fees posted with the ICC. It noted several sections of the Interstate Commerce Act under which the ICC had jurisdiction over questions the BSCP raised, and cited Supreme Court decisions which it contended had established precedent for such investigations. Discounting Pullman's contention that the union wanted only to force the company to raise wages, the BSCP argued that the desire for wage increases was irrelevant to the question of whether the Commission had authority to conduct the investigation requested.[47]

The Brotherhood contended that porters were employees of a public agency, and that tipping heightened the probability that porters would discriminate in the quality of service individual passengers received. It went on to cast porters almost in the role of federal agents, describing them as sanitation officers responsible for keeping communicably diseased passengers off the cars and providing proper means for disposal of the sputum of tubercular passengers; as police officers with the duty of enforcing gambling laws and Sunday regulations in the several states (to say nothing of federal prohibition laws), and with preventing violations of U.S. customs laws on trains which ran to port cities. Above all, porters served as guardians by day and night of passengers and valuable railroad equipment which in the final analysis were public assets. By allowing tipping, Pullman provided opportunity for passengers, publicly and without compunction, to bribe public agents. The Brotherhood claimed, moreover, that not only did Pullman allow tipping, but the company encouraged the practice, and cited instances in which company officials had admitted doing so. Pullman's policy of tying wages to tips was the major reason why porters spent so much time on the road—

[47] The following discussion is based on BSCP Brief on Motion to Dismiss, ICC Case #20,007, ICC Files. Labor Bureau, Inc., *Survey of Working Conditions Among Porters*, placed Pullman's savings on its wage bill through tips at $7,000,000.

they had to "follow the tip" to the end of the line in order to get all their pay. The BSCP requested in its brief that the ICC require the company to refrain from informing applicants for porters' jobs that they might expect increments to their income from passengers; that the Commission force the company to refuse to allow porters to accept tips on its property; and that it forbid Pullman from fixing wages at such a level that porters could not remain in the service without tips.

The brief convinced the ICC to delay the decision on dismissal until it could hear oral arguments.[48] Yet, though it had achieved a favorable ruling from the ICC, the BSCP's bold new stroke was not popular with all porters, and to some extent it played into the hands of the Pullman Company. Decline in tipping, which union officials had noted as early as spring, continued. By striking further at members' earning power without guaranteeing replacement of lost income from a different source, the union's proposal actually produced a groundswell of dissatisfaction. This was the first issue on which there was decided disagreement between the membership and union officials, and the company moved quickly to heighten the division. Pullman circulated petitions among porters requesting the ICC to deny the Brotherhood's complaint because porters did not wish to have tips removed from their earnings.[49] The Pittsburgh *Courier* reported that a certain Pullman Porters' Club, "a pseudonym for a group of company stool-pigeons," actively engaged in securing signatures. One Pullman superintendent, the *Courier* wrote, paid a porter six dollars a day to collect names on the petitions.[50]

A number of mainly non-union porters, meeting at Omaha, addressed a long petition to the ICC and the public in which they expressed their hostility to the anti-tipping campaign, voiced bitter opposition to the BSCP, and vowed to maintain loyalty to their employer. The Omaha group contended that the BSCP was an outside organization, and that its

[48] BSCP Brief on Motion to Dismiss, ICC Files, 3-4, 17-25. The union specifically cited Secs. 1, 2, 3, 6, 10, 12, 13, 14, 15, and 20 to support its contention that the ICC had authority. Among Supreme Court decisions cited to buttress its claims, the union mentioned *Smith* v. *ICC* (245 U.S. 33), in which the Court upheld the ICC's power to investigate any phase of a carrier's business; *ICC* v. *Cincinnati*, *etc*. *Ry*. (167 U.S. 479), which upheld the Commission's power to insure equal treatment of all users; and *ICC* v. *Goodrich Transit Company* (224 U.S. 194), in which the Court expanded on the ICC's right to regulate rates. The BSCP argued that wage costs directly affected rates.

[49] Numerous telegrams and letters, Oct.-Nov., 1927, BSCP ChiPa.

[50] Pittsburgh *Courier*, Nov. 5, 1927. Six dollars a day was far in excess of a porter's regular pay.

utterances on tipping were proving "detrimental to the best interest of the porters" because passengers accepted them as representative of porters' views and refrained from granting tips for services. The group denied that tips placed porters in a demeaning position or made them susceptible to bribes. Brotherhood supporters argued that the company had forced porters to sign the loyalty petitions. They alleged that Pullman agents called on porters in their homes to secure signatures, on occasion pressuring porters' wives to encourage their husbands to sign, and that the company sometimes resorted to more overt acts of intimidation by denying porters access to their runs until they signed the proffered forms.[51]

The BSCP anti-tipping/ICC affair was curious in more than one respect. Not only did it place the union at odds with much of its membership on an issue of fundamental concern; more important, it contradicted the union's avowed goal of being recognized as the porters' sole bargaining agent. Randolph had placed recognition above wages in his public discussions with Robert Mays during January, 1926, and more recently Webster had pointed out that a favorable ICC ruling would do nothing to force the company to recognize the union. Indeed, he warned Randolph that the BSCP would have to strike and "use force to make the company recognize the Brotherhood as the representative of the porters." Webster believed that if the ICC would decide in the union's favor by outlawing tipping and forcing the company to raise wages, the BSCP would be in danger of working itself out of a job without achieving recognition. The porters, receiving higher wages from the company, would think they had no further use for the Brotherhood and refuse to support it in its other aims.[52]

The Brotherhood disregarded opposition of union and non-union porters to its anti-tipping campaign and continued to press its complaint before the ICC. Randolph denied that the campaign was responsible for declining tips, contending instead that the company's announcement after its latest wage conference that porters had received a million-dollar raise had convinced the public that Pullman paid porters well and that

[51] *Messenger*, X (Jan., 1928), 16-17.

[52] MPW to APR, Nov. 11, 1927, BSCP ChiPa. Rienzi B. Lemus made this same point in reference to the members of his union, the Brotherhood of Dining Car Employees. Ira DeA. Reid and Charles S. Johnson, *Negro Membership in American Labor Unions* (New York: Alexander Press, 1930), 122, quotes Lemus as saying of his men, "I am waiting for them to get it into their heads that this is a Brotherhood, not a machine to get increases in pay and improved working rules, only to have them drop out after the accomplishment."

tips were unnecessary. He believed that the lower tips would eventually make the porters understand the disadvantage of depending upon such a capricious system for one's income, and encourage them to support the union's demand for a living wage.[53]

The ICC finally convened to hear oral arguments on Pullman's request for dismissal on January 21, 1928. Hunt, the union's attorney, had little to say in addition to what he had written, though he did point out social questions raised by tipping and brought up the issue of mendicancy. George A. Kelly, the Pullman Company's chief attorney, told a seemingly hostile Commission that it had no authority to grant relief sought by plaintiff. Along the lines of the Omaha Petition, Kelly claimed that the BSCP did not represent the feelings of porters and that as such its request should be thrown out. It is important to point out that at no time did Kelly deny the authenticity of the BSCP's charges. After several questions and statements indicating that they supported the Brotherhood's position, the commissioners retired to deliberate in private.[54]

While the Commission had the case under advisement, Randolph sought all possible support to secure a favorable decision. He encouraged influential individuals, such as Senator Hiram W. Johnson of California and Karl F. Phillips, commissioner of conciliation of the Department of Labor, to express their concern to the ICC, as well as having numerous other noted persons write the Commission on the union's behalf.[55] His activities included a visit to the White House, where he outlined the BSCP's case to the president and requested his backing. President Coolidge received him cordially, expressed interest in and general sympathy with the Brotherhood, and wished Randolph well — but he would not make the public statement Randolph desired.[56]

Though hopeful, BSCP organizers were not confident that the anti-tipping appeal would work, so they spent the waiting time in late 1927 and early 1928 preparing a contingency plan. Randolph was particularly interested in enhancing the union's public image and lining up public support in case the union had to strike. He organized a labor conference

[53] Pittsburgh *Courier*, Dec. 24, 1927.

[54] Stenographer's Minutes on Oral Hearing, Jan. 21, 1928, ICC Case #20,007, ICC Files.

[55] See letters in ICC Case #20,007, *ibid*.

[56] Lancaster to Dellums, Jan. 31, 1928, BSCP Oakland Papers (Manuscripts Division, Bancroft Library, University of California). Hereafter cited BSCP Oakland Pas.

in New York for December, 1927, and emphasized to Webster that such gatherings would strengthen porters' morale and at the same time alarm the Pullman Company.[57] At Randolph's suggestion, Webster and Bradley held similar conferences in Chicago and St. Louis, respectively, during January, 1928. The New York gathering went on record as supporting the porters' aims and promised to provide whatever assistance the union needed in case a strike became necessary.[58]

Some BSCP leaders, particularly Webster, wanted to do more than mobilize public opinion; they insisted that the union's officials come to grips with the full scope of what a strike threat entailed.[59] Webster had insisted that educating porters in what was expected of them was far more important than worrying about public opinion, and that above all the BSCP had to agree on a definite plan of action should the strike come about. In taking such a step the union was doing something too important, and too fraught with danger, to allow planning on a day-to-day basis.[60] Randolph, too, had considered calling a meeting of BSCP leaders to discuss strategy, but he and Webster had different ideas. Characteristically, Randolph was still speaking of a secret conference which would serve only "to alarm the company"; Webster had in mind a meeting of union officials which would lay definite plans for handling a strike.[61]

Webster's views prevailed, and BSCP leaders convened at Chicago during the first week of January, 1928, to map the sort of plans he had in mind. They agreed to establish a central committee to give guidance to all strike activities. This committee of Webster and Randolph had final authority to make all decisions concerning the strike, even to the matter of setting the date, or, at the discretion of the two leaders, postponing it. The Brotherhood's "Instructions for Handling Strike Situation" explicitly forbade district organizers to act on information on the strike from any source other than the Randolph-Webster committee.[62] In a

[57] APR to MPW, Nov. 27, 1927, BSCP ChiPa.

[58] APR Circular to BSCP Organizers, Dec. 15, 1927, *ibid*. Randolph wrote in his circular that this was the first time a community had gone on record in support of a strike before the fact, and added that "public opinion is the most powerful weapon in America." Whites as well as blacks, including workers and professionals, attended the conference.

[59] See, for example, MPW to APR, Nov. 28, 1927, *ibid*.

[60] APR to MPW, Dec. 1, 1927, *ibid*. In this letter APR responds to MPW's proposal. MPW's letter to APR is not available.

[61] APR to MPW, Nov. 8, 1927, *ibid*.

[62] BSCP "Instructions for Handling Strike Situation," Jan., 1928, *ibid*.

companion document, "Creating the Emergency," union leaders laid out specific guidelines for implementing the strike. They informed district leaders that, in the event the ICC issued an unfavorable ruling and the Mediation Board failed to recommend an emergency board, "the next and only step of the Brotherhood [would] be to carry out its threat and actually interrupt Interstate Commerce with the staging of a strike." The Brotherhood believed Pullman would be unable to withstand a long walkout, and the BSCP assured its members that the union would win in a week or ten days.[63]

After the Chicago meeting Webster grew more impatient with the delay occasioned by the ICC hearing; he also grew increasingly critical of the New York leadership. As late as two days before the Commission issued its statement, Webster wrote to Randolph decrying his failure to move boldly. He scoffed at Randolph's insistence upon publicity to accompany BSCP appearances before governmental bodies, characterizing the stratagem as one which did not put the union "any nearer the goal." Mindful of waning spirits among Chicago members, Webster sniped at Randolph's seemingly endless use of legal maneuvers and argued that the union must realize the necessity of following the "policy that will in the quickest manner bring material results to the membership." He reminded Randolph that he had been able to maintain morale in the Chicago area only with extreme difficulty; since he had preached emergency for the past four months, his men were ready to strike and would not accept another legal dodge.[64]

At this climactic moment the ICC issued a statement: by a split decision, the Commission had determined that it had no authority to grant the relief the union requested.[65] Randolph was gravely shocked and disappointed to find that all his efforts had failed. The BSCP had suffered another major rebuke.

Not surprisingly, Webster felt vindicated by the ICC's decision that it had no competence in the BSCP's case. It proved that the porters could

[63] BSCP Document, "Creating the Emergency," Jan., 1928, 2-3, NLCRG Pas.

[64] MPW to APR, Mar. 3, 1928, BSCP ChiPa.

[65] ICC *Reports*, CXXXIX (Mar., 1928), 741-43. It is somewhat strange that on the very day that the ICC issued its decision, the Commission wrote Randolph that the ICC had not yet reached the union's case. See Randolph to ICC, Feb. 29, 1928, and ICC to APR, Mar. 5, 1928, ICC Case #20,007, ICC Files. It is apparent, also, that the commission did not communicate its decision directly to the union. As late as Mar. 7 Randolph wrote the Commission thanking the secretary for information that the case soon would be decided. ICC Case #20,007, ICC Files.

expect no help from government agencies. Now the union could stage the strike he had advocated. Webster advised Randolph that it would be impossible for the Brotherhood to hold its membership over another long wait and insisted that the BSCP "pursue a vigorous program . . . through keeping things active and going."[66] If strikes can be considered a form of warfare, then Webster was the war-monger among BSCP officials. His continuous pressure, and the weight of the ICC decision, combined by the middle of March to force Randolph to move. On March 15, 1928, the beleaguered union leader announced that the BSCP would request the membership to authorize a strike against the Pullman Company.[67] Within days the call also appeared in various areas of the country over signatures of other Brotherhood officials.[68]

Given Webster's state of mind, and his position as leader of the largest and best-organized single group of BSCP members, it is easy to understand why the union moved to put its strike plans into effect after the adverse ICC decision. But even then it was not clear that Randolph intended to go all the way. He continued to hedge on the issue, insisting that a strike vote did not necessarily mean that the union would strike. Instead, he wished to collect porters' signatures on strike ballots and present them to the Mediation Board to force appointment of an emergency board. He wrote Webster that anything less than 90 percent support for the strike would represent failure for the union because the board would be unimpressed with a lesser figure, and he urged BSCP organizers to "execute our Strike Vote Plan with great dispatch, the quicker the better, so that we will be able to get action from the United States Mediation Board in recommending to the President the establishment of an Emergency Board. Let us not permit anything to daunt us in this work," he continued. "We must get the ballots signed."[69]

Randolph apparently failed to recognize that his negative comments harmed the strike effort because they caused both porters and board

[66] MPW to APR, Mar. 15, 1928, BSCP ChiPa.

[67] New York *Evening News*, Mar. 15, 1928.

[68] Pittsburgh *Courier* and Chicago *Defender*, both Mar. 17, 1928. That these announcements carried Webster's and Totten's names, respectively, instead of Randolph's, indicates the union was trying to depersonalize its image. Previously Randolph's name had appeared on everything except occasional statements such as the Totten Circular discussed above. There is no contradiction between the appearance of strike notices over signatures of several officials and the central direction Webster had demanded on the occasion of the Totten Circular.

[69] APR to MPW, Mar. 19, 1928, BSCP ChiPa. In a letter to MPW of Mar. 24, 1928, APR was even more explicit on this point.

members to believe he did not intend for the union to take the final step. Morrow, the Mediation Board member who handled the porters' case, considered Randolph's actions little more than a gesture. He advised his colleagues that "if anything approaching a real strike could have been staged with any hope of success, it would have been done long ago." He went on to say that Randolph's only aim was to get an emergency board.[70] Samuel Winslow, chairman of the Mediation Board, responded that this was "exactly the information we wanted to get."[71]

It is difficult to understand just how Randolph felt about a strike in the early spring of 1928. By his own admission, the responsibility of calling men off their jobs, which they might be unable to regain, pressed heavily upon him.[72] During this same period Randolph suffered a deep personal loss: his brother — closest friend, confidant, and only living relative besides his wife — had recently died. This death, according to intimates, "broke Randolph terribly."[73] Randolph's letters of the time suggest that he was determined to avoid the strike if at all possible; he would call it only if nothing else worked.[74] It must be remembered that he had recently suffered two major defeats at the hands of the Pullman Company and governmental agencies. He had been sharply criticized for these failures, and probably had lost some of his self-confidence. He must have realized that another loss might mean the union's end. The question whether the BSCP deserved to exist if it could not achieve recognition through a strike was beside the point. Randolph believed the union was destined to succeed if only he kept the spark alive.

Webster was still far ahead in private conversation and correspondence, though Randolph moved to bridge the gap in public utterances. Although he was not yet ready to support Webster's view that the union should ignore the Mediation Board altogether and call the strike immediately, thus presenting the company and the board with a fait accompli,[75] Randolph nonetheless rejected further use of litigation to accomplish the Brotherhood's goals. In a bulletin which he sent to porters in late March, he declared that the Brotherhood would tolerate no

[70] Telegram, Morrow to Winslow, Mar. 19, Morrow to Winslow, Mar. 20, 1928, *BSCP* v. *PC*, NA.

[71] Winslow to Morrow, Mar. 20, 1928, *ibid.*

[72] Interview with APR, Jan. 19, 1972.

[73] Lancaster to Dellums, Jan. 31, 1928, BSCP Oakland Pas. See the next chapter for other problems confronting Randolph in 1928.

[74] Several letters, APR to MPW; *e.g.*, Mar. 19, 1928, BSCP ChiPa.

[75] APR to MPW, Mar. 24, 1928, *ibid.*

more red tape; he further affirmed that the porters would walk off the cars if "red tape show[ed] its vicious head," thus displaying a new militancy. Porters, he said, would not only walk off the cars, but they would also refuse to allow anyone else — "black, white, Chinese, Japanese, or Filipino" — to walk onto them.[76]

However, Randolph had not abandoned hope that an emergency board would make the strike unnecessary. On April 24 the BSCP informed the Mediation Board that 6,013 porters, more than 50 percent of the force, had endorsed the union's strike, and requested that the board recommend that President Coolidge create an emergency board to prevent disruption of rail service.[77] The board procrastinated, and the red tape Randolph had vowed he would not tolerate again engulfed him.

During April and May, as the union waited for word from Washington, both the Brotherhood and the company gathered their forces for the anticipated conflict. BSCP sources maintain that the company employed a professional strikebreaker, E. R. MacDonald, to direct its campaign, and another source tells of elaborate steps which Pullman took to insure that it had men available to replace those who went out on strike.[78] At the same time thousands of letters from black men reportedly flooded Pullman offices, offering support for the company and requesting to be used as replacements for porters who left their cars. Throughout May and early June Pullman officials maintained that no emergency existed, continuing their operations as usual.[79]

In all the confusion surrounding the BSCP's strike threat, two things are certain: one is that even though some Brotherhood leaders strongly favored a strike — Webster suggested the union use force to get "obstinant" porters off their cars[80] — Randolph had no intention of calling it; the other is that the Mediation Board had no intention of recommending creation of an emergency board. As early as March Morrow had come to believe that the Pullman Company's appraisal of the situation was accurate.[81] Nothing occurred between that time and

[76] BSCP Bulletin, Mar., 1928, BSCP Oakland Pas.

[77] New York *Times*, Apr. 25, 1928.

[78] BSCP Bulletin, Mar., 1928, BSCP Oakland Pas; New York *Age*, May 5, 1928.

[79] Spero and Harris, *The Black Worker*, 453. Spero and Harris list no sources for this allegation. In his report to the full board on conversations with Pullman officials, Morrow maintained that the company had enough employees in reserve to replace striking porters. See Morrow's report to the board, June 5, 1928, *BSCP* v. *PC*, NA.

[80] MPW to APR, May 4, 1928, BSCP ChiPa.

[81] Morrow to Winslow, Mar. 20, 1928, *BSCP* v. *PC*, NA.

early June to change his mind. For his part, Randolph continued to issue broadsides and other pamphlets insisting to the porters that a strike threat was not necessarily a strike. In addition, the Randolph-Webster committee never came to agreement on a date for the strike.

When Randolph talked with Morrow on June 4 about an emergency board, Morrow informed him that the union must first set a date for the strike. It was then that Randolph, frustrated and angered at the apparent run-around on the part of the board, impulsively and unilaterally decided to announce that the union would strike Pullman at noon on June 8.[82] On June 6 BSCP district officials learned of the strike date by telegram, a copy of which went to the Mediation Board.[83] Randolph announced the date and so informed the board mainly to prod it into action — as if to say, if you want a strike date, I'll give you a strike date. To strengthen his position, he solicited the aid of highly respected black and white leaders to impress upon the board the importance of warding off the strike. James Weldon Johnson and Arthur Spingarn of the NAACP, for example, addressed telegrams to both the president and the Mediation Board on the union's behalf[84] — all to no avail.

Brotherhood leaders did not know that Morrow had talked with Pullman officials on June 5, following his conversations with Randolph the day before. Company management again stressed its view that Randolph was bluffing and that no threat of emergency existed. They convinced Morrow.[85] Consequently, all Randolph's efforts after June 5 were fruitless. The board informed Randolph by letter on June 6 that no emergency existed,[86] and pointed out to Johnson the next day that in its opinion no community would be deprived of essential rail service if Pullman cars stood idle.[87]

The letter from the Mediation Board draped BSCP headquarters in

[82] Morrow's Report to Board of Mediation, June 5, 1928, *ibid*.

[83] Telegram, APR to Mediation Board, June 6, 1928, *ibid*. Webster's name also appears on the telegram, a copy of which went to porters. Whether MPW actually agreed to the strike date is questionable, however, because a few weeks later he protested to Randolph about "ineffective handling of the publicity" on the strike date. See MPW, Self Memo, on back of APR to MPW, June 21, 1928, BSCP ChiPa.

[84] NAACP news release, June 7, 1928, NAACP Pas, C413, LC.

[85] Morrow's Report to Board of Mediation, June 5, 1928, *BSCP* v. *PC*, NA.

[86] Mediation Board to APR, June 6, 1928, *ibid*.

[87] Telegram, United States Mediation Board to JWJ, June 7, 1928, NAACP Pas, C413, LC. See also Brailsford R. Brazeal, *The Brotherhood of Sleeping Car Porters* (New York: Harper and Brothers, 1946), 80-81; Spero and Harris, *The Black Worker*, 454.

New York with a cloak of despair, and served as a severe rebuke to Randolph's literal interpretation of American laws and his idealistic belief that "right will prevail." The board's decision presented BSCP leaders with a dilemma. It was now clear that there would be no emergency board. The Brotherhood's alternatives were either to face Pullman head-on and alone, or to cancel the strike and admit defeat. The major problem was to find a way to save face so that the union would not be destroyed.

On the morning of June 8, a telegram arrived at BSCP headquarters from William Green of the AFL. In his message, which reached the embattled BSCP leader just three hours before porters were scheduled to step down, Green advised Randolph that "conditions were not favorable" for a strike at that moment and suggested that the showdown be postponed.[88] Though Green's telegram allowed Brotherhood officials to claim that they had not been defeated but had simply heeded the best possible advice in deciding to call off the strike, it was not the reason for the postponement. Nor is it possible to construct a clear picture of just how the decision was reached. What is clear, however, is that at least some BSCP officials knew as early as the evening of June 7 that the strike would not come off.[89] Spero and Harris contend that the union made its decision not because of Green, but because leaders knew the porters would not strike.[90] Generally, BSCP correspondence fails to support the allegation that a successful strike could not have been staged. Webster and Dellums, for example, and even Randolph, wrote that the stepdown could have been effective; Webster even emphasized the difficulty with which he had convinced his members in Chicago that they should not go out alone.[91] In any event, indications that the porters would not strike, which Spero and Harris claim poured into Pullman headquarters, may have come from outlying districts. The sad fact is that correspondence from those districts does not exist, and Spero and Harris cite no evidence for their conclusion.

A question of some difficulty is just how and why Green became involved, and whether his actions represent intervention or requested advice. Spero and Harris wrote on this question that Randolph and some of his colleagues went to Washington to ask Green for a statement;

[88] Telegram, Green to APR, June 8, 1928, in New York *Age*, June 16, 1928.
[89] MPW to APR, June 8, 1928, BSCP ChiPa.
[90] Spero and Harris, *The Black Worker*, 454.
[91] MPW to APR, June 8, APR to MPW, June 11, 1928, BSCP ChiPa.

however, the timing between receipt of the Mediation Board's decision and arrival of Green's telegram makes this improbable.[92] Yet it is hard to take at face value Green's explanation that he stepped in because "conditions were not right." Though no specific date had been determined for the Brotherhood's strike before Randolph's statement of June 4, June was one of the peak travel periods in the year.[93] Aside from disruption of peak travel, what could be more damaging to interstate commerce than to tie up the rails during the time when both national political parties were holding conventions in such remote cities as Houston and Kansas City? Even the Pullman Company recognized this as a potential danger. It would have been most helpful to the BSCP if AFL affiliates and other railroad unions had actively supported the strike, rather than advising its postponement. Those unions presumably would have preferred only union men on the trains. Instead, the conductors' union even suggested, after the strike had been postponed, that the BSCP's best efforts should be centered on increasing the porters' loyalty to the company.[94] All things considered, cooperation between the BSCP and other railroad unions was unthinkable in 1928, especially when the latter could act only in a supporting role.

What is certain about the whole affair is that Randolph wanted not a strike, but an emergency board. Having saved face as best it could, the Brotherhood turned to condemn the Mediation Board's decision as racial discrimination. Union leaders and their sympathizers pointed out that the board had recommended an emergency panel in a case involving 600 white railroad workers of the Kansas, Mexico, and Orient Railroad who went no further in their strike threat than the BSCP had gone. Many people, including the Boston Citizens' Committee, a Brotherhood front organization, could not see how the interest of 600 clerical workers could be deemed more important than that of 6,000 porters. The Chicago *Defender*, which now took the Brotherhood's side, accused the Mediation Board of outright racism and called for a congressional investigation to see if porters had been denied equal protection of the

[92] Spero and Harris, *The Black Worker*, 454.

[93] Several letters among BSCP correspondence show the union leaders' emphasis on June as the ideal time for the strike, though they cite no specific date. See esp. MPW to APR, Mar. 15, May 4, 1928, BSCP ChiPa. In letter of May 4 MPW even named specific trains that he thought could be "tied up."

[94] L. E. Sheppard, President of the Order of Railway Conductors, to APR, June, 1928, cited in APR's news release, "Why Pullman Porters' Strike Postponed," June 16, 1928, NAACP Pas, C413, LC.

law.[95] For his part, Randolph, retracting earlier remarks that the Mediation Board was above reproach, privately charged the board with racism. Unaware that a Mediation Board member had taken the initiative to come to Chicago to hear what Pullman had to say, rather than waiting for Pullman to send a man to Washington, Randolph wrote Webster that he was "satisfied that the Pullman Company got a man big enough to go to Washington and tell the Mediation Board and perhaps the President himself, that the Pullman Company was not going to stand for any Emergency Board." Randolph further informed his colleague that the major factor in the board's decision not to support the BSCP was that support would only tend to make blacks cocky and would "cause them to feel their power . . . and cause the business interest to have trouble with Negro workers." Randolph said he had raised this issue with members of the board; they denied that they had been influenced, but he "gave them some straight hard talk."[96]

While Randolph expressed himself quite vehemently in private statements, in his correspondence with the Mediation Board during the weeks after the strike fiasco he was more reserved, and it was left to Totten, the firebrand among BSCP leaders, to openly accuse the board of racism. Instead of straight hard talk, Randolph engaged in a legal debate with the board over the meaning of the Watson-Parker Act.[97] For his part, Totten thanked the board for the "very splendid work you are doing to adjust grievances of *white* workers." He went on to say that such action was only part of what was to be expected by blacks from a board appointed by a Republican administration.[98] In response to Totten's charges, the board's secretary, John Marrinan, explained that the Watson-Parker Act gave the board no coercive powers, and he denied Totten's allegations. Asserting that the time had passed when federal agencies practiced racial discrimination, he criticized Totten, or any man "charged with responsibility for the economic well-being of any racial group," for raising that cry.[99] But Marrinan's protestations do not

[95] Chicago *Defender*, July 14, 1928. Note that this is a new position for the *Defender* on the question of the BSCP. See the next chapter for full discussion of its change of stance.

[96] APR to MPW, June 14, 1928, BSCP ChiPa.

[97] APR to Mediation Board, July 23, 1928, *BSCP* v. *PC*, NA. In this letter Randolph told the board that its decision not to recommend an emergency board was "not calculated to increase the respect of Negro American citizens for the spirit of fair-play of Government agencies where their interests are involved."

[98] Totten to Mediation Board, June 28, 1928, *ibid.*

[99] Marrinan to Totten, July 2, 1928, *ibid.*

explain the board's actions. As outlined above, the board favored Pullman's position all along. Even more indicative of the board's true feelings and of the fact that it had no intention of giving full consideration to the Brotherhood's request was the cover letter which Marrinan sent to the company, accompanying a copy of the letter in which he informed Randolph that there would be no emergency board. Marrinan wrote, "I take pleasure in . . . forwarding for the information of your Company copy of a letter which I have been instructed to send to Mr. A. Philip Randolph. . . ."[100]

The fact is that the BSCP had suffered a major defeat, and (as he had no doubt expected) Randolph experienced considerable press abuse. The *Courier*, now firmly anti-Randolph, wrote that the union had never intended to call a strike in the first place and that the whole episode had been simply another "Randolph bluff."[101] Predictably, the *Argus* joined in the condemnation. Rienzi Lemus, writing in the New York *Age*, which he edited, placed full blame for the porters' plight at the feet of "A. Piffle Randolph." Citing Randolph's "bootleg superiority complex," Lemus called Randolph the most important weapon in Pullman's arsenal against a porters' union. He advised other BSCP leaders to disengage themselves from "All Piffle Randolph, generalissimo of the Afric hustlerati," before he dragged them into the oblivion from which Des Verney and others had snatched him to mislead the movement.[102]

Perhaps the loudest, if not the most effective, criticism of the Brotherhood's handling of the strike affair came from the Communists. Classing Randolph and Webster as bourgeois and false labor leaders, the Communists claimed the BSCP leaders had sold out to the AFL in exchange for the promise of a charter in that organization, and called on porters to reject such leadership.[103] The American Negro Labor Congress became active for a while in trying to bore inside the porters' movement. Communists had made solid inroads into BSCP ranks in Oakland, influencing even C. L. Dellums to criticize the Randolph-Webster decision to postpone the strike.[104] Trying to mobilize all

[100] Marrinan to Pullman Company, June 6, 1928, *ibid*.

[101] Pittsburgh *Courier*, June 16, 1928.

[102] New York *Age*, July 14, 1928.

[103] APR to MPW, June 14, 1928, BSCP ChiPa; American Negro Labor Congress flyer, June, 1928, *BSCP* v. *PC*, NA. In this announcement of a meeting to reject current BSCP leadership, Lovett Fort-Whiteman of the Congress identified himself as a Pullman porter.

[104] Dad Moore to MPW, June 18, 1928, BSCP ChiPa.

possible support for the strike in the Oakland area, Dellums became entangled with Communist organizers. Randolph excused Dellums's apparent siding with the Communists on grounds of political naivete, but he warned Dellums of the ways of those political revolutionaries. The BSCP president closed the case without prejudice after Dellums recognized his mistake and pledged continued loyalty to the union and its work.[105]

Randolph did not care for Communists and their tactics. He warned Webster, as he had Dellums, that the Brotherhood could not temporize with that "sinister and destructive crowd," vowing that the union would kill that "reptile" from the outset before it wormed itself too deeply into the organization.[106] He dismissed the Communists' opposition to postponement of the strike with one paragraph in his major statement on the matter and claimed that the Brotherhood gave no consideration to the merits of their arguments.[107]

As at the time of the BSCP's failure to gain recognition in 1927, Randolph again showed his rare ability to look on the bright side of any issue. He was even able to view the union in shambles after the abortive strike and see a BSCP victory. From his perspective, the strike had not been called off, but simply postponed.[108] He added that the union had actually won a victory by the strike maneuver because it had forced the company to spend an estimated half-million to a million dollars which resulted in free publicity for the BSCP; it had achieved wider recognition of its goals; and it had demonstrated its firm discipline by aborting the maneuver on three hours' notice.[109]

Despite Randolph's claims of victory, the BSCP experienced deep trouble during the summer of 1928. Its membership figures plummeted, the *Messenger* ceased publication, and the union relieved some of its organizers of their duties. Noticing the union's trouble, the Pullman Company did everything in its power to compound the difficulties. It began discharging porters who were known BSCP supporters and circulated loyalty oaths among the rest.[110] Randolph suggested that the union

[105] APR to Dellums, July 3, 1928, BSCP Oakland Pas.

[106] APR to MPW, June 27, 1928, BSCP ChiPa.

[107] APR, "Why Porters' Strike Postponed," 1.

[108] New York *Age*, June 21, 1928. BSCP correspondence supports this public statement. APR probably convinced MPW to go along with the decision of June 8 by promising that the strike would come at a later date.

[109] APR, "Why Porters' Strike Postponed."

[110] MPW to APR, June 19, 1928, BSCP ChiPa.

permit the membership to sign the oaths without prejudice. Webster objected, reminding Randolph that the porters would interpret such statements from the leadership as an indication of weakness. Their thrust would be to weaken the union still more.[111] Webster and Randolph argued about the issue through June and July, with Webster also insisting that the union must eventually strike Pullman.[112] Meanwhile Randolph shied farther and farther away from the idea of a strike, and after mid-July nothing more was heard of it. The Brotherhood was in difficult straits in the summer of 1928, but it would be incorrect to assume that all subsequent troubles resulted from the strike failure. In fact, the malaise of that year was the culmination of many factors operating within the union during the two years of protracted litigation.

[111] APR to MPW, June 19, MPW to APR, June 26, 1928, *ibid.*
[112] APR to MPW, MPW to APR, June-July, 1926, *passim*, *ibid.*

A. Philip Randolph (1889-), president and general organizer of the Brotherhood of Sleeping Car Porters. Photo of early 1930s; original in Chicago Historical Society.

Milton P. Webster (1887-1965), first vice-president and chairman of the International Board, Brotherhood of Sleeping Car Porters. Photo of early 1930s; original in Chicago Historical Society.

BSCP cartoon, *Messenger* (Oct.-Nov., 1925), 351.

BSCP cartoon, *Messenger* (Jan., 1927), 22.

Melvin Chisum's National Negro Conference Group at White House, Nov. 12, 1925. Original in Chicago Historical Society.

Public Mass Meeting

— HELD BY —

Chicago Division

Brotherhood of Sleeping Car Porters

Sunday Afternoon, April 22,

3 P. M.

AT

Metropolitan Community ...Church...

4100 SOUTH PARKWAY

A. PHILIP RANDOLPH

General Organizer,

will discuss every phase of the Strike Situation, and also the **"So called offer to Settle with the Pullman Porters,"** so prominently played up by the Pittsburg Courrier.

The success of the Brotherhood is of vital interest to all Negro workers. Learn more about it at this meeting.

Everybody Welcome **Admission Free**

CHICAGO DIV. HEADQUARTERS

224 EAST PERSHING ROAD

M. P. WEBSTER, Organizer **GEO. W. CLARK, Sec.-Treas.**

101

BSCP flyer, April 22, 1928. Note the appeal for public support which the union made a central part of its work. Original in Chicago Historical Society.

STRIKE
NOTICE

To All Pullman Porters and Maids

On account of the refusal of the Pullman Company to settle the dispute on Recognition of Wages and Rules governing Working Conditions with the Brotherhood of Sleeping Car Porters, a strike has been declared and shall be enforced on all Pullman Cars effective

FRIDAY, JUNE 8th
12 O'clock Noon

For further information call Glendale **6373.** You are requested to attend the meetings to be held each evening from 4 until 6 o'clock at **2382 18th street.**

BENNIE SMITH
Field Organizer

By Order of Strike Committee

BSCP strike notice, Detroit, June 7, 1928. Original in

STRIKE
Postponed

To All Pullman Porters and Maids

Strike - set for

FRIDAY, JUNE 8th
12 O'clock Noon

Has been Postponed this action taken upon advice of Wm. GREEN-PRESIDENT of the American Federation of Labor.

Who promises immediate Co-Operation.

BENNIE SMITH
Field Organizer B. S. C. P.

By Order of Strike Committee
A. PHILIP RANDOLPH and M. P. WEBSTER

BSCP strike cancellation flyer, Detroit, June 8, 1928.

BSCP negotiating team, 1937. *Left to right*: L. O. Manson, Bennie Smith, A. L. Totten, T. T. Patterson, Randolph, Webster, C. L. Dellums, and E. J. Bradley. Original in Chicago Historical Society.

BSCP convention, ca. 1940. Photo includes Webster and Randolph seated near center. Seated to Webster's right are E. J. Bradley, C. L. Dellums, and L. O. Manson. To Randolph's left, seated, are A. L. Totten, T. T. Patterson, and Bennie Smith. Original in Chicago Historical Society.

CHAPTER V

Tempest: Within and Without

Reports are being circulated around the headquarters of the Brotherhood of Sleeping Car Porters and other points where porters congregate, that the movement has now reached the point where no further progress can be made under the present leadership. It is even hinted among some of the staunchest followers that Mr. Randolph, the leader should step aside if he is sincere in his desire to see the porters secure some kind of consideration from the Pullman Company.

— "Is Randolph to Resign?" Pittsburgh *Courier*, April 7, 1928

I think we should immediately proceed to reorganize completely and carry on a campaign that will reach the men, as well as an organized publicity campaign. I suggest that it be directed from two strategic points, Chicago and New York. . . .

— Webster to Randolph, June 8, 1928

The BSCP encountered severe internal crises at the same time that it suffered humiliating public defeats. In early 1927 Webster threatened to resign because of his inadequate pay, and later he considered leaving in order to save his position in Chicago politics. Twice during 1927-28 secretary-treasurers absconded with large sums of BSCP money. Powerful interests in the black press accused Randolph of being the sole impediment to the union's success and called for his resignation so that the BSCP could gain recognition. In addition, differing assumptions on Brotherhood policy touched off power struggles within the union, while its outside support was shifting. Faced with repercussions from the strike fiasco, and with instability within as well as pressures from the Mediation Board and the ICC, BSCP leaders were forced to change the union's organizational structure. By 1930 they were extending participation in union policy decisions to leaders outside New York and spreading the feeling among the rank and file that the BSCP was more representative of the members' aspirations. Through it all, shared failures had forced such strong bonds among surviving leaders that a small group of dedicated men remained to continue the work.

The key developments within the BSCP during 1927-30 were the efforts on the part of certain regional organizers to reduce the influence of New York. As leader of the strong Brotherhood unit at Chicago, Milton P. Webster became the central figure in the movement for reform, and his activities stand out above those of all other leaders. Besides leading what appeared to be a recalcitrant union in making much-needed organizational changes, by 1930 Webster had engineered the move to dismiss Roy Lancaster as national secretary-treasurer, thus removing an individual whom some had considered a source of discontent since the union began.

Deep animosity and distrust existed between BSCP leaders in New York and those in other parts of the country. These stemmed from the tendency on the part of New York officials to see the union as their own private club, a feeling that derived partly from the facts that the Brotherhood had been founded in New York and that all the national officers were from that city. The reaction of Chicago leaders to monthly audits of local finances, which the national office had instituted as early as 1926, is symptomatic of the low opinion which Webster and his associates held toward some of Randolph's colleagues in New York, especially Roy Lancaster. Chicago officials, particularly the division's secretary-treasurer George W. Price, saw the audit as a form of espionage, since they never saw New York financial records and did not have first-hand information on the fiscal status of the union at large. In December, 1926, Webster protested to Randolph and suggested that the audit be stopped as a way to save meager BSCP funds.[1] Randolph did agree to stop the procedure, but he denied that spying was the original intent, adding that such thoughts were "wholly unnecessary and offensive to me."[2]

While Webster's complaints to Randolph were couched in terms of regional independence, the Chicagoan did have personal interests in mind. As early as December, 1926, believing he was being grossly underpaid in view of the "intrinsic value of the service" he was performing for the union in Chicago, Webster had demanded that his $50 monthly salary be doubled. He even suggested that the additional money could come from what the union paid the auditing firm.[3] His demand clouded much of the Brotherhood leaders' joy on the occasion of their initial meetings with the Mediation Board. The union could not afford to lose Webster at this crucial time, but it could hardly afford to

[1] MPW to APR, Dec. 27, 29, 1926, BSCP ChiPa.
[2] APR to MPW, Dec. 29, 1926, *ibid*.
[3] MPW to APR, Dec. 27, 1926, *ibid*.

double his salary. Randolph offered Webster a fifteen-dollar raise and assured his colleague that the increase represented the absolute maximum the union could pay under current conditions. He pointed out that the Mediation Board case was putting a considerable drain on BSCP resources, and reminded Webster of the Brotherhood's responsibility to provide for porters who had lost their jobs because of union activities.[4] Webster rejected Randolph's offer and, supported by the Chicago organizing committee, resubmitted his demand for $100, effective January 1, 1927. Noting that he understood the union's financial problems as well as any man, Webster insisted that his request was just and added with an air of finality that further discussion would be pointless.[5] John Mills, chairman of the Chicago organizing committee, tried to impress upon Randolph his group's feeling that Webster was indispensable to Chicago operations. Mills argued that though the union had little money, it could better afford to make retrenchments elsewhere than risk losing Webster.[6]

Randolph refused to budge and again turned down Webster's demand. He repeated his statements about the union's serious financial problems and informed Webster that he asked no one to make greater sacrifices than he was willing to make himself. The BSCP chief explained that though many were "under the impression [he] received some fabulous salary," his own pay was only $150 a month.[7] Webster was not impressed. Although he realized that Randolph would have difficulty living on his meager pay, he did not think Randolph was worth three times as much to the union as he was. Webster had resolved that he would be paid what he asked or would find work elsewhere.[8]

The two titans reached an impasse over Webster's pay during mid-January, 1927. It is interesting to speculate what would have happened had it not become imperative that they resolve the issue immediately or risk destroying the union. Just then startling news broke that George W. Price, secretary-treasurer of the Chicago division, had embezzled more than $400 of BSCP funds during the first three weeks of January. Webster telegraphed Randolph of the alleged theft on January 21, and

[4] APR to MPW, Dec. 28, 1926, *ibid.*

[5] MPW to APR, Jan. 8, 1927, *ibid.*

[6] Mills to APR, Jan. 7, 1927, *ibid.*

[7] APR to MPW, Jan. 10, 1927, *ibid.*

[8] Absence of papers from New York headquarters makes it impossible to determine what salaries other BSCP leaders received. Webster may have known that others earned more than he did, insisting on his own demand in order to reach parity.

later ordered an audit of Chicago books to confirm his suspicions and the amount taken.[9] It now became clear why Price had insisted to Webster that the New York audit was espionage. Unwittingly, Webster had provided an opportunity for Price to steal from the union.[10]

The Price affair terrified Randolph and caused him and Webster to work closely together, forgetting their differences for the moment. They immediately fired Price, but since the BSCP stood to lose its whole Chicago operation by the adverse publicity that could result from such a scandal, Randolph suggested to Webster that he keep the incident quiet and not initiate legal action against Price. Instead, he should use other means to recover outstanding funds from the former official. Randolph also recommended that Webster tell Price what to say if Chicago members questioned him about his absence from the post.[11] Webster did not attempt to use the union's difficulties to enhance his position vis-à-vis Randolph, and he did not mention his pay during the whole period of the Price affair. He simply stayed at his job to insure that the union suffered as little as possible. For his part, Randolph admitted Webster's value to the union, and on January 28 had the latter's salary raised to $100 a month, retroactive to January 1, 1927.[12]

In explaining to Webster why he did this, Randolph denied that the union's financial condition had improved or that the increase had been granted under pressure; rather, he claimed that he had agreed to the increase in recognition of Webster's executive ability. Webster should be aware, he added, that even after the raise his salary did not represent his worth to the union. Randolph refused to connect the Price affair to his decision, although he discussed Price at length in the letter telling Webster about the raise. With characteristic vanity, he also denied that the Chicago organizing committee's recommendation had affected his decision on the matter. He stressed that he had changed his mind on his own, and that he had done so even before receiving word of the

[9] Telegram, MPW to APR, Jan. 21, Audit Report, W. D. Alimono and Company for Chicago BSCP, Jan. 29, 1927, BSCP ChiPa. The report for Jan. 29 showed a shortage of $472.09. A subsequent report for the same period, filed Feb. 5 by the same firm, showed a shortage of $527.18. Correspondence between APR and MPW refers to the accountants' later finding $165. How much money Price took cannot be definitely known.

[10] See esp. MPW to APR, Dec. 27, and APR and MPW, Dec. 29, 1926, BSCP ChiPa, for indications that Price supported the idea of New York espionage.

[11] APR to MPW, Jan. 28, 1927, *ibid.*

[12] *Ibid.*

committee's feelings. This is at best a dubious assertion, because Mills had communicated the committee's desires to Randolph as early as January 7.[13]

Webster fully justified Randolph's confidence in him. He handled the Price situation so effectively that by February he could write that it would cause no harm to the movement.[14] No mention of the scandal appeared in the newspapers, and Randolph wrote later that he had heard nothing of the affair among New York porters who went into Chicago, except from those whom he had delegated to receive information from Webster.[15] Few BSCP members missed Price, and after an unsuccessful attempt to return to the union he disappeared from BSCP circles and the affair was forgotten.[16] Randolph then moved to reinstitute the monthly audit of Chicago finances, claiming that quarterly audits of the union's general books were incomplete without statements from Chicago. Webster accepted the decision without protest.[17]

A crisis-ridden organization full of dynamic tensions, the BSCP had little time to savor the new Webster-Randolph detente. Randolph's handling of a serious problem involving Bennie Smith, the BSCP organizer at Jacksonville, Florida — or at least Webster's perception of how Randolph handled it — soon placed the two men at odds again. Smith had first become prominent among BSCP leaders in 1926, when he got himself elected to the ERP wage conference and refused to sign the agreement which Pullman reached with the porter representatives. This action cost him his job, and he then went to work full-time with the BSCP, first as Totten's assistant at Kansas City. Smith's troubles in Jacksonville developed when city officials and Pullman representatives began to harass him for trying to organize porters and for selling the *Messenger*. Branding the magazine radical, they accused Smith of trying to stir up racial troubles. Randolph saw the attack on the *Messenger* as a diversionary issue and insisted that the major reason for Smith's difficulties was his union work. He advised Smith either to refrain from selling the magazine or to leave town, and solicited the aid of the American Civil Liberties Union to guarantee the organizer's safety.[18] Smith refused, declaring that he was willing to "make the

[13] *Ibid.*; Mills to APR, Jan. 7, 1927, *ibid.*

[14] MPW to APR, Feb. 7, 1927, *ibid.*

[15] APR to MPW, Feb. 14, 1927, *ibid.*

[16] APR to Price, Mar. 5, MPW to APR, Mar. 8, 1927, *ibid.*

[17] APR to MPW, Mar. 28, 1927, *ibid.*

[18] APR to MPW, May 19, 1927, *ibid.*

supreme sacrifice" and remain at his post, whatever the consequences.[19] But conditions for Smith worsened rapidly, and during the night of May 26 he wired Webster requesting funds with which to leave Jacksonville immediately.[20] Smith's decision to leave Jacksonville was understandable, for, as Randolph wrote to Webster, there was a big difference between "denouncing the South from long range and being down there and persecuted by those crackers."[21] What was surprising, and significant, is that Smith went from Jacksonville to Chicago, rather than to New York. When he got there he told Webster that he had appealed to Chicago in desperation when the New York office refused his request for aid. Webster angrily protested this neglect to Randolph.[22]

Smith's accusation was strange. As Randolph pointed out to Webster, there "was no earthly reason" to deny Smith funds to leave a place which he had been advised to leave. Terming the charge "ridiculous," Randolph admitted that he had not sent travel money, but emphasized that he had not done so because Smith did not request funds. He said it never occurred to him that Smith might not have money with which to travel.[23] The explanation did not fully convince Webster. The problem was that Randolph had previously written to Webster about the splendid publicity the union had received from the Smith incident.[24] Such comments angered Webster because he did not see the affair in terms of publicity; and, given the union's past interest in getting its name in the newspaper, it seemed likely that the New York group wished to use Smith's difficulties as part of a major publicity stunt. For his part, in an apparent attempt to alleviate the situation, Randolph portrayed Smith as a martyr in the next issue of the *Messenger*, writing that all blacks owed him a vote of thanks for the sacrifices he had made on their behalf. But at the same time Randolph took credit for his own handling of the affair,

[19] Telegram, Smith to APR, May 26, 1927, *ibid.*

[20] MPW to APR, May 27, 1927, *ibid.*

[21] APR to MPW, May 29, 1927, *ibid.*

[22] MPW's original letter to APR is not available, but APR responded to the charges in APR to MPW, June 13, 1927, *ibid.* Jervis Anderson, *A. Philip Randolph: A Biographical Portrait* (New York: Harcourt Brace Jovanovich, 1972), 182-83, gives a totally different version of these events. He writes, for example, that rather than a telegram of desperation from Smith to Webster requesting money, MPW in fact initiated Smith's decision to leave Jacksonville and come to Chicago. Evidence among BSCP ChiPa does not support his version.

[23] APR to MPW, June 13, 1927, BSCP ChiPa.

[24] APR to MPW, May 26, 1927, *ibid.*

adding that Smith left Jacksonville only "after he was advised to do so by the General Organizer."[25]

Argument over the handling of the Smith affair symptomized the tensions between BSCP officials in New York and in outlying areas, while pointing to the lack of unanimity within the New York group itself. Randolph noted a "dead-level period in the general spirit of the membership" and admitted that the Brotherhood was going through a crisis.[26] Webster's overt actions to change the union's power structure began shortly after the Smith incident.

Webster and Smith believed some New York leaders were interested more in their own welfare than in that of the porters. As Webster wrote Smith in June, officers in New York apparently intended to maintain "their little closed corporation . . . and give only as much [information] as they feel disposed to."[27] The secrecy and lack of involvement of which they complained existed even within the New York circle; some members of the New York organizing committee had no knowledge of union policies until after they were promulgated. Those people turned to Webster for support. In June, after talking with a member of the New York committee who complained that Randolph and others had not informed him on recent issues, Webster wrote Smith that this represented "just another blunder." Such blunders, he added, emphasized the need for diversified management of the union, and he was "going to insist upon that being done."[28] He saw diversified control and expanded input as imperative, because the porters had more confidence in their local leaders than in central headquarters. If district organizers wanted to maintain that confidence, they needed hard information on the union's activities.[29]

Determined to press for improvements, Webster used the issue of finances as the basis for his attack on the "closed corporation." For two years the Chicago office had sent money to New York without receiving any accounting of it. Accordingly, Webster and his associates did not know what relative percentage of the union's operating expenses they paid, especially in comparison with New York. Webster informed Randolph on June 20 that he recognized the union's financial problems,

[25] *Messenger*, IX (July, 1927), 226.

[26] APR to MPW, June 13, APR Circular Letter, June 17, 1927, BSCP ChiPa.

[27] MPW to Smith, June 17, 1927, *ibid.*

[28] MPW to Smith, June 21, 1927, *ibid.*

[29] *Ibid.*

but that he would feel "much more secure" if he had "authentic information relative to the general financial situation."[30]

Randolph shared Webster's concern about the district organizers' lack of information. He wrote that greater coordination among the several branches of the organization was "indispensable and imperative," and assured Webster that "nothing would be left undone to make coordination as faultless as possible."[31] In an effort to make good on this pledge, the Chief promised to bring Webster the accountant's statements of BSCP finances on his next trip to Chicago.[32] Although Randolph provided the fiscal report, Webster and the Chicago organizing committee were not satisfied. The Chicago group and Randolph meant different things by "financial statements" — Randolph referred to a fiscal record of receipts and expenditures, whereas Webster wanted an itemized accounting of all Brotherhood funds. Furthermore, Randolph's determination to widen involvement in union policy decisions did not materialize in other aspects of BSCP activities. The New York office continued to run things on its own, and as late as September, 1927, Randolph wrote Webster that "the various plans the organization has for securing recognition . . . cannot be revealed to you at this time."[33]

After the commotion from the Mediation Board's handling of the BSCP case subsided, and probably because the union lost, Webster renewed his request for a financial statement, making clear that he wanted an itemized account covering the period from August, 1925, to September 1, 1927, and asked that "this matter be given immediate attention."[34] Webster's renewed request for the financial report spread the discussion beyond the usual sparring between him and Randolph, raising serious problems for the union. Other men, especially in New York, joined the fray. Among other things, the discussion underlined Randolph's difficulties in pacifying the leader of the Brotherhood's strongest local, while at the same time maintaining a working relationship with men in New York. In addition, the argument, coming shortly after the union's failure to force Pullman to arbitrate the dispute, allowed outsiders to step in and deepen the dissatisfaction. For example, a

[30] MPW to APR, June 20, 1927, *ibid*.
[31] APR to MPW, June 22, 1927, *ibid*.
[32] APR to MPW, June 23, 1927, *ibid*.
[33] APR to MPW, Sept. 19, 1927, *ibid*.
[34] MPW to APR, Sept. 9, 1927, *ibid*.

Pullman representative approached Webster during September and suggested that if he would leave the union he "could write [his] own ticket."[35] Webster rejected the offer as a sign of company weakness and continued his efforts to gain access to the union's inner circle. At last Randolph agreed that Webster should see the financial reports.[36]

The dispute over the issue of financial reporting between officials in Chicago and some members of the New York committee, particularly Ford and Lancaster, reached crisis proportions during October. While Randolph was away from New York on union business, Lancaster and Ford refused to send the reports Webster had requested and which Randolph had promised. Randolph's lieutenants in New York claimed that they refused to send Webster the financial reports on recommendation from the union's accountant and fiscal advisor. The consulting firm believed it would imperil the secret nature of the BSCP to send union records to Chicago.[37]

This insinuation of distrust, or of Chicago's inability to maintain the union's confidentiality infuriated Webster, coming soon after Randolph's "things that cannot be revealed to you" comment. He wrote Randolph that Lancaster and Ford had made it appear that some calamity would befall the BSCP if the Chicago committee received the financial report, and added that he could not "concur in that opinion." Webster reminded Randolph that the auditing firm could not have recommended so negatively if Lancaster and others had told its officials that the Chicago committee was an important link in the BSCP. The dispute clearly was greater than just that between Randolph and Webster. The latter was convinced that the Chief wished him to see the papers he requested, but that Lancaster had refused to obey direct orders. Webster warned Randolph of the seriousness of such insubordination, emphasizing that, in the event the union had to strike, it was imperative that the leader's wishes be obeyed without question. The Chicago committee had lost confidence in Lancaster's ability to carry out his duties and obligations as directed. If the situation continued, Webster wrote, it would cause a "break in the organization."[38]

Charges and countercharges between Webster and Brotherhood offi-

[35] MPW to APR, Sept. 27, 1927, *ibid*.

[36] See MPW to APR, Oct. 12, 1927, *ibid*.

[37] The original letter from New York to MPW is not available, but in MPW to APR, Oct. 12, 1927, *ibid*., MPW outlined the reasons why he had not received the information he needed.

[38] *Ibid*.

cials in New York almost ruptured relations between the two districts. When Randolph tried to minimize the differences by discussing Webster's charges with his New York colleagues, members of the New York inner circle turned the charge of insubordination back on Webster. One even protested directly to Webster, writing what Webster called "a rather bitter letter" criticizing the entire Chicago operation.[39] Unwilling to see this as fair response to his criticisms of New York, Webster denied that he had been insubordinate, arguing instead that his only interest was in strengthening the union. He termed the charges of deliberate miscarriage of instructions "absolutely false" and told Randolph he did not "care to have any more insinuations" of that kind.[40] Randolph apparently heeded Webster's warning and muzzled his New York subordinates, for they launched no further assaults.

More important, Webster had won the right to see the general office accountbooks. Although the records contained nothing that on the surface disturbed the Chicagoans, and Webster raised no questions even though Randolph promised to answer any such, the Chicago committee's receipt of the financial report represented a major change in BSCP operations. Henceforth the Chicago group would have a much stronger voice in running the union. Webster's victory on this issue gave him sufficient leverage to press for still more changes in operating procedures.

Quickly grasping the changes in the power relationship between New York and Chicago, Webster wasted no time in moving to consolidate his new position. He convinced Randolph to call a meeting of the several BSCP organizers from around the country to discuss the current status of the Brotherhood and to decide whether organizational changes were necessary. Randolph agreed but wanted to hold the meeting in New York, shortly after the ICC issued its findings on the BSCP petition. Webster objected on both counts. Insisting that Chicago was a better site, Webster pointed out that the city's central location would make it possible for many more leaders to attend. On the matter of the conference's timing, Webster believed it would be to the union's advantage to hold the meeting before the Commission's decision. That would enable Brotherhood leaders to make plans and be back in their home districts to handle whatever problems might materialize. Randolph eventually con-

[39] MPW to APR, Oct. 25, 1927, *ibid*.
[40] MPW to APR, Nov. 15, 1927, *ibid*.

ceded both points. He even offered to bring Lancaster along to explain the union's finances to the whole network of leaders.[41]

BSCP chiefs met in Chicago on January 12, 1928, to discuss the future of their organization. The most important single development of the meeting was the delegates' decision to set up a permanent body through creation of a policy committee. The new committee brought men from district offices into the inner councils of BSCP operations, thus reducing the power of Randolph and his New York associates. The Policy Committee was much stronger than Randolph's earlier Advisory Committee, a body that had given only semblance of involvement to chairmen of organizing committees. After the Chicago meeting, official power to run the Brotherhood resided in the Policy Committee, whose duty was "to formulate policies and work out methods for their execution in co-operation with the General Organizer." Set up so that the BSCP's policies would "reflect the actual conditions as they touch the life and work of the porter," the Policy Committee represented another major Webster victory. He consolidated this victory by getting himself named chairman of that committee, which also included Lancaster and Des Verney from New York, Totten from Kansas City, Smith from Pittsburgh, and Randolph.[42]

In addition to widening participation in decision-making, the group at Chicago moved to streamline the union by dividing the BSCP into four zones and placing a supervisor over each. Local organizers would report to zone supervisors, rather than directly to New York. This new arrangement further diminished the power of New York leaders and at the same time improved coordination by providing a smoother method for the general organizer to direct affairs, since he could more easily communicate union strategy to zone supervisors than to numerous local leaders.[43]

Despite their efforts, internal problems did not entirely disappear,

[41] APR to MPW, Nov. 22, MPW to APR, Dec. 3, 1927, *ibid*. Chicago was not picked solely for its central location. Probably Webster did not want to hold the meeting in New York because he hoped to minimize the input of New Yorkers in the deliberations. With the exception of Lancaster, Randolph was the only New York representative who appeared. Others included Totten of Kansas City, Bradley of St. Louis, Paul Caldwell of St. Paul, Smith of Pittsburgh, and Webster.

[42] Memorandum on Brotherhood Chief's Strategy Conference, Jan. 12, 1928; issued Feb. 2, 1928, over APR's signature, BSCPChiPa. Policy Committee powers were not fully defined until after failure of the strike threat.

[43] *Ibid*.

especially those at St. Louis and Oakland. As early as November, 1927, Webster had complained to Randolph that St. Louis had the lowest morale of all the union's districts, pointing out that the problem lay with the district organizer. He told Randolph that it would be in the union's best interest to replace E. J. Bradley because the city was "too big a field to be left destitute."[44] Fully confident that his district would some day be one of the better ones in the BSCP, Bradley suffered no delusions about his current situation and admitted that "at present it [was] the worst." Unable to raise enough money to keep his office going, Bradley appealed to Webster for funds to "tide me over."[45] The *Argus*'s intense opposition to the union caused some of Bradley's problems. In addition, Pullman representatives in St. Louis took an exceptionally hard line against BSCP porters. But Bradley's own political flaws — such as threatening porters with suits and garnishments if they did not pay dues, appealing to the public for funds, and announcing that the union was broke — worried Webster more.[46] Randolph, at times more charitable than Webster, agreed that Bradley did not produce the desired results, but allowed that he seemed "to be doing his best."[47] Nonetheless, the St. Louis situation did not improve, and well into the following year Webster was still pushing for Randolph to remove Bradley before he could "kill what little spirit there [was] in St. Louis and make it utterly impossible for somebody else."[48]

In Oakland the problem was of a somewhat different order. In January, 1928, R. D. Jones, the local secretary-treasurer, stole $780 from the BSCP, causing problems for both the district and the union at large. On the local level, the loss depleted Oakland's operating funds

[44] MPW to APR, Nov. 19, 1927, *ibid.*

[45] Bradley to MPW, Dec. 9, 1927, *ibid.*

[46] *Ibid.*; Flyer, Bradley to St. Louis Business Community, Dec., 1927; MPW to Bradley, Dec. 11, 1927; MPW to APR, Aug. 1, 1928, *ibid*. C. L. Dellums in a telephone interview (Mar. 12, 1975) spoke of the harshness with which Pullman superintendent Burr at St. Louis treated porters who showed interest in the BSCP. MPW called the threat to sue porters for dues "a ridiculous document."

[47] APR to MPW, Nov. 21, 1927, BSCP ChiPa. Anderson, *A. Philip Randolph*, 212, pictures Bradley as a hard-working BSCP organizer who suffered tremendously for the union, losing his automobile, his home, and even his family. Though Bradley was undoubtedly hard working, Webster considered him incompetent.

[48] MPW to APR, Oct. 10, 1928, BSCP ChiPa. Bradley apparently did not know what a low opinion Webster had of his work. Bradley confided in the Chicago leader, and on one occasion wrote Webster that "such information . . . that comes from your office is more direct and exact than from elsewhere, and I will appreciate your view on this matter." See Bradley to MPW, Dec. 9, 1927, *ibid.*

and forced Dad Moore to appeal to Webster for money with which to pay rent. More important, it created a crisis of leadership for the national union when Oakland officials failed to keep reports of the theft out of the newspapers.[49] Some BSCP opponents called the Oakland incident a common occurrence and alleged that Brotherhood representatives often ran off with the porters' money. Since such comments caused an erosion of confidence among the public and the porters, Randolph was exuberant when the Fidelity and Casualty Company of New York, the BSCP's bonders, paid the union a check to cover the full amount. Randolph used the occasion for a major publicity announcement in which he declared that the porters' money was safe.[50] Despite the hard times which the Oakland district experienced financially, it reaped one positive benefit from the Jones theft: Jones's departure created a place in the Brotherhood's leadership for C. L. Dellums. He became secretary-treasurer of the Oakland division in February, 1928, and brought to the Bay Area the dynamic leadership the union needed to complement Dad Moore's charisma. Dellums demonstrated excellent abilities and soon became a major figure in the national organization.

As Brotherhood leaders grappled with these internal problems, their external support also changed in a way which some of them, particularly Randolph, believed would significantly improve the BSCP's public image. In November, 1927, one of the strangest incidents in the Brotherhood's history took place. The Chicago *Defender*, whose support Randolph had long deemed vital, completely reversed its position and came out in support of the union. It would be tempting to explain the change by saying the paper suddenly realized its errors and wanted to mend its ways, or that perhaps some new union action brought the *Defender* to its senses. These were not the real reasons, however, nor are those real reasons entirely clear.

The first public indication that the *Defender* was having trouble because of its opposition to the BSCP came on November 2, 1927, when Randolph issued a flyer in New York claiming that the porters would destroy the paper. On November 8 he addressed a mass meeting in which he "denounced in scathing language the Chicago *Defender* in particular and Robert S. Abbott, its editor-owner."[51] Randolph claimed

[49] Several letters, MPW to APR, Feb. - Mar., 1928. See particularly MPW to APR, Mar. 7, 1928, *ibid*.

[50] New York *Age*, May 26, 1928.

[51] Pittsburgh *Courier*, Nov. 12, 1927. BSCP sources later claimed that the porters

that the porters had made the *Defender*, and that now they could break it. Those attacks, coming after Randolph had already entered into conversation with Nathan K. McGill, managing editor of the *Defender* and Abbott's personal attorney, show Randolph's use of publicity to enhance the BSCP's image of power. Randolph informed Webster that McGill "followed me to New York, [and] begged for a statement on the Brotherhood."[52] During their conversations McGill told Randolph that neither he nor Abbott had been aware that the paper was anti-BSCP.[53] Not surprisingly, Randolph did not believe the claim. Indeed, it is unlikely that the paper's chief officials were ignorant of such a major policy position, especially when it provoked the *Messenger* into almost monthly counterattacks, such as labeling the newspaper the "Chicago *Surrender*, misnamed *Defender*" or the "World's Greatest Weakley," and deriding its editors as "idiot-ors."

Brotherhood officials had long alleged that the *Defender* accepted payments to support the Pullman Company. Webster wrote Randolph that he believed McGill approached the BSCP because the company had taken the *Defender* off its payroll, and claimed that Abbott was experiencing additional financial woes because the *Defender* had suffered a sharp decline in circulation during the period shortly prior to McGill's visit. Webster wanted to let the *Defender* people "sweat for a while."[54] He credited his Chicago sources with proving that the *Defender* changed

---

themselves carried on an unofficial boycott of the *Defender* and forced it to change. See Roy Lancaster, "Porters Smash a Company Union," *Labor Age*, XVII (Jan., 1928), 16. If it occurred, the boycott probably took the form of porters discontinuing their practice of delivering the *Defender* to small outlying towns.

[52] APR to MPW, Nov. 11, 1927, BSCP ChiPa. Randolph had indicated to Webster in a letter of Nov. 3, the day after he issued the New York flyer, that something was going on between the *Defender* and himself. N. K. McGill had at one time been a major force in the NAACP in Jacksonville. In Feb., 1921, McGill had been among a party of NAACP local representatives who visited President-elect Harding while he vacationed at St. Augustine. The delegation wanted to sound out Harding on his views concerning the conditions of blacks in the South. See NAACP *11th Annual Report* (1921), 8-9. Some sources spell the editor's name Magill.

[53] Roi Ottley, *The Lonely Warrior*: *The Life and Times of Robert S. Abbott* (Chicago: Regnery Press, 1955), 259-65, supports part of this allegation in his official biography of Abbott. He absolves Abbott of any knowledge of or responsibility for the paper's position and holds McGill fully responsible. Ottley asserts that McGill made his peace mission to Randolph in New York after Abbott learned of the paper's position and insisted that he do so.

[54] MPW to APR, Nov. 11, 1927, BSCP ChiPa; Ottley, *Lonely Warrior*, 265, speaks of the *Defender*'s decline in circulation, yet he suggests that Abbott initiated the change more out of concern for the Brotherhood's verbal darts than for financial reasons. Part of

its position because the company "unexpectedly dropped [it] from the payroll." He added that the paper had made several unsuccessful attempts to regain its favored position at Pullman, but, because BSCP attacks had made it useless to the company, the editors "got down on their knees" to the union.[55] Loss of money through a drop in circulation was perhaps the prime reason for the *Defender*'s change of heart. The *Argus* had been effective in holding down porter participation in St. Louis and thus could justify its alleged retention by the company; at least Pullman would continue to buy numerous copies of the journal and make them available to the porters. The *Defender*, however, was in the hotbed of porter unionism, and since it had ineffectively opposed the BSCP for two years, Pullman management had undoubtedly decided the company simply could no longer afford such support. Randolph got away with the charges he leveled in November, 1927, so the Brotherhood's claim may be accurate. The *Defender* remained silent while he used its own pages to accuse the paper of treason against black people; nonetheless, it later came to the union's side as a staunch supporter.

Randolph handled the *Defender* affair in a rather curious fashion. The paper published its new position on the BSCP in an article and an editorial, both of which Randolph wrote and sent to the paper with instructions that amounted to an ultimatum. He informed Webster that he had written

> an article and an editorial and sent it to Mr. N. K. McGill. I also told him not to change a word in the article or the editorial, and that I want both to be carried in the same edition of the Chicago and National sections of the paper, and if that were not done, I did not want them to carry anything. I also pointed out that I want the article on the front page of the *Defender*. Since we have them down on their knees to us, I thought we would drive a

the reason for the loss in circulation might be that the Pullman Company no longer bought the paper to place at the porter's disposal, as it had done earlier. Andrew Buni, Robert Vann's biographer, writes that black newspapers depended upon circulation for 80 percent of their income in 1920s. See Andrew Buni, *Robert L. Vann of the Pittsburgh Courier: Politics and Black Journalism* (Pittsburgh: University of Pittsburgh Press, 1974), 134.

[55] MPW to APR, Nov. 11, 1927, BSCPChiPa; Ottley, *Lonely Warrior*, 266, quotes Randolph, some years after the incident, as saying that McGill told Randolph and Webster that the *Defender* had received money from Pullman for its support, probably in the form of advertising. According to Ottley, Randolph claimed that McGill cited figures as to how much money the paper got from the company. The fact is, however, that the *Defender* never carried an ad for Pullman — although it did get accounts from Melvin Chisum's National Negro Advertising Agency, which was established in Chicago in

hard bargain, otherwise we don't need them to come to our side. I told them that we could get along well without the *Defender,* but that the *Defender* could not get along without the Brotherhood.[56]

When the November 19, 1927, issue of the *Defender* hit the newsstands, it carried the required front-page article as well as the editorial. It treated its readers to the unprecedented spectacle of a newspaper denouncing itself it terms approaching libel. Randolph wrote in the article:

There were those who elected to oppose the movement. Some prominent men of color hired their souls for Pullman gold to lie and deceive. In one of America's most sinister sinful and sordid chapters of industrial crime, debauchery and deviltry, black men, alleged leaders, conscienceless, crooked, and corrupt, seeking to redden their hands in the blood of their brothers for greed and gain, clutched the pulsing throats of innocent black babes with their filthy murderous fingers of graft, vouchsafed by the labors of their fathers. In pulpit and press, like mad dervishes howling for the blood of their victims, they hunted, hounded and harassed, libeled and slandered those militant men who stood their ground for the right of the porters to organize and be men.

In announcing the new editorial stance, Randolph let it be known that the *Defender* was "a four-square red blooded race paper," and that "after a careful survey and review of the determined and lawful struggle of the Pullman porters, led by the brilliant and fearless A. Philip Randolph over a period of two years, the *Defender* herewith announces its determination to stand with the porters, arm in arm, shoulder to shoulder, for a living wage and better working conditions."[57]

Although Randolph played tough with the *Defender* people, he was overjoyed that the paper joined the Brotherhood's supporters. Calling the *Defender*'s decision "the most significant change ever made in American journalism,"[58] he believed the paper's new stance would cause a sensational reversal in the attitude of porters toward the union

---

1925 to coordinate advertisements in black papers. Chisum's earlier episode as an agent for Pullman heightens the possibility that he used his agency as a conduit of Pullman funds into the black press. The main problem with Ottley's quotation of Randolph is that Randolph said McGill made the revelations at a meeting in which Randolph and Webster represented the BSCP. But the Brotherhood/*Defender* peace meeting took place in New York, and Webster never participated in the negotiations. In correspondence with Webster during the crisis Randolph did not mention that McGill had made the admissions to which Ottley refers.

[56] APR to MPW, Nov. 8, 1927, BSCP ChiPa.

[57] Chicago *Defender*, Nov. 19, 1927.

[58] *Messenger*, X (Jan., 1928), 21.

and would bring its membership and dues up to about 90 percent of all the porters. He urged Webster to "check about the reaction of the people in Chicago to the *Defender*'s change of front."[59]

Not sharing Randolph's enthusiasm for the *Defender* and its officers, Webster answered that he had "absolutely no confidence in Abbott or McGill." He reminded Randolph of McGill's attempts to poison the Webster-Randolph relationship during the early days of the movement and indicated that the *Defender*'s opposition had not been against the porters' union, but against Randolph personally.[60] He did not want the BSCP to give the *Defender* any further consideration. After all, porters "paid the *Defender* no attention anyhow." Webster pointed out to Randolph that instead of enhancing its value to the union, the *Defender*'s change had placed the paper "in the most ridiculous light," because "everybody in Chicago considers Abbott dumb, anyhow."[61]

Like so many issues, the *Defender* affair soon placed Randolph at odds with Webster. Though he knew Webster hated Abbott, Randolph insisted that Abbott participate in Webster's labor conference scheduled for January, 1928. He even suggested that Webster stop in at *Defender* offices to talk with Abbott about it, explaining that, though he knew Webster's feelings, the union should endeavor at all costs to profit from Abbott's influence.[62] Webster repeated his belief that Abbott's change was insincere. Arguing that the Brotherhood should not have Abbott appear at any event it sponsored, he suggested that the rank and file would not look favorably upon the editor's participation. This man whom Randolph could not control, and probably did not understand, wrote that it would be most embarrassing to him to have to introduce Abbott, and quietly added that he did not "feel like participating [in the labor conference] if it is insisted that Mr. Abbott be a speaker."[63] His comment left Randolph little choice. Abbott did not appear and Webster hosted the labor conference.

As the BSCP reeled from the effects of the adverse ICC decision of early 1928, and despite newfound support in the *Defender*, the con-

[59] APR to MPW, Nov. 19, 1927, BSCP ChiPa.

[60] MPW to APR, Nov. 19, 1927, *ibid.*

[61] MPW to APR, Nov. 21, 1927, *ibid.*

[62] APR to MPW, Dec. 19, 1927, *ibid.* APR had already proposed the talk to Abbott.

[63] MPW to APR, Dec. 19, 1927, *ibid.* MPW indicated in this letter that evidence supporting his charge that the paper's change was insincere had appeared in Chicago during the month after the *Defender*'s change. He does not make clear what issues he had in mind.

stantly beleaguered organization found itself in still another public embroilment when the Pittsburgh *Courier*, once the BSCP's staunchest supporter, shifted its position as radically as the *Defender* had done. As fortune would have it, the Brotherhood had converted an enemy but had also lost a powerful friend.

It is not certain if there was any connection between the *Defender*'s recruitment and the *Courier*'s defection. Clearly, however, the two papers were in sharp competition, and Randolph might have precipitated the *Courier*'s action when he wrote the article which the *Defender* published. He sent a copy of the article to the *Courier* and led the newspaper to believe it had exclusive rights to it. The *Courier* printed the piece over Randolph's name, complete with his picture, on the same day that the *Defender*'s identical story appeared.[64] One can easily imagine the disgust of Robert Lee Vann, the *Courier*'s editor-owner, when he learned he had been deceived. The Vann-Randolph relationship probably began to erode; soon after Randolph's article of November 19 appeared in the *Defender* and the *Courier*, Vann backed away from his previous position of printing everything Randolph asked him to run. Refusing to publish one of Randolph's stories, Vann wrote the union leader on January 30, 1928, that the BSCP should exercise a little silence while the union's petition was before the ICC. He further pointed out that the *Courier* "hate[d] to carry columns after columns of useless propaganda."[65]

The *Courier*'s action, especially given its long support of the BSCP, calls into question claims by Randolph and others that the Brotherhood had forced the *Defender*'s change of heart. In any event, the new Vann-Randolph relationship had deep and troublesome consequences for the BSCP during the spring of 1928. On March 31 Webster alerted Randolph that the Pullman Company had approached an eastern newspaperman friendly to the Brotherhood, asking him about acting as an intermediary to discuss with Randolph ways to settle the BSCP-Pullman dispute.[66] Assuring Webster that his only aim was to win recognition for the BSCP, Randolph answered that he would gladly discuss methods of

[64] Pittsburgh *Courier*, Nov. 19, 1927. The editor's note which accompanied Randolph's article read: "A. Philip Randolph, general organizer of the Brotherhood of Sleeping Car Porters, has written this article setting forth the intimate details of the courageous fight for economic justice, exclusively for the Pittsburgh *Courier*."

[65] Vann to APR, Jan. 30, 1928, Vann Papers. All material cited from Vann's papers was obtained through the courtesy of Andrew Buni, Vann's biographer.

[66] MPW to APR, Mar. 31, 1928, BSCP ChiPa.

achieving that goal with anyone. He considered this new activity, along with the *Defender*'s change, as evidence that the company was ready to meet with the Brotherhood and negotiate in earnest. Randolph pointed out to Webster that, since most eastern newspapermen were friendly to the union, he could not determine who the agent would be; he asked Webster whether the man was "colored or white."[67]

Webster did not know who the agent was, but the fact that he heard of the mission in Chicago four days before Randolph received the contact indicates the accuracy of his suggestion that it originated at Pullman headquarters. The perplexing question is why the company would be interested in settling with the BSCP a month after the union had lost the ICC decision. Perhaps it believed the adverse ruling had left the union shattered, and that the time was propitious for it to step in and settle the dispute to its advantage. Likewise, the company might well have wished to ward off the threatened strike.

Although the company's involvement cannot be proved, the proposal which came forth was a classic example of an attempt to divide and conquer. Vann approached Randolph and asked if he would be willing to resign from the union's leadership if the company in turn agreed to negotiate with the BSCP. The request that he resign must certainly have been crushing to Randolph and must have brought memories he wished to forget. The situation closely paralleled the one in which he had been involved in organizing elevator operators in New York, only to see the group coopted by a larger union. Yet he seemed to accept the proposal graciously. Randolph indicated to Vann, and so informed his colleagues by telegram, that he would resign if Pullman made a bona fide offer that would help the union.[68] He repeated the offer in a letter to Webster on the same day. But despite his response to Vann and his colleagues, Randolph decided to stay in his position. As he told Webster, his resignation would not be necessary, since Vann's approach meant that the company was willing to negotiate and simply wanted to save face.[69] Webster supported the Chief and passed on to him information which Bennie Smith, from his post in Pittsburgh, had collected from Vann. The editor had informed Smith that if Randolph did not step down and allow the company to enter into negotiations with the union by June 1,

[67] APR to MPW, Apr. 2, 1928, *ibid*. For APR's opinion of the significance of the *Defender*'s action, see APR to MPW, Nov. 8, 1927, *ibid*.

[68] See, *e.g.*, Telegram, APR to MPW, Apr. 5, 1928, *ibid*.

[69] APR to MPW, Apr. 5, 1928, *ibid*.

Pullman would force all porters to sign "yellow-dog" contracts as prerequisites for continued employment.[70]

Until now the discussion had been private, but Vann made it public with the *Courier* of April 7. The paper's banner headline read "Is Randolph to Resign?" and the accompanying story said that porters were spreading the story that he would. In answer to its own question, the *Courier* alluded to Randolph's known Socialist affiliations as the reason why he should step aside, asserting that no American corporation would do business with a Socialist. Vann discussed Randolph and the union in an amicable fashion. He printed the essence of his conversation with Randolph about resignation, and praised the union leader for his hard work on behalf of the porters. Vann asserted that Randolph had worked himself sick for the union and praised his willingness to give way now so that a negotiating session could be assured. News that Randolph would resign, he concluded, had more "significance for the company and men than any other news story published within the past year."[71]

Vann was mistaken in his belief that his low-key appeal to Randolph would be effective. In response to Vann's account of the conversation with Randolph and his suggestion that Randolph resign, the BSCP published a statement declaring that it was the wish of the rank and file that Randolph remain as general organizer. Porters, it declared, believed that if the company was willing to recognize the union without him, there was no reason why it would not do so with him as leader.[72] With that declaration began a debate which grew increasingly hostile and which, as Webster suggested to Randolph, would make Vann the Brotherhood's enemy "purely and simply."[73]

In a personal letter to Randolph on the very day when the *Courier* asked whether he would resign, Vann reemphasized his opinions about Randolph's socialism being the reason for the *Courier*'s defection. The editor pointed out that Randolph saw himself as the only person through whom the porters could achieve their goal of recognition, but emphasized that he was "just as convinced as long as you are in the picture

[70] MPW to APR, Apr. 7, 1928, *ibid*.

[71] Pittsburgh *Courier*, Apr. 7, 1928.

[72] It must be emphasized that the BSCP took no poll of the rank and file on this matter. APR notified MPW, and apparently other district organizers, that they should issue such statements. See Telegram, APR to MPW, Apr. 6, 1928, BSCP ChiPa; Special BSCP press release, Apr. 7, 1928, NAACP Pas, C414, LC.

[73] MPW to APR, Apr. 7, 1928, BSCP ChiPa.

you will never get anywhere with these porters." Vann noted that he understood how difficult and embarrassing the matter must be for Randolph, and went on to say that a man of Randolph's leadership abilities and potential was too valuable to black people to be "crushed because you cannot see that your history is the strongest militating force against your efforts to succeed."[74]

With this letter Vann made his last attempt to handle the dispute in a friendly manner. The next week's edition of the *Courier* carried a front-page open letter from the editor to Pullman porters and maids; in it he placed full responsibility for the union's failure to gain recognition at Randolph's feet. He described the BSCP leader as a "school child" and a "socialistic dreamer" who was "whistling in the dark to keep up courage" when he made comments about bringing Pullman to its knees. Claiming that Randolph simply wanted a good fight, Vann emphasized that the porters and maids wanted results. He ridiculed the general organizer's pledge to "die in his tracks" before he would let the porters down and affirmed that the *Courier* was tired and would not continue to support such vainglory.[75]

Aside from Randolph's personal fears of seeing another dream shattered, he and other BSCP leaders saw the perils which could befall the organization if Vann succeeded in forcing Randolph to resign under fire. The Brotherhood was then in the middle of its strike vote, and a change in leadership would bring the entire effort tumbling down around those who remained. Furthermore, Randolph astutely realized that if Pullman could tell the porters who to put out as leader, it could tell them who to put in. In the final analysis, the BSCP would be just another company union.[76] In order to prevent this calamity, the BSCP Policy Committee met in New York on April 13 to map ways of countering the Vann offensive. The group concluded that "there was no one in sight . . . that could lead as successfully and as effectively the fight of the Pullman porters as A. Philip Randolph."[77] Discussing Vann's open letter point by point, the committee made specific responses to his charges, denying (among other allegations) Vann's claim that other individuals had urged Randolph to resign. The committee added that Vann had known for

[74] Vann to APR, Apr. 7, 1928, Vann Papers.

[75] Pittsburgh *Courier*, Apr. 14, 1928.

[76] For an example of Randolph's comments on this point, see New York *Age*, May 19, 1928.

[77] Lancaster to Dad Moore, Apr. 20, 1928, BSCP Oakland Pas.

years that Randolph was a Socialist and charged that the editor either had malicious intentions against the union or totally misunderstood what the BSCP's fight was about.[78] Few papers supported Vann on the resignation issue, and even those which remained neutral denied that Randolph's socialism had anything to do with the company's refusal to recognize the BSCP.

As the debate deepened, the *Courier*'s statements showed how important the matter of destroying the union had become. It launched continuous tirades against Randolph and the Brotherhood; indeed, the paper even reversed its position on trade unionism altogether and urged porters to sign loyalty oaths.[79] Vann, writing in his personal front-page column, summed up the *Courier*'s new position:

> As between labor and capital in this country: let it be known that it has always been the policy of the *Courier* to cultivate a friendly feeling between the colored workingman in this country and American capital. Labor unions may be all right for white men — and there are times when we doubt their efficiency even for white men; but so far as the American Negro is concerned, the labor unions offer him no hope. As between labor unions and American capital the colored man ought to be able to choose capital without the slightest hesitation. The labor unions not only fight the colored worker and keep him out of the unions, except in rare and inconsequential occasions, but they fight to keep him and capital apart so that the colored man profits nothing from forming a union, but loses the possibility of a profitable contact with capital.[80]

The publisher's defection from the BSCP was easier to understand than his casual rewriting of his previous position. In speaking of what had "always" been the *Courier*'s policy, he overlooked the fact that the paper had been the BSCP's primary supporter for more than two years. Vann's chameleon-like political tendencies have been noted, and his biographer points out that he occasionally changed his editorial stance when it suited his interests, or those of the *Courier*.[81] Now, during April and May, 1928, he was exhibiting the same traits in his dealings with the

[78] *Ibid*. Though dated Apr. 14, the *Courier*, being a weekly, appeared on the newsstand in New York one or two days earlier. The national edition had to be available throughout the country by Saturday.

[79] Pittsburgh *Courier*, May 5, 1928.

[80] *Ibid*., May 12, 1928.

[81] James H. Brewer, "Robert Lee Vann, Democrat or Republican: An Exponent of Loose-Leaf Politics," *Negro History Bulletin*, XXI (Feb., 1958), 101-3. Brewer explains that Vann supported Hoover in 1928, Roosevelt in 1932 and 1936, and Willkie in

Brotherhood. Andrew Buni writes that Vann had set out in the early 1920s to make the *Courier* the leading black newspaper in the country, both in influence and in circulation. He suggests that Vann supported the BSCP during the early years because of blacks' widespread interest in the union: their interest would heighten *Courier* circulation. Indeed, Vann employed several *Messenger* staff members in 1925-26; George Schuyler became the *Courier*'s chief editorial writer, and Randolph often plugged the paper in the *Messenger* and instructed porters and *Messenger* salesmen to advertise and buy the *Courier*. By 1928 both the Brotherhood and the *Messenger* were experiencing difficulties. Vann might well have decided he no longer needed either of them. True, when he began his attack on April 7 he aimed it specifically at Randolph, while reaffirming his desire to see the union succeed. But by May 12 he came out in opposition to all trade unionism for blacks, a position for which he had criticized Kelly Miller in 1925.[82]

Another possible explanation for Vann's turnabout, and his persistent attack on Randolph, is that the company had made him a proposition he could not refuse. The *Courier* itself had long maintained that the Pullman Company could buy any support it desired. That Webster in Chicago knew of Vann's mission ahead of time increases the company's culpability. Buni cites an anonymous source as saying that Vann received $50,000 from Pullman for his opposition. Money could explain why Vann carried his opposition so far. When he could not get Randolph to resign, he had to bring the whole union down to justify the fee.[83]

1940. He depicts Vann as a farsighted black leader who switched allegiances in the best interest of black people.

In his recent biography, Buni (*Vann*, ch. 7) presents a different picture of the editor. He discusses in detail Vann's attack on the NAACP hierarchy in 1926 over handling of monies contributed by the public and the Garland Fund for the defense of Ossian Sweet, a black doctor accused of murder for defending his home in Detroit in 1925. This argument also represented a switch in Vann's position on the NAACP and toward NAACP leaders. The hard feelings lasted for almost three years.

[82] See Buni, *Vann*, 162-71, for his discussion of the *Courier*-BSCP affair. Buni also writes about Vann's ability to hold a grudge against an enemy. If Randolph angered him by the article he sent to both the *Defender* and the *Courier* in Nov., 1927, it would have been characteristic of Vann to want to retaliate. Vann's reaction on the death of James Weldon Johnson shows the extent to which he carried his anger when he felt he had been insulted. Buni quotes Vann as having told Walter White: "You know, Walter, I must be frank about this. . . . Jim and I were not friends when he died, and had not been friends for some time. I have never forgiven him for the way he treated me over my difference with the NAACP. . . . And so I say about his funeral the same thing I said about Huey Long's funeral — 'I shall not be present, but I am glad it happened.' "

[83] Buni writes that the allegation of a payoff, though unprovable, was a "general

A further point to bear in mind is that Vann was a leading black Republican, and 1928 was a presidential election year. A contemporary observer wrote that the *Courier* tried to rid the BSCP of Randolph so that the dispute could be settled before the election.[84] Webster firmly believed that Vann wanted to push Randolph out of the leadership and set himself up as spokesman for the porters' union. By so doing, he could make a deal with Pullman and then go to the Republican convention as a major supporter of Frank O. Lowden of Illinois.[85] In addition to private political aims, Vann was publicity chairman in what Webster called the "Jim Crow end" of the Republican party in 1928. He had abundant reason to want to squelch a black movement that could harm the party.[86]

Though no direct relationship can be made with Vann's activities, Republican politicians did express concern about the BSCP. On the same day that Vann published his first suggestion that Randolph resign, Webster wrote Randolph that he was having trouble holding onto his position in Chicago Republican circles.[87] By the first of May he was being constantly besieged about the BSCP by a man whom he called the "big Negro boss in Chicago" who was himself under pressure to get Webster out of the union. Webster refused to resign, suggesting that to do so would be "nothing less than treachery."[88]

Despite union regulations to the contrary, the BSCP was doing everything in its power to create political unease among its enemies, even disregarding BSCP bylaws that explicitly forbade connections between the union and political parties. As early as April union officials had proposed to a segment of the Democratic party that they would "give assurance that the entire influence of the Brotherhood of Sleeping Car Porters, built up over three years of intensive educational work would be thrown on the side of Governor Smith and Democratic victory" in exchange for a contribution of $97,000 over a seven-month period to support a union publication. Such a grant, the union's memorandum continued, "would put the Brotherhood over the top and

---

kind of story that got around" among BSCP leaders. According to Buni, if Vann did receive the money, he probably used it to build a new printing plant for the *Courier*. *Ibid*., 170.

[84] New York *Age*, May 12, 1928.

[85] MPW to APR, Apr. 7, 1928, BSCP ChiPa.

[86] Buni, *Vann*, ch. 7, n. 136, refers to others who pictured Vann as a calculating politician who saw himself as "the greatest race politician that ever came along."

[87] MPW to APR, Apr. 7, 1928, BSCP ChiPa.

[88] MPW to APR, May 1, 1928, *ibid*.

swing a large section of the Negro voting public to the Democratic side.''[89] The BSCP had an inflated vision of its influence, but at least some high-ranking Democratic campaign officials were willing to listen to its proposal. Neither group of BSCP leaders succeeded in soliciting national party support. As Randolph and Webster lamented to each other, neither party paid any attention to black voters because blacks were politically unorganized.[90] Their attempts only added up to another union failure.

The Pullman Company not only brazenly dropped the *Defender* and equally cultivated the *Courier*, but company management, emboldened by the Brotherhood's failure to carry through on the strike threat, also encouraged non-BSCP porters to find a way for Pullman to meet with representative porters under ERP. To facilitate such action the porters, at the company's suggestion, organized committees who talked with Pullman officials and tried to convince other porters to denounce the Brotherhood and pledge support to the company. Such groups were particularly strong and effective on the West Coast.[91]

All these problems — the abortive strike, Vann's opposition, the *Messenger*'s failure, and defection of once-loyal porters — had grave consequences for the BSCP by mid-1928. Membership figures, which had reached a peak of 4,632 shortly before the aborted strike (a figure that would not be attained again until 1936), fell off sharply to 2,368 by early 1929. Conditions deteriorated so much that Randolph felt compelled to change the union's traditional position and allow porters to submit to company demands and deny any relationship with the Brotherhood. On informing Webster of his views, Randolph wrote:

> Unquestionably, our strategy must be to protect the men from being exposed to sniping by the company. It is sound policy for us to advise the

[89] Undated, unsigned memorandum to Mr. [Howard S.] Cullman [Apr., 1928], NLCRG Pas. In an article in St. Louis *Argus*, Feb. 22, 1929, Frank Crosswaith accused Roy Lancaster of having written the memorandum. Howard S. Cullman was a high-ranking assistant to George van Namee, Smith's campaign manager in 1928. The governor had appointed Cullman a member of the Port Authority of New York in Feb., 1928. Crosswaith might be right in stating that Lancaster wrote the memorandum in question, but it is unlikely that he wrote it without Randolph's knowledge and consent. Correspondence between APR and MPW proves that both men approached political parties in violation of union regulations. See, *e.g.*, MPW to APR, Oct. 1, 1928, and APR to MPW, Oct. 4, 1928, BSCP ChiPa.

[90] MPW to APR, Oct. 1, and APR to MPW, Oct. 3, 1928, BSCP ChiPa.

[91] Minutes of a conference between Pullman officials and porters at Los Angeles, July 28, 1928, *ibid*.

> men when questioned by Pullman Company officials, whether white or black, whether they are members of the union, to say no; whether they are going to strike, to say no; whether they are going to work, to say yes; and whether they are with the company, to say yes. This gives the men definite assurance and the feeling that the Brotherhood is trying to protect them and their jobs. For discharged men not only weaken the Brotherhood numerically, but financially and spiritually.[92]

Not seeing this as "sound policy" at all, Webster disagreed vehemently. He insisted that any program of passive resistance would sap what little strength and morale the union still possessed and would deprive it of a following. He wrote Randolph that "if we are not able to produce something which can be held out to the men to look forward to, I do not see how we can hold them any length of time."[93] Webster considered Randolph's comments evidence that the union was falling down around him and that desperate measures must be taken to save it. He saw the responsibility as falling particularly upon himself, because Randolph seemed to have lost his nerve after the strike fiasco. That humiliation, as well as the stress of the Vann incident, apparently had left Randolph with a feeling of inadequacy.

Randolph's letter of June 21 convinced Webster that the Chief had lost courage and that he could now press for the changes he wished to make in the union. Webster immediately drew up his own "things-to-be-done" memorandum, jotting his notes on the back of Randolph's letter. Having steadily complained since February, 1928, that the New York office got too few results for too much in salaries, Webster decided to insist upon an investigation of the New York payroll.[94] This was an important issue: some officers in New York, particularly Lancaster, occasionally overdrew their salaries while field organizers drew nothing. For example, the BSCP owed Bennie Smith $500 in salary in June, 1928 (a problem Webster thought "should be taken care of"). But more than the inequitable distribution of funds available for salary payments, Webster was concerned about the emphasis which BSCP leaders at headquarters placed on organizing the public, as opposed to spending their time among porters. Webster argued this point through the spring of 1928, emphasizing to Randolph his belief "that upon the Pullman

[92] APR to MPW, June 21, 1928, *ibid*.

[93] MPW to APR, June 21, 1928, *ibid*. As on numerous other occasions, APR and MPW addressed each other on the same subject on the same day. Apparently they discussed these issues by telephone before writing about them.

[94] MPW Self Memorandum, June 21, 1928, *ibid*.

porter lies the responsibility of financing this movement and that if we are not successful in educating him up to financing it, it is not going to be done by outsiders.''[95] While criticizing the general organizer, Webster reemphasized his belief that no one man should be responsible for determining the union's policy. He wanted to place real power in the hands of the recently constituted Policy Committee, a step which might also improve what he saw as the Brotherhood's ineffective public relations efforts. Premature announcement of the strike plans was only one example of the need for more effective control. Webster made clear to Randolph that he had discussed these matters with other BSCP representatives, all of whom agreed that a change from the union's usual militancy and continued concentration on organizing the public would be a major tactical error that would cause porters to place little faith in the leadership in the future. He warned his colleague that ''if [the porters] get away from you this time, I don't believe you will ever be able to get them back again within any reasonable length of time.''[96]

Webster made his most important, and potentially most disruptive, proposal when he suggested that the union's organizational work be directed ''from two strategic points, New York and Chicago.'' He told his New York colleague that he would come there in early July, along with other ''western men,'' to discuss the merits of his concerns. He had hinted at such a reorganization before, but this was the first time he allowed himself to suggest that the Chicago district was as important to the union's success as New York headquarters.[97] The feudal lord was reminding the king where power now lay.

At Webster's request, BSCP chiefs met in New York to debate his proposals. As it turned out, they adopted most of them.[98] The most significant action at the meeting centered on the questions of long-range development and regional access to information on the union's general financial condition. The leaders decided to require that the national secretary-treasurer supply regional organizers with quarterly financial statements. Likewise, the officials hampered Randolph's freedom of action by requiring that matters of policy be determined in advance, and that Randolph cease making major decisions on his own. They also discussed the question of the union's stance in face of increased Pullman

[95] MPW to APR, June 26, 1928, *ibid.*

[96] *Ibid.*; MPW Self Memorandum, June 21, 1928, *ibid.*

[97] MPW Self Memorandum, June 21, MPW to APR, June 8, MPW to APR, June 26, 1928, *ibid.*

[98] APR to Dad Moore, Aug. 7, 1928, *ibid.*

pressure on porters, deciding in the end to reject Randolph's proposal of passive resistance and reaffirming the union's militancy. Brotherhood porters should refuse to cooperate with the company on the issues of "yellow dog" contracts or loyalty oaths.[99]

Such decisions enabled Webster to leave New York as the strongest man in the BSCP. But more important than Webster's new strength was the fact that, through all this debate and reorganization, the Chicago organizer had not challenged Randolph's right to continue in his role as national leader of the Brotherhood. On the contrary, Webster realized that he functioned better in a behind-the-scenes role, working directly with the porters, and he recognized Randolph's excellence at operating on a more public level. Although the work of making porters into BSCP members was crucial, Webster realized the importance of a good public image and understood that no one could better serve as a moral force for the porters and more effectively articulate their interests to the public than Randolph. Though Webster kicked and complained about Randolph's leadership and the latter's positions on certain matters, the two men had developed deep mutual respect. Webster exercised wide latitude in the union not only because of his powerful position in Chicago, but also because Randolph valued his opinions. For his part, Webster was a good organization man and always carried out union policy, even when he disagreed with it.

After spending several days debating the union's future, Webster was determined that the New York leaders would live up to the agreements reached at the conference, especially those concerning finances. Lancaster omitted from the minutes any mention of the requirement that regional organizers have regular access to financial reports, but Webster had it inserted.[100] Despite the fact that the leaders had discussed assignments for regional directors, within a month Randolph wanted to reassign two of them. Again Bennie Smith was involved. Webster objected, pointing out that this represented a return to snap decision-making, and Smith remained in Pittsburgh.[101]

The long-standing issue between Randolph and Webster over the relative merits of organizing porters as opposed to organizing the public soon cropped up again when Randolph, as usual, endeavored to line up public support for the BSCP. On this occasion he sought aid from three

[99] *Ibid.*
[100] MPW to APR, July 27, 1928, *ibid.*
[101] MPW to APR, Aug. 13, APR to MPW, Aug. 16, 1928, *ibid.*

specific and diverse sources: the Improved and Benevolent Order of Elks of the World, one of the largest black fraternal organizations in the country; the conservative wing of black leadership represented by Dr. Robert Russa Moton, president of Tuskegee Institute; and the Socialist labor unions in the needle trades.

During August, 1928, Randolph tried hard to carry the Brotherhood's message before the annual meeting of the Elks. He hoped to persuade the fraternal order to award the BSCP a thousand-dollar grant and endorse its program.[102] Randolph had even gone so far as to join the Elks, after which he wrote Webster that the initiation "nearly killed me."[103] But by joining the organization in order to feel welcome at the convention, Randolph made a tactical error. He had joined a New York lodge which intended to challenge the Grand Exalted Ruler in his bid for reelection.[104] Though Randolph succeeded in getting the Order's endorsement, he did not come away from the convention with a check. His maneuver did not impress Webster, who pointed out that the union had "passed the point of stirring up things" and added, "you and I both know that we are not going to get a terribly lot of support from Negroes outside the Organization." Reminding his colleague that the porters had brought the union as far as it had come, Webster insisted that it was up to them to "take it the rest of the way."[105]

It was not mere annoyance at Randolph's appearance before the Elks that caused Webster to speak out. He also objected to Randolph's carrying Crosswaith, the BSCP's Socialist organizer, along on his tour. Since Crosswaith had spent most of his time with the Brotherhood speaking to the public and helping Randolph to create a favorable image for the union, Webster believed porters associated Crosswaith too closely with the general trade union movement. Webster warned Randolph that Crosswaith's presence on the trip would indicate to porters that the union cared more for public opinion than for membership, and he encouraged the Chief to select someone who identified more closely with the rank and file.[106]

Still searching for outside support, Randolph had come almost full circle to the point of betraying his past. By September he was flirting

[102] APR to MPW, Aug. 8, 1928, *ibid*. One should recall the Elks' policy decision concerning unions at their 1925 meeting in Richmond. See the first chapter.

[103] APR to MPW, Aug. 20, 1928, BSCP ChiPa.

[104] APR to MPW, Aug. 23, 1928, *ibid*.

[105] MPW to APR, Aug. 31, 1928, *ibid*.

[106] *Ibid*.

with Robert R. Moton, whom he called the "most powerful single Negro in the country"[107] — a far cry from his dismissal of the educator in 1926 as a "hidebound conservative." Apparently Moton knew several members of the board of directors at Pullman, and Randolph wanted him to gain the BSCP a hearing with the company. Though Moton pledged his services, nothing came of this proposition, as Webster had predicted when he reminded Randolph that Moton was "on the charitable end of corporations."[108]

Instead of trying to whip public opinion into line behind the union, Webster busied himself with trying to maintain the porters' interest in the BSCP. He suggested to Randolph that the leadership draw up a wage scale and present it to the men for their approval, so the porters would feel they were participating in the union's operation.[109] A group of active Pullman porters could then present the proposal to the Pullman Company, disproving company charges that the BSCP did not represent the porters. Randolph agreed and submitted the wage scale to the membership, but the scheme broke down when New York leaders failed to persuade their local BSCP members to participate on the committee of porters. Webster lamented that the "men in the East [were] so conservative," as were their leaders. He declared that he could get the necessary number of men in Chicago, but lamented they would not constitute a representative group.[110]

Not only did eastern leaders fail to maintain an effective following among the porters during late 1928, but they were also feuding among themselves. In October the backbiting took a turn that soon had the union's private matters before the public: BSCP general officers, whom Frank Crosswaith described as a "little group of five, all friends of Lancaster," dismissed Crosswaith and William Des Verney from their places as union organizers. Crosswaith bitterly objected to his dismissal, especially to the manner in which it had occurred. In a letter to Harry Laidler of the League for Industrial Democracy, he requested an impartial investigation of the union's finances. He accused Lancaster of having personally enriched himself at the union's expense during the past three years, and implied that he had done so with Randolph's knowledge, if not with his consent.[111] Randolph, undoubtedly anxious

[107] APR to MPW, Sept. 24, 1928, *ibid*.

[108] MPW to APR, Sept. 18, 1928, *ibid*.

[109] MPW to APR, Sept. 10, 1928, *ibid*.

[110] MPW to APR, Sept. 18, 1928, *ibid*.

[111] Crosswaith to Laidler, Oct. 15, 1928, NAACP Pas, C413, LC. Ironically, although the union had been founded in Des Verney's home, the reason given for his

to maintain public support, convened an independent three-man committee headed by the Socialist-oriented Robert W. Bagnall of the NAACP, with Laidler and I. A. Shiplacoff of the International Pocketbook Makers Union as members, to conduct the investigation. The committee ultimately exonerated Lancaster of any wrong-doing and supported the union's decision to release the two organizers.[112]

The firings and subsequent investigations occurred in private, but in February, 1929, Randolph and Lancaster informed the press that Crosswaith and Des Verney had been fired, provoking the two men to break their previous silence by speaking out in their own defense. They accused Lancaster of theft, implied that Randolph was aware of it and perhaps had benefited from the corruption,[113] and further elaborated on their charge in a later statement in the St. Louis *Argus*. They claimed that four of the union's six general officers (excluding Randolph and Lancaster) had tried to maintain the union on the "high plane of honor, responsibility and integrity" on which it had been founded. That they had failed, Crosswaith and Des Verney concluded, would constitute an "eternal challenge to Mr. Randolph's claim to a [high] place" among black leaders.[114]

Sensing the Brotherhood's difficulties, Pullman stepped in to administer what it thought would be the union's death blow. After the Crosswaith–Des Verney crisis became public, the company acceded to earlier requests by non-union porters and authorized a wage conference under the ERP, announcing that the company union would hold elections during March and April to elect porter-delegates to a conference scheduled for May. The BSCP protested the wage conference and solicited AFL support in its efforts to mount a porters' boycott of the

---

dismissal was that he was acting as a spy. Crosswaith claimed that Lancaster's friends had met without his and Des Verney's knowledge and decided on the dismissal. He did not say whether Randolph attended the meeting but lamented to Laidler that the Chief had not extended the courtesy of sending him a letter informing him of the reasons for his dismissal. The whole Crosswaith affair defies explanation, especially since Randolph and Crosswaith had enjoyed a long friendship and since it came so shortly after Randolph wanted to carry him along on a major organizing tour. Crosswaith apparently did not know how Webster felt about him, for he insisted that Webster sit in on any investigation. If Randolph did not favor the action, at least he accepted the decision to dismiss his two associates.

[112] Brailsford R. Brazeal, *The Brotherhood of Sleeping Car Porters* (New York: Harper and Brothers, 1946), 58.

[113] Chicago *Defender* and Pittsburgh *Courier*, both Feb. 16, 1929. The account in the *Courier* explicitly identifies Randolph and Lancaster as having released information on the dismissals of Des Verney and Crosswaith.

[114] St. Louis *Argus*, Mar. 1, 1929.

election.[115] Raising its familiar cry that the company was forcing porters to participate in the election, the Brotherhood protested to the Mediation Board. The board reminded Pullman of Watson-Parker regulations governing relations between employers and employees in the matter of electing representatives and cautioned that board members would observe the election for irregularities.[116]

Although the Brotherhood had always maintained that Pullman operatives used intimidation, coercion, and violence in arranging wage conferences and in removing BSCP opposition, it had been unable to prove the allegation. But they thought they had the proof in late April, 1929, when Ashley L. Totten suffered a severe beating in Kansas City. The Brotherhood immediately charged Pullman with responsibility for the attack. When authorities arrested Totten's assailant, who had escaped to Oklahoma City, and brought him back to stand trial, he corroborated that charge. Admitting that he had attacked Totten for pay, the suspect claimed that he had been hired by a black nightclub owner and a white Kansas City police captain. His mission had been to kill the BSCP leader for "a large sum of money," only five dollars of which he received. According to newspaper accounts, the police captain had known connections with the Kansas City office of the Pullman Company, but the judge refused to allow that information as evidence. The court gave the assailant a light sentence and fined Eddie Burton, the nightclub owner.[117] For his part, Totten suffered greatly from the attack. Union officials moved him from his organizing work in Kansas City to a desk job in New York headquarters, and Spencer Watson, a close associate of Webster's, took over the reins in Kansas City.

After this episode, the BSCP again appealed to the Mediation Board to disallow the results of the ERP election. The board did not see the assault on Totten as evidence of Pullman intimidation; it replied that it had received tabulations of the results of the election, and that all evidence showed that the porters had voted overwhelmingly to participate in the wage conference. The board informed Randolph that of 12,301 porters and maids eligible to vote, 11,382 participated in the primary and 11,586 in the general election to choose the final twenty-four porter-delegates — more than a 92 percent turnout in each case.

[115] New York *Age*, Mar. 30, 1929.

[116] Samuel B. Winslow, Mediation Board Chairman, to Pullman Company. The Board sent a copy of the letter to BSCP organizer A. L. Totten, which he made available to the Chicago *Defender*. See *Defender*, Apr. 13, 1929.

[117] New York *Age*, Aug. 3, 1929.

Furthermore, it pointed out that the BSCP had not exercised its right to put forward its own representatives in the elections, and that the company had piled up these impressive totals despite the Brotherhood's efforts to induce porters not to vote. Accordingly, the Mediation Board could find no fault with the ERP's elections.[118]

At the conference in 1929 the porters received a monthly pay raise of five dollars, which brought a starting porter's pay to $77.50. However, the company made no attempt to improve working conditions. BSCP officials charged that Pullman tried to tie the porters to a long-term "yellow dog" contract and warned that a strike might occur if the contract went through.[119] Though nothing came of the "yellow dog" issue, the conference did have a debilitating effect on the union. Coming in the wake of the strike fiasco and at a time when the BSCP's impotence was public knowledge, it contributed to the defection in membership.

BSCP leaders, sadly viewing the decline which now affected their once-proud movement, noted that internal dissension increased as their outside problems mounted. One problem, especially for some non–New Yorkers, involved the continued presence of Lancaster, the man Webster had long accused of being the center of dissension. Besides having allegedly taken more than his share of salary funds, Lancaster had recently harmed the organization by forcing out Crosswaith and Des Verney, thus provoking charges of graft and corruption that reflected adversely on the union's leader.

This was hardly a new occurrence for Webster. The Chicagoan had criticized Lancaster as crooked and insincere as early as October, 1927, and during mid-1928 had accused him of taking the union's money while other organizers went without their regular pay.[120] In fact, Webster, and perhaps a few others, thought Lancaster was downright dishonest. This feeling stemmed partly from the fact that the union rarely received what some considered appropriate income from major fund-raising events under Lancaster's direction. A prime example was an exhibition baseball game in 1929, during which thousands of people crowded Yankee Stadium to watch the festivities and pledge support for the BSCP. Lancaster explained the poor financial return by pointing out that not everyone in the stadium had actually bought a ticket; he had awarded numerous courtesy tickets in exchange for publicity.[121] His

[118] George A. Cook of the Mediation Board to APR, Apr. 23, 1929, PC Pas.

[119] Chicago *Defender*, June 1, 1929.

[120] MPW to APR, Oct. 12, 1927, July 24, 1928; BSCP ChiPa.

[121] Discussion of events surrounding Lancaster's removal from office is based largely on telephone interview with C. L. Dellums, Mar. 12, 1975. Dellums points out

explanation was unconvincing, and Webster determined at long last that Lancaster must go.

Webster failed in his first overt attempt to deny Lancaster reelection as secretary-treasurer at the BSCP's first national convention in Chicago in September, 1929. Lancaster had powerful friends in the New York office, including Randolph and Totten, as well as BSCP field officials who would support Randolph on most issues.[122] Dellums describes the discussion over election of the secretary-treasurer as heated. This was especially true on the crucial issue of whether delegates would vote by secret ballot or voice vote. Lancaster's hopes depended on the votes of two delegates from Chicago who, according to Dellums, would never have publicly voted against Webster's position. Randolph let it be known that he supported Lancaster's reelection and secured necessary votes for a secret ballot. Lancaster retained his office for another term.[123]

Between the 1929 meeting in Chicago and the convention in St. Louis the following year, Webster worked among Brotherhood leaders in other districts — Bradley, Smith, Spencer Watson, and Paul Caldwell — to get the votes he needed. By the time the delegates arrived in September, 1930, Webster had sufficient backing. To avoid appearances of a power struggle that could split the union, he had even convinced important and influential people at union headquarters, including Randolph and Totten, that Lancaster was the source of many of the union's problems. The St. Louis gathering denied Lancaster reelection and replaced him with Totten, Webster's choice.[124] Lancaster did not protest his ouster and quietly retired from the union.

Few porters noticed this change in leadership, although one newspaper spoke of the shock with which Lancaster's friends received the news. As with the dismissal of Crosswaith and Des Verney, the *Courier* accused Randolph of having self-serving reasons for engineering Lancaster's ouster. The paper alleged that the union had removed Lancaster because he had criticized Randolph for his laziness, his lack of business acumen, and his undue interest in publicity rather than in organizing

---

that he had not met Lancaster before the convention in Chicago in 1929, but he believes it possible that Lancaster did incur many of the expenses he enumerated and perhaps was not as dishonest as Webster believed.

[122] MPW to Spencer Watson, BSCP Kansas City organizer, Sept. 9, 1930, BSCP ChiPa.

[123] Telephone interview with Dellums, Mar. 12, 1975.

[124] *Ibid.*; MPW to Watson, Sept. 9, 1930, BSCP ChiPa. Dellums confirms that APR

porters. It portrayed Lancaster as a man of high character and ability who had suffered a terrible wrong.[125] Randolph simply explained that Lancaster had been replaced for the good of the union.

With Lancaster gone, Webster could at last feel that he had achieved his goal of making the BSCP responsive to the views of union leaders outside New York. But since the victory had come at a time when the union was too weak to change the porters' working conditions, it was in some ways hollow. Indeed, the abortive strike, Vann's public outcry against Randolph, Crosswaith's and Des Verney's implication that Randolph was involved in graft, and the pay raise which porters received at the wage conference of 1929 all augered the union's doom. The only props holding it up were Webster's changes in its organizational structure. After the 1929 Chicago convention the BSCP had a constitution which for the first time explicitly spelled out where power lay and provided procedures necessary to sustain the union through the worst of times. The new constitution provided for election of national officers from around the country, ending New York domination of the national BSCP. For example, Webster was now a national vice-president and chairman of the executive board — a significantly different position from his earlier role as Chicago division organizer, and one from which he could wield official power.[126] These changes were essential for ultimate success. It is true that as the Great Depression worsened, so did the fortunes of the Brotherhood. Yet the BSCP's three public defeats at the hands of Pullman and government agencies during 1927-28, which left the union seemingly prostrate, had not fatally damaged its internal structure. Beneath adversity was an amazing resilience that would one day bring the union hard-earned success.

---

and others recognized the difficulties for the union which were inherent in continued opposition to Webster on this issue.

[125] Pittsburgh *Courier*, Sept. 27, 1930. Spencer Watson implied in a letter to MPW (Sept. 30, 1930, BSCP ChiPa) that part of the reason for removal of Lancaster was that the secretary-treasurer had been the source of BSCP leaks to Vann of the *Courier*.

[126] Throughout the remainder of his career with the BSCP, Webster spoke of himself as "first vice-president," and referred to other vice-presidents as second, third, and so on. Dellums maintains that the union never officially made numerical designations for its vice-presidents, but that MPW simply appropriated the title of "first." It was probably a mark of his power that he succeeded in convincing others that he was indeed the second man in the Brotherhood. Telephone interview with Dellums, Mar. 12, 1975.

CHAPTER VI

Maintaining a Lease on Life

> Regardless of what may be one's personal feelings about the organization known as the Brotherhood of Sleeping Car Porters, there is one phase to it everyone will have to admire whether one wants to or not. This is the persistent way in which it keeps alive. Every time the prophets start presaging its demise, and the I-told-you-so's begin to shake their heads, the unexpected happens — it bobs up with a fresh lease on life.
>
> — James Hogans, New York *Age*, July 12, 1930

The aborted strike of 1928 caused BSCP leaders to take direct action to diminish internal tensions; it also engendered major strains on union officials as they struggled to keep their doors open, in order eventually to revitalize the Brotherhood as an organization. After June, 1928, the BSCP lay in shambles, its leadership apparently bankrupt and totally powerless to improve conditions of the porters and maids. No one suffered more adverse publicity than Randolph from this sorry state of affairs. Yet, through the public pressures and internal demands for change, he maintained a sense of the importance of the BSCP. Employing a combination of creativity, innovation, and daring, Randolph succeeded by 1933 in reestablishing the Brotherhood of Sleeping Car Porters as a vigorous union ready once again to press the porters' grievances with the Pullman Company. The magnitude of the accomplishment is underlined when one recalls that during much of this period the United States was experiencing an economic depression that had a serious negative impact on the membership of the BSCP, and on the willingness of porters to risk their jobs by involvement with a labor union. But Randolph and his colleagues were convinced that if they could keep the union's doors open and maintain the trappings of permanence, they could rekindle porters' interest. Referring in later years to this distressing period, C. L. Dellums summed up the union's plight when he said, "doors were about all we did have actually open, too."[1]

The Brotherhood's public activities during these years centered on

[1] Dellums to author, Aug. 16, 1972.

three main goals: to gain recognition from Pullman as the bargaining agent for porters and maids, to establish itself in the councils of organized labor, and to win respect among influential black individuals and organizations. Winning Pullman recognition remained the union's primary aim, but BSCP leaders astutely recognized that the Brotherhood was in no position to accomplish this goal on its own. Accordingly, the union pressed its struggle against Pullman mainly through the federal courts, maintaining a low profile with the porters; at the same time it turned the bulk of its attention to attaining charter recognition from the American Federation of Labor, and to maintaining support from organizations like the NAACP and the National Urban League. Characteristically, Randolph still maintained that assiduous courting of black advancement organizations and leaders of the white American labor movement would redound to the Brotherhood's advantage in later years.

In the weeks following the abortive strike of 1928, Randolph decided to make BSCP affiliation with the AFL a central part of his program. This was not entirely a change in direction; rather, it marked an increase in the union's effort to acquire recognition from the House of Labor. The BSCP had applied for an international charter from the AFL as early as 1927, but that application had foundered on a jurisdictional claim of the International Bartenders and Beverage Dispensers of America regarding the right to organize porters. The bartenders' union based its claim on a decision of the AFL Executive Council that dated from 1920.[2] Through 1927 and the spring of 1928 William Green, president of the Federation, had endeavored to break down the waiters' opposition to an independent charter for the porters' union. When his efforts failed, he offered Randolph and his colleagues affiliation with the AFL through the Bartenders' League. Of course, the BSCP adamantly refused the Jim Crow arrangement, preferring to go it alone rather than give up its independence.[3]

[2] For origin of BSCP interest in an AFL charter, see Henry T. Hunt to JWJ, Apr. 14, 1927, NAACP Pas, C414, LC. History of bartenders' jurisdiction over porters is outlined in AFL Convention, *Report of the Proceedings* (Nov., 1929), 137-38.

[3] Several letters, Green to Edward Flore, president of the International Bartenders League, and Green to APR, Feb.-May, 1928, Green Copy Books, AFL-CIO Headquarters, Washington, help to unravel Green's part in trying to settle the controversy. Those letters also cover the BSCP's uncompromising attitude on maintaining its independence, as does APR to MPW, Apr. 30, 1928, BSCP ChiPa. On this point, see also AFL Convention, *Report of the Proceedings* (Nov., 1929), 137-38, and New York *Age*, May 5, 1928. In Aug., 1929, the official title of the hotel workers' union was changed to Hotel and Restaurant Employees and Beverage Dispensers International Alliance.

Randolph found Green reserved when the BSCP renewed its application for a charter in mid-1928. Green's coolness stemmed largely from two complaints that had surfaced against Randolph during the period of the proposed strike: that he had close connections with Communists, and that he had mismanaged the business of the *Messenger* magazine. Informing Randolph that the AFL would "not tolerate communism in any form," Green advised the BSCP leader to clarify his position on this point. Moreover, he warned Randolph that he should submit to the AFL a "complete reply to the statement which has been circulated reflecting upon you and your administration of your publication," action Green deemed "of very great importance to the welfare and future progress of the Brotherhood of Sleeping Car Porters."[4]

Randolph's reply to charges against him apparently satisfied the AFL leader. In October Green again carried the BSCP's request for a charter before the Executive Council, and he invited both Randolph and Edward Flore of the Bartenders' League to come before the Council to resolve the matter of jurisdiction over porters. The resulting conference failed to produce an agreement, but Green promised Randolph that he would continue his efforts on the BSCP's behalf.[5] Webster condemned the AFL for the delay. He wrote Randolph that certain Federation officials wanted to keep the Brotherhood out of the organized labor movement, because admission of the BSCP would "open up the door" and make the union "quite a power in the organization. I believe they prefer having us in there under the control of a white organization."[6] Whatever the validity of Webster's charge, AFL leaders had undoubtedly decided that it would be advantageous to grant a charter to the BSCP. After subsequent talks with Flore at the AFL convention in November failed to convince him to withdraw his claim, the Council decided in February,

---

Green to Flore, Aug. 28, 1929, Green's Copy Books No. 404, p. 859. Green's Copy Books are hereafter cited GCB.

[4] Green's reticence is noted in several letters from Green to APR, summer, 1928, GCB. See, for example, Green to APR, June 5, GCB No. 390, p. 215; July 6, GCB No. 390, p. 431; July 31, GCB No. 391, p. 79; Aug. 27, GCB No. 392, p. 131; and telegram, Aug. 1, GCB No. 391, p. 97. See letters of June 5 and July 6 for references to communism and APR. Quote is from letter of Aug. 27. Webster charged (in MPW to APR, Aug. 24, 1928, BSCP ChiPa) that "the Pullman Company sent a lot of propaganda to the A. F. of L. in order to keep us out of there." He referred to allegations to BSCP-Communist connections that were current at the time.

[5] Green to APR, Sept. 25 and Oct. 25, 1928, GCB No. 393, pp. 11, 869; Nov. 8, 1928, GCB No. 394, p. 339.

[6] MPW to APR, Oct. 6, 1928, BSCP ChiPa.

1929, to charter BSCP locals as federals directly affiliated with the AFL, thus temporarily dodging the question of international jurisdiction.[7] The Bartenders' League, which learned of the Council's action only after it became final, asked the convention to overrule the Executive Council at the 1929 session, but the delegates sustained the leadership.[8]

Chartering of the BSCP locals as independent federal unions raised questions about the AFL leadership's attitude toward the Brotherhood, for the Council did not grant the BSCP an international charter. Instead, the BSCP entered the House of Labor under a system that had been established largely to accommodate blacks who could not gain membership in the regular unions of their crafts — a substitute for real unionism that had long been resented by Afro-Americans.[9] Critics pointed out that black workers admitted under this arrangement had no control over their working conditions, since all authority rested with the parent white union. But the BSCP's position was somewhat different, mainly because Randolph's organization would not have to deal with another porters' union. Since all porters were black, the BSCP could enter the AFL and still maintain its autonomy.

Though Randolph was clearly aware of the difficulties imposed by the federal charters, and of the fact that the BSCP had not received full recognition from the AFL,[10] he was nonetheless pleased with the Council's action. The BSCP needed permanence and publicity, and Randolph saw affiliation with the American Federation of Labor as the best way to

[7] Green to APR, Dec. 20, 1928, GCB No. 395, p. 565; Green to APR and Green to Flore, both Feb. 23, 1929, GCB No. 397, pp. 524, 525. During the fall of 1928 Flore had begun to sense that AFL leaders favored the BSCP in the dispute. Flore complained to Green that AFL organizers were spreading the word that the Federation would charter the BSCP, but Green denied that AFL headquarters was responsible for the rumor. See Green to Flore, Sept. 18, 1928, GCB No. 397, p. 592.

[8] AFL Convention, *Report of the Proceedings* (Nov., 1929), 137-38. The Bartenders' Alliance renewed its attempt to gain control of the BSCP in 1930 when it asked the convention to approve a resolution granting it jurisdiction over porters. The resolution failed. *Ibid.* (Oct., 1930), 152, 255.

The AFL's interest in having the BSCP in the Federation is highlighted by the Executive Council's decision to wrest jurisdiction of porters from the Bartenders' Alliance at the very time when members of the Council pontificated on the sanctity of jurisdictional decisions. The Council was unequivocal in its support of the established group when problems arose in the United Mine Workers in 1930. See Philip Taft, *The AF of L from the Death of Gompers to the Merger* (New York: Harper, 1959), 18-20.

[9] See the first chapter for discussion of origin of federal union system in 1900.

[10] For an example of APR's negative comments about the federal union system, see AFL Convention, *Report of the Proceedings* (Oct., 1934), 705.

gain them. He quickly accepted Green's offer and applied for charters for nine BSCP locals.[11] Moreover, he prevailed upon President Green to come to New York to dedicate the charter for that local and to personally welcome the BSCP into the Federation.[12]

On June 30, 1929, Green showed up at the Abyssinian Baptist Church in Harlem to address a huge meeting of porters and black leaders on the question of the relationship between blacks and organized labor. Randolph, with his rhetorical flair, introduced Green as "the second Abraham Lincoln, come to relieve industrial bondage"; the AFL leader then went on to deliver what one black newspaper described as "probably the most significant speech ever made by a white leader" to a black audience.[13] But if the speech was important, Green had to contend with hecklers who demanded to know whether his presence in Harlem represented a new direction for the AFL; they also asked Green to explain his part in calling off the BSCP's proposed strike of the previous spring.[14] Green tried to meet the challenge. He deplored the working conditions at Pullman and defended the Federation's racial policies. Though admitting that some international unions affiliated with the AFL did refuse to admit blacks, Green pointed to the recent association between the Federation and the BSCP as evidence of change; he also announced that, under circumstances where black workers could not find membership in the unions of their crafts, the AFL would charter them directly. Asserting that the "heart of labor beats with sympathy for Colored workers' efforts to secure a better life," he assured black New Yorkers that the AFL would do everything possible to aid in those endeavors.[15]

[11] Green to APR, May 8, 1929, GCB No. 400, p. 435; June 18, 1929, GCB No. 409, p. 534. The BSCP eventually received seven additional charters for a total of sixteen locals.

[12] Green to APR, June 18, 1929, GCB No. 409, p. 534. Randolph asked Green to appear in each BSCP city to dedicate its local charter, but Green declined.

[13] Quote from Randolph in New York *Times*, July 1, 1929. Quote from black newspaper refers to Chicago *Defender*, July 6, 1929. The *Times* estimated the crowd at about 700 persons.

[14] New York *Times*, July 1, 1929; Pittsburgh *Courier*, July 6, 1929.

[15] Chicago *Defender*, July 6, 1929; New York *Times*, July 1, 1929. Just how much Randolph had to do with determining what Green had to say at the New York meeting is uncertain, but it is clear that Randolph undertook to suggest ideas to the AFL leader. Randolph's June 25 letter to Green is unavailable, but Green refers to the letter and thanks Randolph for his suggestions in Green to APR, June 26, 1929, GCB No. 402, p. 833.

Randolph had achieved his goal in attaining the charters and getting Green to come to New York. He had succeeded in focusing attention on the BSCP; in addition, he and the union both stood to gain from the publicity that surrounded the affair, for the Brotherhood's receipt of the charters caused widespread debate in the black press and among black organizations. Not surprisingly, the *Argus* cautioned the porters that the only way the BSCP could aid their cause was through a strike. But since the AFL would not support such a strike, the only ones who stood to gain from the new arrangement were Randolph and his colleagues. There was nothing in it for the porters, let alone the general pool of black workers.[16] The *Defender* disagreed. It saw the issuance of the charters as just reward for the BSCP's persistence and prophesied that henceforth the union would be treated with new respect by government agencies and the Pullman Company.[17] Even the Pittsburgh *Courier* spoke of the significance of Green's "going out of his way to address a Negro labor union," and added that though white labor unions had in the past been derelict in their duties to black workers, "colored people should not forget that the majority of white employers whose plants are organized do not offer the Negro any more cordial reception than white unions, and frequently less."[18]

The leading black advancement organizations were also divided. A careful survey by Dr. Abram L. Harris of previous AFL activities and of the alternatives available to black workers summarized the NAACP's position. Harris concluded that the BSCP had taken a positive step by aligning with white organized labor, and he predicted that the Brotherhood would eventually receive an international charter, an achievement that would go a long way "toward bridging the gap between white and Negro workers."[19] But the National Urban League did not agree. The

[16] St. Louis *Argus*, Apr. 26, 1929.

[17] Chicago *Defender*, Feb. 23, 1929.

[18] Pittsburgh *Courier*, July 13, 1929. This comment must be read in connection with the *Courier*'s statement of May 12, 1928, when the paper was trying to force Randolph's resignation from the presidency of the BSCP. It said then that it had always favored management over unions. The different tone a year later adds credence to the argument that the *Courier* had been paid for its attacks on the union and Randolph.

[19] Abram L. Harris, "Why the Brotherhood of Sleeping Car Porters Should Organize Under Separate International Charter" (1930), 16, prepared for the NAACP, NAACP Pas, C413, LC. This report appeared when the waiters renewed their jurisdictional claims over the porters. Harris adamantly opposed the BSCP's affiliation with the AFL through the waiters' union because that group had a color clause in its constitution and had never endeavored to organize black waiters.

Federation's failure to remove bars against black workers in unions at its 1929 convention heightened the League officials' pessimism and brought about a discussion between AFL and Urban League leaders that provided further publicity for the BSCP.

The League's opposition to the AFL rested on two main issues: distrust of the federal union system, and the Federation's insistence upon maintaining its craft orientation. Discounting the AFL's allegation that it had not signed up more black workers because blacks were unorganizable, the League pointed out that more than 100,000 Afro-American workers belonged to labor unions, despite the opposition of white unionists. The AFL could not hope to improve the standing of black workers, and its own standing among blacks, until it abandoned its outmoded emphasis upon craft unions, a system that left out the "great mass of unskilled labor with which the bulk of black workers is identified."[20] Moreover, the AFL could take no credit for organizing porters, and affiliation of BSCP locals with the Federation did not prove that the AFL intended to take an active and vigorous role in organizing black workers, particularly those employed in competitive positions with whites.[21] In an open letter to Green the League's director of industrial relations, T. Arnold Hill, took specific exception to the issuance of federal charters as an efficient way to organize Afro-Americans. Calling the system an escape rather than a solution, Hill claimed that it gave black workers "the badge but not the protection of unionism." If anything, federal unions handicapped black workers by placing them under the jurisdiction of an Executive Council made up of vice-presidents of the AFL, many of whose unions had color clauses in their constitutions.[22]

Responding to such charges, Green reaffirmed his conviction that the AFL had done all it could in trying to organize blacks. If few blacks belonged to international unions, the fault lay with Afro-Americans themselves, largely because they had not yet gained a labor consciousness. "The Federation," he wrote, "cannot effectively carry the gospel of unionism until workers [are] ready to hear and act." Green admitted that the attitude of blacks toward unions was changing, and he pointed to the work of Randolph and the BSCP as a hopeful sign for the future.[23]

[20] *Opportunity*, VII (Nov., 1929), 335.
[21] *Ibid.* (Dec., 1929), 367.
[22] *Ibid.*, VIII (Feb., 1930), 56.
[23] *Ibid.*, VII (Dec., 1929), 381-82.

When he learned that his statement had failed to quiet *Opportunity* and the Urban League, Green alleged that the magazine and its editors were set in their opposition to organized labor and that they would "refuse to consider any information or any facts supplied by representatives of organized labor." He wrote his new comrade, Randolph, that "this publication *Opportunity* and its editorial policy should be dismissed from consideration on our part."[24]

The AFL's decision to charter individual BSCP locals rather than grant the Brotherhood a national charter caused difficulties for BSCP leaders. The BSCP now found it difficult to maintain a national structure. Under terms of the charters, BSCP district organizers had to place their major efforts on maintaining the solvency of their particular locals. AFL officers looked to them, and not to the national BSCP, for payment of taxes. Indeed, these officials actually became presidents of the various BSCP locals. A major feat of leadership for Randolph and Webster, who recognized the impossibility of organizing the porters for effective action against Pullman without a national structure, was to withstand the divisive effects of the AFL charters during the difficult period between 1929 and 1933.

Brotherhood leaders received little support from the AFL in this matter. Green was convinced that the only way for the BSCP to proceed was through the local structure. For example, he strongly disagreed with Randolph's decision to call a BSCP national convention in the fall of 1929, terming such action premature. Rather than a national convention, Randolph and his colleagues should bend their efforts toward "establishment of strong local unions in every community where Pullman porters reside." Referring to this same theme in a later statement, Green wrote that through its experience

> the American Federation of Labor has found that workers are better protected and their interests more rapidly advanced, through continued and persistent organization of local unions directly affiliated with the American Federation of Labor until such time as the strength and numeri-

[24] Green to APR, Dec. 12, 1929, GCB No. 407, p. 96. This whole debate must have placed Randolph in a difficult position. For Green to dismiss *Opportunity* was one thing, but Randolph could hardly consider disregarding the collective opinion of a leading black organization whose support he needed. GCB do not include incoming correspondence, and BSCP Headquarters Papers are unavailable for this period. Thus we cannot determine what Randolph said in his letter to which Green responded on Dec. 12. It is clear from the context, however, that the Chief had discussed the debate between the AFL and *Opportunity*.

> cal number of these local unions would warrant formation of a national union. The prospects for an eventually strong and prosperous active international are retarded through the premature organizing of a national body. Time and again in the early years of the Federation, when a national union of a small membership, and thus not truly representative of the trade or industry was formed, the organization eventually languished and fell by the wayside, and the work of organizing the workers had to be done all over again.[25]

Despite the difficulties between the BSCP and the AFL, it is likely that both the Federation and the Brotherhood profited from the relationship. Randolph flooded AFL headquarters with applications for an international charter for the BSCP almost every month after the federal charters became effective; the Executive Council turned down each request. Green explained the action by pointing out to Randolph that the BSCP did not have sufficient financial strength to justify issuance of an international charter. In fact, between the end of 1931 and mid-1932 the AFL suspended several BSCP locals, including New York and Chicago, for failure to pay per capita tax to the Federation.[26] But the explanation breaks down when one considers that, rather than grant the BSCP an international charter after it demonstrated renewed strength in 1933, the Council endeavored to restrict the union even further by granting jurisdiction over porters to a white union of sleeping car conductors.[27] It is probable, then, that the AFL interest in the BSCP centered on the Federation's need for a black spokesman to serve as an ambassador

[25] Green to APR, June 5, 1930, GCB No. 416, p. 333. See also Green to APR, Aug. 22, 1929, GCB No. 404, p. 836; Aug. 28, 1929, GCB No. 405, p. 92.

[26] Green to APR, June 10, 1932, GCB No. 444, p. 617; APR to Frank Morrison, June 1, 1932, BSCP ChiPa. The status of BSCP locals as of June, 1932, was as follows:

Suspended locals and date of suspension			Locals in good standing	
18068	New York	Nov. 24, 1931	18076	Detroit
18070	Chicago	Nov. 24, 1931	18080	Washington
18075	St. Louis	May 24, 1932	18085	Los Angeles
18077	Kansas City	May 24, 1932	18086	Cleveland
18078	St. Paul - Minneapolis	May 24, 1932	18088	Denver
18079	Oakland	May 24, 1932	18089	Fort Worth
18082	New Orleans	Mar. 25, 1932	18097	Boston
18159	Louisville	May 24, 1932	18104	Omaha

The Illinois Federation of Labor was also considering expelling the Chicago local for failure to pay taxes. See John Fitzpatrick to George Clark, Sept. 10, 1930, BSCP ChiPa.

[27] See discussion in the next chapter.

among Afro-Americans and to help mute some of the criticisms leveled by blacks against the leaders of the American labor movement. For his part, Randolph tolerated the difficulties imposed upon the BSCP by the Federation's charters because he needed the moral support and publicity accruing from affiliation with the general labor movement. Though the AFL officially suspended BSCP locals and Green lectured Randolph on the importance which organized labor placed on dues payment, AFL and BSCP leaders demonstrated mutual respect and continued to work together.[28] In effect, the BSCP paid its membership dues in part by serving as the AFL's ambassador among blacks; it also used its affiliation to press for wider participation of Afro-Americans within organized labor.[29]

The BSCP's efforts to secure permanent affiliation with the American Federation of Labor came during a difficult period for the union. The onslaught of the Great Depression had immediate and devastating effect upon the porters, and consequently affected their union. Worsening

[28] Victor Olander to MPW, Mar. 28, 1932, BSCP ChiPa. Tangible results that accrued to the BSCP from its relationship with the AFL are discussed below in this chapter. Olander wrote MPW: "If there are any two men of your race who are doing better work than you and your associate, Mr. Randolph, in giving to your people the right view of sound Americanism, then I'd give a good [bit] to meet them."

[29] APR served as Green's expert on black labor. When blacks appealed to the AFL leader for assistance in organizing a group of black workers, Green turned their requests over to Randolph and asked him to help solve whatever difficulties were involved. See, *e.g.*, the Reverend P. Colfax Rameau to Green, July 7, 1931, GCB No. 431, p. 475; Green to Rameau, July 9, 1931, GCB, p. 749; Green to APR, July 9, 1931, GCB, p. 746; July 17, 1931, GCB, p. 749; Green to APR, July 9, 1931, GCB, p. 746; July 17, 1931, GCB No. 432, p. 40. APR undertook Green's assignments. In Green to APR, July 17, 1931, Green referred to APR's action as "just the kind of letter I wished you would send Rev. Rameau. The communication you sent him will be productive of good results." For another example of appeals of blacks for aid that Green turned over to Randolph, see Green to APR, Aug. 16, 1929, GCB No. 404, p. 494.

But Randolph did more than serve as Green's special trouble shooter. Green apparently valued Randolph's ideas, and though Randolph represented only a local union in the AFL, in early 1930 Green invited the BSCP leader to join a committee of national and international union spokesmen to help map plans for a major organizational drive in the South. Randolph's special expertise would be valuable to the AFL in efforts to organize Afro-Americans. As Green wrote Randolph, "We are interested in organizing the Negro workers of the South and for that reason I am sure the national union officers who will be in attendance at this conference will deeply appreciate such assistance and information you may be able to give relating to the organization of Negro workers." Green to APR, Nov. 8, 1929, GCB No. 407, p. 918.

economic conditions caused a decline in travelers, which meant fewer people to tip porters, as well as fewer jobs for them. Moreover, Randolph pointed out as early as 1930 that travelers were disinclined to tip with their former generosity, or to tip at all. The quarters which had once changed hands were now only nickels and dimes.[30] Randolph warned that the only solution was for porters to support the union's demands for a living wage so they would not have to depend upon handouts. But the porters were less than impressed: rather than rallying in support of the Brotherhood, they left the union in droves. The BSCP's membership plummeted from its peak of 4,632 before the aborted strike in 1928, to 771 in 1932, and eventually bottomed out at 658 in 1933, shortly before the resurgence.[31]

The porters' refusal to heed the union's message convinced Randolph and his colleagues of the urgent need to educate Afro-Americans on a sustained and systematic basis concerning the meaning of trade unionism. Much of the porters' lack of interest stemmed from advice from their preachers and other community leaders. Discussing the problem in an article written in 1929, Randolph had claimed that black ministers did not understand the differences between company unions and trade unions. Even when these differences were explained, they supported company unions because they accepted industrial paternalism and depended upon white philanthropy for many of their activities.[32] The problem for the BSCP seemed clear. Before substantial gains could be made by porters or any other group of black workers, the union would have to educate all Afro-Americans — a racial group composed overwhelmingly of laborers — regarding their self-interest.

Though representative of the importance which Randolph had long placed on public opinion and propaganda, the BSCP's bold new front of active involvement with the black community developed largely from the Brotherhood officials' recognition that they needed to demonstrate

[30] *Black Worker*, Jan. 1 and Mar. 15, 1930. This publication should not be confused with the Spero and Harris book of the same title. It is a newspaper that succeeded the *Messenger* as the BSCP's official journal. Victor Weybright, "Pullman Porters on Parade," *Survey Graphic*, XXIV (Nov., 1935), 573, supports Randolph's allegation of the decline in tips during the early 1930s.

[31] Brailsford R. Brazeal, *The Brotherhood of Sleeping Car Porters* (New York: Harper and Brothers, 1946), 222.

[32] A. Philip Randolph, "Negro Labor and the Church," in Jerome Davis, ed., *Labor Speaks for Itself on Religion* (New York: Macmillan, 1929).

effective leadership in order to stave off the union's collapse. They realized that one way to distract attention from the union's weaknesses was to keep the Brotherhood involved in a wide range of public issues; achievements in other areas would reflect favorably on the BSCP and its leaders at a time when they were being castigated as failures. Good publicity was of fundamental concern because influential individuals, and not just hostile newspapers, had begun to name A. Philip Randolph as the person mainly responsible for the union's demise. Some critics had even begun to point to the Brotherhood's setbacks as signifying a loss for black labor in general, despite the union's recent affiliation with the AFL. Indeed, in some circles the BSCP had been written off as dead. As Spero and Harris observed: "The great pity of the virtual collapse of the porters' union lies not merely in its effect upon the porters who have grievances which sorely need correction but in its effect upon Negro labor generally. The hope that this movement would become a rallying point for Negro labor as a whole is now dead."[33]

The BSCP's first response to the challenge was to employ the National Negro Labor Conference, the educational arm which the union had established as a permanent adjunct in 1929. Grounded primarily on the premise that the interests of both black and white workers were identical and that blacks should thus align with organized labor, the Labor Conference received favorable publicity from both the black press and officials of the labor movement.[34] William Green extolled the activities of the Labor Conference and praised BSCP leaders for the "practical and constructive" manner in which they approached the problems of blacks and organized labor.[35] Though emphasizing the relationship between the problems of black and white workers, speakers who participated in the conferences under BSCP auspices agreed that responsibility for improving economic conditions of black workers lay

[33] Sterling D. Spero and Abram L. Harris, *The Black Worker: The Negro Worker and the Labor Movement* (New York: Columbia University Press, 1931), 459-60. See the next chapter for discussion of Harris's efforts to prod the NAACP into a stronger position on economic matters.

[34] For examples of comments by white labor officials, see Clarence O. Senior, "The Negro Labor Conference," *American Federationist*, XXXVI (July, 1929), 800-802; William Green, "Editorial on Negro Labor Conference," *ibid.*, XXXVII (Jan., 1930), 21-22. Green also opened the pages of *American Federationist*, the AFL's official magazine, to BSCP leaders so they could write about the Negro Labor Conference. See Randolph's article on the subject *ibid.* (Sept., 1930), 1054-57.

[35] Green, "Editorial," 21-22.

in their own hands. The Conference maintained, moreover, not only that most black people were members of the working class, but also that their problems in American society were essentially economic. Low wages and poor working conditions lay at the root of many social inequities besetting blacks, and the only remedy lay in trade union education.[36] The Negro Labor Conference accepted as a further part of its responsibility the challenge of teaching black professionals that they too should be interested in the economic advancement of the masses of Afro-Americans. Through its conferences the BSCP tried to convince them that they could not establish their own practices and businesses on solid foundations until their clients had economic security. Webster believed that the most significant contribution of the National Negro Labor Conference was its success in converting to the side of organized labor numerous black leaders who previously had been hostile or indifferent.[37] The BSCP, the "guardian of black labor," stood as an example for other black workers to follow.[38]

In January, 1930, the NAACP announced in a policy statement on labor that it would conduct a nationwide campaign on behalf of the rights of blacks to industrial jobs and admission to exclusive labor unions. In characteristic NAACP style, the Association threatened to go to court, if necessary, to achieve that goal.[39] Hoping to make the NAACP an active participant in efforts to solve the labor problems of Afro-Americans, Randolph moved quickly to capitalize on what he perceived as the Association's new position. He asked Walter White, who was serving as acting secretary during James Weldon Johnson's leave of absence, to attend a BSCP-sponsored conference in New York which would focus public attention on the plight of unemployed blacks and investigate ways to ease the problems caused by unemployment.[40] Randolph made the

[36] *American Federationist*, XXXIX (Mar., 1932), 302-3.

[37] MPW, "The National Negro Labor Conference," Illinois Federation of Labor *Newsletter*, Feb. 28, 1931.

[38] Chicago *Defender*, Jan. 25, 1930. The *Defender*'s support was so unstinting on the occasion of the Labor Conference in 1930 that BSCP leaders voted the paper a special thanks. Just two years earlier Webster had threatened to resign from the union if the *Defender* or its publisher had anything to do with the Conference. See the preceding chapter.

[39] New York *Age* and Pittsburgh *Courier*, both Jan. 8, 1930. The *Courier* welcomed the Association's comments, calling its position statement "a good New Year resolution."

[40] APR to White, Mar. 11, 1930, NAACP Pas, C413, LC.

same appeal to the leaders of the Urban League. Both groups agreed to participate; White attended the sessions as representative of the NAACP, and James H. Hubert, executive secretary of the New York Urban League, appeared on behalf of his organization. The conference, which met on March 20-21, 1930, adopted a platform calling for the five-day week and the eight-hour day as means of getting people back to work. It also advocated a drive to organize black workers into labor unions under the AFL, and a continuing fight against company unionism. These resolutions represented an endorsement of the BSCP's own program; in addition, the union reaped further gains when the conference established a permanent joint committee to keep statistics on the employment crisis among blacks and to provide a ready agency to deal with specific situations as they arose.[41] The fact that Randolph sat on the committee, which also included White, Hubert, and the Reverend John W. Robinson of St. Marks Methodist Episcopal Church, gave the Brotherhood a working relationship with the two leading civil rights organizations and renewed its contacts with an influential segment of the black church. Randolph's rising prestige among NAACP leaders was apparent by mid-1930, when he became a consultant to the Association on labor matters.[42]

Nevertheless, the extent of the gains should not be overemphasized. Though BSCP officials did not realize it at the time, the expressions of support from the two civil rights organizations were superficial and did not represent basic reassessments of the need for trade unions among blacks. During late 1929 and early 1930, both organizations were competing for money from the Garland Fund. The NAACP wanted the Fund to support a long-range program of civil rights activity through the courts, while the League put forth a plan emphasizing job placement for Afro-Americans. Given the personnel of the Garland Fund board and the political views of the donor, the two organizations faced a difficult task. In October, 1929, the NAACP had presented to the Garland Fund a proposal to improve the overall conditions of blacks in the United States. Terming its plan "radical," the Association requested up to $314,000 to fight discrimination in education and housing, to guarantee the right of blacks to participate in elections and serve on juries in the South, and to

[41] APR to White, Apr. 2, 1930, *ibid*.

[42] See several letters, APR to White and Robert Bagnall, and White and Bagnall to APR, June-Oct., 1930, *ibid*. The AME Zion Church also endorsed the BSCP's fight at its convention in 1930. Chicago *Defender*, June 28, 1930.

put an end to lynching. Such reforms, it argued, must be accomplished before trying to increase the involvement of blacks in trade unionism.[43] The Urban League agreed, contending that the problems involved in organizing black workers should be taken up later.[44]

Neither proposal received immediate funding, for the Garland Fund was considering making contributions to other groups, including the Communist-dominated American Negro Labor Congress and the BSCP. The NAACP issued its statement in favor of trade unionism in January, 1930, partly to ward off the Garland Fund's flirtation with the ANLC and to make its own proposal more palatable to the foundation. Assuring the Fund that the work of the Congress duplicated its own, the Association denied that there was much to be gained by attempting to organize black workers, ''the overwhelming majority of whom are still agricultural workers or domestic servants,'' and dismissed the BSCP as a union unlikely to be of service to Afro-American laborers. It saw no promising organization in the field, and advised the Fund to withhold money from the Brotherhood and other black unions and union organizers because further support of such groups would be ''like pouring money down a sink.''[45] The opposition of the two organizations, combined with the Fund's previous experience with the Brotherhood, had the desired effect. The Garland Fund refused to make further grants to the BSCP, while both the NAACP and the NUL received part of what they requested.

In March, 1930, President Herbert Hoover provided the BSCP with an opportunity to bring together the relationships it had cultivated with organized labor and black protest organizations when he appointed Judge John J. Parker of the Fourth Circuit Court in North Carolina to the Supreme Court. The appointment horrified labor leaders and blacks, particularly NAACP officials, but for different reasons. The Association attacked Parker because he had declared years before (in an unsuccessful campaign for the governorship of North Carolina) that he opposed political participation by blacks, either as voters or as office-

[43] Report of the Joint Committee on Negro Work to the Garland Fund, Oct. 18, 1929, NAACP Pas, C196, LC. Members of the committee were Morris Ernst, Lewis S. Gannett, and James Weldon Johnson.

[44] Eugene K. Jones of NUL to the Garland Fund, May 26, 1930, NUL Pas, 4-1, LC.

[45] Joint Committee on Negro Work to the Garland Fund, May 28, 1930, p. 17, NAACP Pas, C196, LC.

holders. Organized labor opposed Parker because of his support of "yellow dog" contracts and his general hostility to trade unions. Neither group wished to have its opposition linked to that of the other. Walter White wrote bitterly of Green's lack of respect when the two men appeared before the Senate on the same day to testify against Parker's confirmation. Consequently, the NAACP never mentioned Parker's labor opinions and, as White put it, the AFL "abstemiously refrained from mentioning Parker's anti-Negro stand."[46] It fell to Randolph to connect Parker's attitudes toward labor and black people, and to point out that Parker had clearly demonstrated his sympathy for the higher classes of American society. Emphasizing that no American corporation had spoken out against Parker's discriminatory comments about blacks (implying that the AFL had), Randolph insisted that this was a clear example of where the issues of blacks and labor were specifically linked. He urged Senator Robert Wagner to vote against confirmation of Parker on both grounds.[47] Randolph probably had little influence on the Senate, but the episode shows the BSCP's leader in action.

The Senate eventually voted down Parker's nomination, and in the fall of 1930 Randolph joined labor and civil rights leaders in efforts to unseat senators who had supported Parker's confirmation. At Green's request, Randolph worked particularly hard to defeat Senator Roscoe McCullough of Ohio, a leading Parker supporter whom the NAACP also

[46] Walter White, *A Man Called White: The Autobiography of Walter F. White* (Bloomington: Indiana University Press, 1970), 106. Richard L. Watson, "The Defeat of Judge Parker: A Study in Pressure Group Politics," *Mississippi Valley Historical Review*, L (Sept., 1963), 213-34, is a fine study of the NAACP's activities in the defeat of the judge. Spero and Harris condemned the Association for its refusal to make an issue of Parker's labor views. Organized labor's major complaint against Parker stemmed from his decision in the Red Jacket case of 1927, when he virtually outlawed the UMW in West Virginia through use of anti-labor injunctions. See Irving Bernstein, *A History of the American Worker, 1920-1933: The Lean Years* (Boston: Houghton Mifflin, 1960), 406-9.

[47] *Black Worker*, May 1, 1930; Bernstein, *The Lean Years*, 550, n. 12, cites APR to Wagner, Apr. 24, 1930, Wagner Papers, as evidence of Randolph's appeal to the senator. Wagner was among those senators who spoke of the recognition of the relationship between Parker's views toward labor and those toward blacks. Watson, "Defeat of Judge Parker," quotes Senator Wagner as having said that "Parker's sympathies apparently flowed to those on top, whether economically or racially" (p. 227). It is not clear from Watson's account whether Randolph made his appeal before or after Wagner's statement.

opposed. Yet Randolph alone linked the issues of black people and labor as oppressed groups.[48]

Activities such as involvement in the Parker affair were particularly suited to Randolph's talents, and he used these abilities most effectively whenever the direct interests of the porters and maids were concerned. It suited Randolph's style, and the union's needs, to keep highly emotional issues of the BSCP and porters before the public. Issues that involved the wider interests of black people in general doubly pleased BSCP leaders, because they permitted the Brotherhood to demonstrate its involvement with the general black population and its willingness to undertake causes that the ERP would not and could not accept. The BSCP wanted to impress upon porters — members and non-members alike — that it would defend them when they encountered trouble from any source, not just from the Pullman Company.

An event occurred in April, 1930, that allowed the BSCP to demonstrate its determination to act on behalf of its members, while at the same time arousing interest in the movement among both blacks and liberal whites. On April 5 porter J. H. Wilkens of Kansas City disappeared from his Pullman car near Locust Grove, Georgia. When Georgia authorities found Wilkens's body hanging from a tree near the railroad track, the Pullman Company disavowed any knowledge of how Wilkens had left or been taken from the train, since it had not stopped near where officers found his body. The Brotherhood reacted immediately to Wilkens's murder. The union retained Frank P. Walsh, a white New York labor attorney, to lead an intensive investigation into the circumstances surrounding Wilkens's disappearance, and it announced that it intended to bring civil suit against Pullman and the State of Georgia on behalf of the porter's widow.[49] Randolph personally wrote Governor L. G. Hardman of Georgia urging that he use the powers of his office to insure that Wilkens's lynchers be brought to justice; he also appealed to the Department of Justice to help apprehend Wilkens's murderers, because his employment in interstate commerce justified

[48] Green to APR, Oct. 22, 1930, GCB No. 421, p. 349; Nov. 7, 1930, GCB No. 422, p. 153; Nov. 14, 1930, GCB No. 422, p. 414. Green also asked AFL leaders in Ohio to extend APR every possible courtesy while he was in their state. See Green to APR, Oct. 22, 1930, GCB No. 421, p. 349. See also Chicago *Defender*, Nov. 1, 1930, and Pittsburgh *Courier*, Nov. 14, 1931.

[49] Walsh to APR, Apr. 9, 1930, BSCP ChiPa.

federal intervention.[50] Meanwhile, the union organized mass protest demonstrations in New York, bringing in (among others) that unrelenting crusader against lynching, Walter White of the NAACP, and initiating a Wilkens Investigation Defense Fund to finance its probe. Warning porters that any one of them could have met death in the performance of his duties, the union appealed to both porters and the public for contributions to the fund to track down Wilkens's murderers.[51]

The BSCP used the tragedy as an occasion to castigate the Pullman Company. Throughout the spring and into the summer the *Black Worker* kept the Wilkens incident prominently before the porters; BSCP officials accused the company of negligence in the case, claiming that Pullman had reassigned porters who had served with Wilkens on that fateful night so they would be unavailable to testify.[52] According to the Brotherhood, the company was trying to maintain that Wilkens had suffered a "natural death" so that it would not be liable for damages accruing to an employee who had died accidentally.[53] Wilkens's death remained an unsolved mystery, but the BSCP's involvement helped to sustain the Brotherhood when it had little else to recommend itself to either the porters or the public.

The BSCP's highly publicized activities during the early 1930s — such as lobbying against confirmation of Judge Parker, holding labor education conferences, and staging demonstrations against lynching — kept the union's name before the public and served to draw attention

[50] *Black Worker*, May 1, 1930. The BSCP published Hardman's reply, in which the governor vowed to do everything in his power to secure justice for Wilkens. For APR's appeal to the Department of Justice, see Mary Frances Berry, *Black Resistance/White Law: A History of Constitutional Racism in America* (New York: Appleton-Century-Crofts, 1971), 161. Berry contends that APR's premise that the federal government had authority to investigate deaths of workers involved in interstate commerce was sound.

[51] Pittsburgh *Courier*, Apr. 24, 1930. BSCP papers do not show an accounting of the money raised for the Wilkens Fund, nor do they show how much money the union raised. Several porters later charged that Randolph and other BSCP officials diverted Defense Fund monies to other BSCP activities, particularly to finance the BSCP's convention at St. Louis in 1930. See, *e.g.*, Pittsburgh *Courier*, Sept. 27 and Oct. 18, and Seattle *Enterprise*, Oct. 22, 1930. The porters did not prove their case, but, like other similar allegations, this one clouded the BSCP's public image.

[52] Chicago *Defender*, Apr. 24, 1930. One porter claimed to have seen a Pullman conductor remove three bloody sheets from the car on which Wilkens had served. He alleged that the porter had been killed aboard the train.

[53] *Ibid.*, Apr. 19, 1930.

away from its inability to reach agreement with Pullman. However, such moves hardly carried the Brotherhood to its goal of replacing the ERP as bargaining agent for porters and maids. Randolph and his colleagues realized that any achievements in other areas would be meaningless if in the end they failed to reach agreement with Pullman. Thus, while they continued to maintain a high propaganda profile, in private they soberly and carefully outlined a program to bring together the forces of organized labor and the federal courts in order to rid the porters of the ERP. Moreover, they accepted the damper which the Depression placed on the militancy of porters. Rather than call non-BSCP porters Uncle Toms and stool pigeons, as in the past, Brotherhood leaders carried on a secret campaign to maintain the core of their membership and lay the base for rapid increases whenever the union regained its effectiveness. Intermittent failures and the drawn-out three-year process proved taxing for the union; at times old regional antagonisms flared anew. But through it all, Randolph's will to succeed infected his lieutenants, carrying the organization through its most troubled period.

Between 1930 and 1933, the federal courts were to serve as the BSCP's major vehicle in its struggle to gain recognition from the Pullman Company. Failure to gain support from the Mediation Board at the time of the aborted strike marked the end of the Brotherhood's long and bitter attempt to obtain justice through administrative agencies, and the union turned to the courts instead. Webster had recommended that the BSCP take Pullman to court to enjoin the company from interfering with the BSCP through maintenance of the company union and by coercing porters to stay away from the legitimate union. But the BSCP had not brought suit, because its attorneys advised that conditions were unfavorable under existing interpretations of railway labor laws.[54] Now in 1930, when the Supreme Court handed down a decision forbidding the Texas and New Orleans Railway from interfering with the right of the Brotherhood of Railway and Steam Ship Clerks to organize employees on its lines, the BSCP found the way clear to challenge

[54] MPW to APR, Feb. 17 and 25, APR to MPW, Mar. 7 and June 19, 1928, BSCP ChiPa. Webster based his recommendation on a U.S. District Court decision in *Brotherhood of Railway and Steam Ship Clerks v. Texas and New Orleans Railway* (281 U.S. 548). The district court decision came in 1927 and is discussed in the Supreme Court decision of 1930 herein cited. BSCP attorney Henry T. Hunt advised that the BSCP's dispute differed from that of the Steam Ship Clerks, and thus that the Brotherhood should delay filing suit against Pullman. See APR's letter to MPW of June 19.

Pullman in the courts.[55] Erroneously interpreting the Court as having outlawed company unions, the BSCP immediately announced plans to bring suit against Pullman in federal district court to enjoin the company against operating the ERP.

The Brotherhood's decision left Pullman management unperturbed. The company maintained that the Court's ruling in no way affected the ERP, and Pullman superintendents warned porters that the company still had no intention of recognizing an outside union.[56] On July 17 Pullman headquarters issued a statement clarifying the company's position on the Supreme Court's *Texas and New Orleans* decision; the Pullman statement gave official sanction to the superintendent's warnings that the company would not recognize the BSCP. The company pointed out that the BSCP's interpretation of the Court's decision was erroneous and informed its employees that both the "company and the employees have done and are doing everything which the Railway Labor Act contemplates and requires."[57]

In so arguing, Pullman stood on solid ground — the ruling did *not* require that a company negotiate with a particular union. The Court had only prohibited the Texas and New Orleans Railroad from interfering with the right of employees to form independent organizations; it had not said, as the Brotherhood believed, that the railroad had to deal with whatever union its employees might form. The Supreme Court had issued a strict interpretation of Watson-Parker, which guaranteed the right of railroad workers to organize. The act did not give courts power to enforce Mediation Board decisions or the right to force carriers to submit to arbitration, nor did the Supreme Court attempt to claim such powers. In fact, the decision left the BSCP in no better position than before.[58]

[55] *Brotherhood of Railway and Steam Ship Clerks* v. *Texas and New Orleans Railway* (281 U.S. 548); *Black Worker*, Mar., 1930, expresses BSCP's joy with the Court's decision.

[56] Pittsburgh *Courier*, July 12, 1930.

[57] Pullman Company Statement to Employees, July 17, 1930, copy in BSCP ChiPa.

[58] *Brotherhood of Railway and Steam Ship Clerks* v. *Texas and New Orleans Railway* (281 U.S. 548). The district court injunction which the Supreme Court upheld read: "Nothing in this injunction shall be construed as authority to prevent any employee of said defendant railroad company, in classes referred to, from joining, promoting, or fostering as many unions as he or they . . . may desire, and in any way he or they may desire, and with the assistance and aid of his fellow employees in any way and to any

The Brotherhood refused to concede the point. When Pullman announced plans in October to hold its annual ERP election the following month, the BSCP petitioned the U.S. District Court for the Northern District of Illinois, requesting an injunction temporarily restraining the company from holding the election on grounds that it interfered with the BSCP's right to organize porters.[59] In addition to its chief counsel, Henry T. Hunt of New York, and C. Francis Stradford, a black Chicago lawyer who served as the union's regular attorney, the BSCP also brought in two other prominent railway lawyers, Walter F. Lynch and David Lilienthal, to help prosecute the case.[60] Nonetheless, the court denied the Brotherhood's appeal on grounds that the ERP was legal under the Watson-Parker Act of 1926, and it ruled that the BSCP had not shown that Pullman's union had been detrimental to BSCP efforts to organize the porters and maids. But the judge assured the Brotherhood that, if it could prove during the ERP election that the company coerced porters to vote against their will, he would invalidate the returns and issue a permanent order against Pullman and the ERP. When the BSCP failed to present satisfactory proof (always hard to obtain in such cases) after the election, the court allowed the original decision to stand.[61]

Rather than abandon its legal efforts after this setback, the BSCP continued to press its case before the district court, with protracted litigation that lasted through 1933. By August, 1931, Webster believed the union had a reasonable chance of winning. He wrote Spencer Watson that the BSCP was on the verge of rejuvenation and added that

---

extent that said fellow employees . . . may desire; nor shall anything in this injunction be considered or construed as authority or permission for any officer or agent of said company, or any employee, acting for or on behalf of the defendant Railroad Company, attempting to influence or interfere with said selection or designation of their said representatives, or their right to self-organization as herein referred to, upon any pretext that they are acting individually and not as representatives of said defendant corporation."

[59] Chicago *Tribune* and Chicago *Herald and Examiner*, both Oct. 15, New York *Age*, Oct. 25, St. Louis *Argus*, Oct. 17, 1930. Brazeal, *The Brotherhood*, 95-100, has a good discussion of the injunction proceedings. Neither the *U.S. Reporter* nor the Clerk of the U.S. District Court for the Northern District of Illinois has files of the BSCP cases.

[60] Chicago *Defender*, Mar. 7, 1930. Lilienthal went on to serve in the administration of President Franklin D. Roosevelt and became one of the original directors of the Tennessee Valley Authority.

[61] Chicago *Herald and Examiner*, Oct. 16, New York *Age*, Oct. 25, MPW to Spencer Watson, Oct. 20, 1930, BSCP ChiPa.

"everything depends upon the case."[62] Randolph actually moved to Chicago almost full time to help push the effort. He and Webster were so caught up in their legal maneuvering during late 1931 that they had to miss the AFL convention lest a sudden development occur that might require their immediate attention.[63]

Though the BSCP's position vis-à-vis Pullman hardly improved, the union's court activity seemed to revitalize the organization. While the national office pressed for an injunction against the ERP as a whole, individual porters showed a new militancy in their dealings with the company. With the help of local BSCP leaders, some porters brought suit in state courts against Pullman for alleged intimidation in recent elections. In other instances they demanded reinstatement and back pay for the time lost since the company fired them because of union activity.[64] One such suit in Kansas City resulted in the company paying a porter a year's salary in back wages and returning him to work and to his position on the seniority roster. Pullman reacted to this mounting litigation by adjusting its previous position and by beginning to compensate porters at the national rate for accidental injury suffered while on duty.[65]

Although not yet the porters' official representative, the Brotherhood often interceded for them in their suits against the company.[66] The union even carried the fight into new areas. It contended, for example, that Pullman should compensate illegally discharged porters for loss of tips as well as for loss of regular wages, since Pullman regarded tips as part of porters' income.[67] Above all, the Brotherhood was concerned to secure restitution for porters who had been paid below the regular rate or laid off on sick leave without compensation; it succeeded in some

[62] MPW to Spencer Watson, Aug. 10, 1931, *ibid*.

[63] Telegram, APR and MPW to Green, Oct. 7, 1931, printed in AFL Convention, *Report of the Proceedings* (Oct., 1931), 273. In Green to APR, Oct. 12, 1931, GCB No. 435, p. 36, Green responded that he was "very much disappointed" that the BSCP leaders could not attend the convention. Green was undoubtedly sincere in his expression of regret, since he took time out from his busy schedule to answer from the convention site while the meeting was still in session.

[64] Chicago *Defender*, May 24, 1930.

[65] Spencer Watson to MPW, Feb. 21, 1931, BSCP ChiPa.

[66] See, *e.g.*, numerous letters, MPW to Watson and Watson to MPW, 1931, BSCP ChiPa; Chicago *Defender*, May 24, 1930. BSCP officials were particularly interested in the cases of twenty-nine porters who filed suit against Pullman in St. Louis for alleged illegal firings. Many of the cases were settled out of court in the porters' favor.

[67] Chicago *Defender*, Mar. 14, 1931.

instances. A signal victory in this regard came in January, 1932: BSCP leaders won a settlement on behalf of porter George Harris which brought him $600 in back pay for injuries sustained during 1928.[68]

Of course, these victories did not mean that the union had really put Pullman on the defensive. The company, for example, remained adamant in its refusal to recognize the Brotherhood as the porters' legitimate representative. To make matters worse, Pullman unilaterally cut porters' monthly pay by five dollars in February, 1932. The company negotiated the new wage rate with the big railroad unions at a Washington conference from which porters were excluded. Nor did Pullman bother to inform them officially of the decision — porters learned that their pay had been reduced when they read newspaper accounts of the meeting. Pullman used the Depression to justify the step and told Chicago reporters that company officials had taken a 10 percent pay cut, "as though," said A. Philip Randolph, "you could compare the salaries of officials with wages of porters."[69]

The union vehemently protested the wage cut, but without success. It organized respected leaders and organizations — including the NAACP and the NUL — in writing letters of protest to the company on the porters' behalf and influenced Green to issue a public statement condemning the wage cut.[70] In an open letter to J. P. Morgan, who sat on the Pullman board of directors, Randolph berated the action and accused the company of cutting porters' pay in order to maintain its record of meeting dividend payments throughout the Depression.[71] Morgan did

[68] *Ibid.*, Aug. 1, 1931, and Jan. 8, 1932. Pullman settled the Harris case out of court.

[69] APR to R. R. Matthews, Feb. 17, 1932, BSCP ChiPa. This wage cut, coupled with the cutback in tips caused by the Depression, brought tremendous hardships for the porters. BSCP officials estimated that the total loss in income amounted to approximately a third of what porters had previously earned. The financial squeeze contributed to the Brotherhood's loss of membership in 1932-33.

[70] Green to APR, Mar. 24, 1932, GCB No. 441, p. 611. Green's statement against PC wage cut was in keeping with the AFL's stance on this question — a position that stemmed from President Hoover's White House Conference between labor officials and industrial leaders in 1930, in which management agreed not to use wage reductions as a method of cutting industrial losses. See Taft, *The AF of L from the Death of Gompers,* 32-33.

[71] Printed in *American Federationist*, XL (1933), 705. See also statement on behalf of BSCP which the Congregational Ministers Union of Chicago issued, in Chicago *Defender*, Feb. 20, 1932.

not deign to reply. Nor were those who wrote on behalf of the Brotherhood any more successful; their letters, like those of the union, went unanswered.

Thus the Brotherhood limped along during 1930-32, throwing verbal darts at the ERP as it sought issues to use in advertising its cause. Its leaders condemned the company for allegedly bringing black men up from the South on the pretext of providing them with jobs, at the very time when there was no work available for some porters already on Pullman's rolls. Week after week they continued to attack the racist policies of the company, but to no avail. Moreover, the union sought Green's assistance in efforts to convince the Hoover Administration to institute an official investigation of Pullman's hiring policies. Though Green agreed to undertake the assignment and did appeal to the Department of Labor for the study Randolph desired, his efforts, too, ended in failure.[72] The BSCP also worked hard to sustain the porters' morale by sponsoring fund-raising parties and soup kitchens for those who had been put out of work by the Depression or because of their union activities.[73] BSCP sources do not reveal how much money these benefit functions raised or how many men and women they helped. What is important is that the union showed that it cared about its members. Such gestures would redound to its advantage in later years.

Actions such as these were necessary for the union's survival, for, as the Depression deepened, the porters feared more than ever for their jobs. Since little visible headway was being made against Pullman, the idea spread that any conditions of work were better than no work at all. Brotherhood officials found it difficult even to talk with porters, save under the most stringent rules of secrecy; one way involved slipping into town on organizing tours days ahead of their announced time of arrival and arranging clandestine appointments.[74] The union's financial resources were almost exhausted. Even Webster, presiding over the best-

[72] Green to APR, Mar. 24, 1930, GCB No. 413, p. 219, and Sept. 3, 1931, GCB No. 433, p. 902. Representative of the change that occurred in national policy with the advent of the New Deal is the fact that, while Green failed to get a survey commitment from the Hoover Administration, FDR's Secretary of Labor, Frances Perkins, agreed in Mar., 1933, to investigate Pullman on behalf of the porters. Subsequent developments made the investigation unnecessary. See Green to APR, Mar. 31, 1933, GCB No. 455, p. 828, and May 23, 1933, GCB No. 458, p. 305.

[73] See, *e.g.*, Chicago *Defender*, Dec. 13, 1930.

[74] MPW to Spencer Watson, May 23, 1931, BSCP ChiPa.

endowed BSCP district, had to hold mass meetings to finance his trips around the country on union business.[75] And, as often happens, financial difficulties bred internal dissension, causing the old rift between New York and outlying districts to reappear. Webster wrote that everything the New York office had tried to do had "been a flop," and he spoke of New York as "they" and the rest of the union as "we."[76]

Given the circumstances, the union was helpless to arrest the continued deterioration in porters' working conditions during the early 1930s. In addition to lowering porters' wages, the company had dismissed many of its car cleaners and forced porters to perform that task along with their regular work; officials instructed porters to "leave the cars as you found them."[77] Far from being able to help, the union was hard put just to survive. The New York office was even in danger of losing its semblance of permanence when Randolph and his New York associates, unable to meet the mortgage note on BSCP headquarters, suffered the humiliation of eviction.[78] It is amazing how Randolph maintained his air of confidence, a spirit that affected his colleagues as well.[79] Rather than acting as president of a union of slightly more than 600 members, Randolph carried himself as if he were a labor leader of the magnitude of John L. Lewis of the United Mine Workers. He seemingly willed that the BSCP would succeed.

There was still some progress in this generally bleak period of the BSCP's development. An important victory for the Brotherhood developed out of an event that occurred in April, 1931. Railroad detectives and city police arrested porter James E. Smith at Utica, New York, on April 29 and charged him with first- and second-degree assault for his

[75] Several letters, MPW to Watson and Watson to MPW, May-June, 1931, *ibid.* A BSCP document, "Injunction Fund–Petty Cash" (Sept.-Nov., 1932), *ibid.*, reflects the BSCP's financial plight during this period. The fund, which APR, MPW, Dellums, and Totten used to sustain themselves while they were in Chicago to help press the injunction suit, showed an average daily balance of approximately ten cents. They took in barely enough money to keep themselves going from day to day.

[76] MPW to Watson, Oct. 29, 1931, *ibid.*

[77] Chicago *Defender*, Jan. 21, 1933.

[78] APR to Robert Linton, June 9, 1932, BSCP ChiPa. Moreover, the BSCP was being sued for failure to pay its printing debt. See Vincent Mannino to APR, Feb. 26, 1932, *ibid.*, re: BSCP debt to Liberal Press, Inc., of New York City. The BSCP had "made no attempt toward the reduction of [its] indebtedness in the last seven or eight months."

[79] BSCP Bulletin, APR and MPW to Eastern Members, Sept. 26, 1932, *ibid.*

part in disturbances that occurred aboard his train on the run from Lake Placid to New York City. He was arraigned in Utica and jailed in lieu of $5,000 bond.[80] The Brotherhood, claiming that the Pullman Company had framed Smith because of his union work, immediately hired counsel for his defense and posted bond to secure his release from jail.[81] The BSCP's charge against Pullman, and its statements to porters that the *Smith* case showed how the Brotherhood would support them when the ERP would not, forced the company to abandon its normal stance of ignoring the union. In a statement of June 1, 1931, Pullman explained its reluctance to come to the porter's aid by pointing out that, unlike the irresponsible BSCP, the company intended to uphold the law.[82] But this statement proved ineffective, especially after Congressman Fiorello La Guardia of New York defended Smith and won acquittal, though failing to prove the company's complicity.[83] Randolph wrote that the BSCP's action in the *Smith* case demonstrated that the porters were helpless as individuals, but strong as an organized group. It proved even to skeptics that the Brotherhood could and would defend its members.[84]

The BSCP often achieved illusions of success that were sufficient to stimulate its leader's boundless faith that justice would prevail. Just prior to the 1932 AFL convention, the BSCP's protracted litigation against Pullman resulted in its first legal victory. Federal District Judge George E. Q. Johnston, of the Northern District of Illinois, upheld the union's right to sue on the porters' behalf under rights granted by Watson-Parker and agreed to hear oral arguments in the case. The way was now clear to challenge the legitimacy of the ERP. Randolph and Webster went to the convention convinced that victory was near.[85]

[80] APR in St. Louis *Argus*, June 26, APR in Chicago *Defender*, Aug. 1, 1931.

[81] Chicago *Defender*, Aug. 1, 1931. Sources do not explain how the broke BSCP got funds for the bail money.

[82] PC public statement on Smith Case, June 1, 1931, copy in BSCP ChiPa.

[83] Letters, APR to La Guardia, La Guardia to APR, Apr.-May, 1932, *ibid*. APR's success in getting La Guardia to take Smith's case, which went to trial in 1932, is representative of his effectiveness in bringing influential individuals to his side. During early 1932 La Guardia was involved in pressing passage of the Norris–La Guardia Anti-Injunction Act, which both Houses of Congress approved overwhelmingly. See Bernstein, *The Lean Years*, 410-15. APR and La Guardia had apparently already begun what was to develop into a long friendship. APR addressed the congressman as "My dear La Guardia" and La Guardia addressed the BSCP Chief as "My dear Randolph."

[84] Chicago *Defender*, Aug. 1, 1931.

[85] AFL Convention, *Report of the Proceedings* (Oct., 1932), 398.

Randolph proposed a resolution requesting that the AFL issue a public endorsement of the Brotherhood's fight, since the BSCP had just won a major victory against company unionism. Reminding the delegates that the number of company unions had increased to more than a thousand since employers instituted the system shortly after World War I, Randolph warned that under depression conditions they would continue to proliferate at the expense of honest unions unless the AFL took an immediate and definite stand against them. The Federation endorsed the BSCP's activities.[86] United Mine Workers President John L. Lewis, contending that verbal support was not enough, proposed and carried a resolution calling upon member unions to make financial contributions to assist the BSCP in its struggle.[87] President Green circulated an official request for funds to aid the BSCP in January, 1933, and member unions responded by raising $660 for the Brotherhood during the ensuing year (although, because of the banking holiday of 1933, the BSCP saw only $240 of it prior to 1936).[88]

Soon after the convention, in November, 1932, the Brotherhood was back in federal court for hearings on its petition that the court permanently enjoin Pullman from operating the ERP. The judge issued only a temporary order restraining the company from interfering with the BSCP's right to organize porters, yet this decision tremendously bolstered the BSCP's morale. The union announced that its days of undercover operations were over and that henceforth it would work publicly.[89] But the Brotherhood's joy was premature: the court had enjoined Pullman against interfering with the BSCP, but it had not required the company to cease operating the ERP. Adding to the Brotherhood's disadvantage, the case passed from the hands of the judge who was favorable to labor unions, George Johnston, into those of an anti-labor judge, Charles Woodward. Pullman and the BSCP argued before Judge Woodward through 1933 and into 1934. The BSCP lost

[86] *Ibid.*, 399.

[87] *Ibid.*, 402.

[88] Green to Victor Olander, Jan. 6, 1933, BSCP ChiPa; Green to APR, June 3, 1933, GCB No. 458, p. 632; AFL Convention, *Report of the Proceedings* (Oct., 1936), 251. *Report of the Proceedings* (Oct., 1937), 289, shows that the BSCP eventually received the full amount. In Green to APR, cited herein, Green explained that the AFL placed no restraints on how the BSCP should spend the money.

[89] BSCP broadside, Nov. 14, 1932, BSCP ChiPa; St. Louis *Argus*, Nov. 18, Chicago *Defender*, Nov. 19, 1932.

skirmishes along the way, failing to have the ERP declared illegal in June, 1933, and losing its plea for relief through equity in January, 1934.[90]

Continued legal setbacks forced Randolph and his colleagues to seek support from any source. On February 8, 1933, Senator Clarence C. Dill of Washington introduced a bill requiring railroad companies to employ only American citizens in service positions in interstate commerce.[91] Randolph was undoubtedly pleased with Dill's effort. When Walter White asked Randolph for his thoughts on the measure, Randolph had a ready answer. White questioned whether the NAACP should support such blatantly exclusionist legislation, soliciting Randolph's frank opinion "both insofar as it affects Negroes and in the larger question as to whether we as Negroes can afford to support exclusionist legislation."[92] Randolph replied that the BSCP favored the bill because it placed before the public the question of why Pullman had hired foreigners in the first place. He claimed that when the BSCP was organized in 1925, the Pullman Company had announced it would hire Filipinos to show black porters that they could be replaced if they joined the union. The BSCP would oppose any group — including blacks — who attempted to displace its members in violation of seniority rights. He pointed out that the Dill bill restricted porter service to American citizens, not simply to black men, and with notable self-contradiction assured the NAACP leader that he was "personally . . . opposed to any exclusion legislation based upon race, creed, nationality or color."[93]

[90] St. Louis *Argus*, June 26, 1933; Brazeal, *The Brotherhood*, 98. Throughout 1933 Green manifested a close interest in the BSCP's legal activities. He wrote Randolph on several occasions expressing the AFL's interest in the case and offering to "render all financial and moral support possible." See Green to APR, Feb. 9, 1933, GCB No. 453, p. 416; July 7, 1933, GCB No. 460, p. 406. Court records for the Northern District of Illinois do not contain files of the BSCP's cases, but Green summarized Woodward's January decision in *BSCP* v. *Pullman* in a letter to Randolph of Jan. 31, 1934, GCB No. 482, p. 554. According to Green, the judge ruled against the BSCP because: a) the Supreme Court decision in the *New Orleans Railway* case did not apply to porters; b) the BSCP presented no evidence of its membership; c) existing railway labor legislation provided ample procedures for the BSCP to employ in solving its difficulties without resorting to the courts.

[91] Draft Copy, Senate Bill S5064, U.S. Senate, 72nd Cong., 2nd sess. (Feb. 8, 1933), copy in NAACP Pas, C414, LC.

[92] White to APR, Feb. 23, 1933, NAACP Pas, C414, LC.

[93] APR to White, Mar. 2, 1933, *ibid*.

Randolph's explanation did not convince White, and the NAACP refused to place its weight behind the restrictionist bill. White informed Randolph that in his opinion the Association could "never end prejudice against one group by indulging in prejudice against another."[94] Nonetheless, Randolph heartily supported the Dill bill and persistently argued that his only interest was in protecting the porters' seniority rights; he even attempted to organize mass support for the proposal, bringing Dill to New York to speak under union auspices.[95] Much of the black press, notably the *Courier*, backed Dill's proposal enthusiastically. Like Randolph and the BSCP, the *Courier* chose to disregard the racist overtones of the bill and Dill's subsequent comments.[96] The bill was never reported out of committee. For all its work the Brotherhood garnered only a little publicity from the affair, although it did make a valuable friend in Dill, who, as chairman of the Committee on Interstate and Foreign Commerce, would be of value at a later date.

The BSCP was fortunate that by 1933 it could base its hopes on legislation stronger than the Dill bill. During the period of prolonged litigation, a sweeping change had occurred in national politics. And though the Brotherhood's failure to force the company to abandon the ERP under provisions of the Watson-Parker Act had come as a disappointment, it was far from fatal to the union. The New Deal had pushed through a torrent of reform legislation during the Hundred Days, including two labor acts that explicitly did for railroad unionism what the BSCP had claimed Watson-Parker should do. These laws, the Bankruptcy Act of March, 1933, and the Emergency Transportation Act (ETA) of June, forbade carriers to use company funds to maintain unions and outlawed "yellow dog" contracts. They also declared null and void those "yellow dog" contracts which already existed.[97]

[94] White to APR, Mar. 3, 1933, *ibid*.

[95] Pittsburgh *Courier*, Apr. 22, 1933. Randolph took pains to assure Green that his actions re: Dill did not represent racism, but a simple desire on the BSCP's part to protect the seniority rights of its members. Green did not commit himself as favoring Dill's bill, but he wished Randolph luck in his parade. Green to APR, June 3, 1933, GCB No. 458, p. 632.

[96] Pittsburgh *Courier*, Feb. 25, 1933. The *Courier* editorial for Feb. 18 shows that the paper shared many of Dill's racist views.

[97] Joseph Eastman, co-ordinator of transportation under the Emergency Transportation Act, denied before the Senate Committee on Interstate and Foreign Commerce that the act outlawed company unions. *Senate Hearings*, S3266, Act to Amend the Railway Labor Act, Apr. 10, 1934, p. 12.

Brotherhood officials recognized how, on the surface, conditions had changed in their favor. In mid-July, 1933, Randolph announced the union's intention to press for relief through the coordinator of transportation, Joseph B. Eastman.[98] The union requested Commissioner Eastman to investigate porters' wages and working conditions to determine if company activities violated the transportation act. Eastman had first become acquainted with the BSCP's case in 1927, when he was a member of the ICC that heard the union's anti-tipping appeal; he accepted the assignment and sent questionnaires to the porters and the Pullman Company soliciting the necessary information.[99]

Soon after Eastman began his investigation, Randolph again wrote to Pullman requesting a conference. As a result he learned that a significant change had occurred in the company's administration.[100] This change in personnel renewed hope among BSCP leaders that Pullman would eventually recognize the Brotherhood as bargaining agent for porters and maids. When Randolph's letter arrived at Pullman headquarters, the old-line officials who had been involved in the dispute since 1925 — Hungerford, Simmons, Kelly — were adamantly opposed even to acknowledging it. They refused to admit that it was a legitimate union question and preferred to call the BSCP dispute "the Randolph matter." But D. A. Crawford, who had succeeded to the presidency, initiated a new policy of dealing with the Brotherhood. Insisting that Randolph's request for a conference was a business matter to which the company should respond, though it had no intention of recognizing the union, Crawford ordered F. L. Simmons, director of employee relations, to reject Randolph's request. Crawford instructed Simmons to tell the union that the company did not consider the BSCP the representative of porters and maids. Moreover, Randolph should be informed that Pullman had sufficient machinery to handle grievances among those classes of employees. When Simmons procrastinated, Crawford demanded that his directive be carried out. On September 18, 1933, Simmons addressed a letter to Randolph as instructed.[101] The BSCP had

[98] Chicago *Defender*, July 15, 1933.

[99] AFL Convention, *Report of the Proceedings* (Oct., 1933), 521.

[100] *Ibid.*; APR to D. A. Crawford, Sept. 8, 1933, PC Pas.

[101] Various memoranda: Crawford to Kelly, Sept. 11, Crawford to Hungerford, Sept. 15, Hungerford to Crawford, Sept. 15, and letter, Simmons to APR, Sept. 18, 1933, all in PC Pas. APR happily referred to this changed state of affairs at the 1933 AFL convention. See AFL Convention, *Report of the Proceedings* (Oct., 1933), 521.

not gained company recognition, but it had finally established direct contact with Pullman officials.

Despite the courtesy which Pullman showed and the pleasure which BSCP leaders must have enjoyed from corresponding directly with company officials, the Brotherhood soon learned that its gains were more illusory than real. The crushing blow to the union's hopes for a quick settlement came within a week after Randolph received Simmons's letter. BSCP leaders learned from Commissioner Eastman that in his judgment the Emergency Transportation Act did not cover porters, because the Pullman Company technically was not a railroad.[102] Thus sweeping legislative changes had left the Brotherhood with no protection other than Watson-Parker, which had proven woefully inadequate to solve the porters' problems. The union could only hope that future laws would correct this oversight. As yet, no new deal had come for the porters.

Brazeal, *The Brotherhood*, 105, mistakenly referred to Simmons as a minor black official whom the company used to communicate with the BSCP. Simmons was neither black nor a minor official; he was the man responsible for handling Pullman negotiations with employees. See the first chapter, above, for discussion.

[102] Eastman to APR, Sept. 25, 1933, BSCP ChiPa. It is not certain if the company was aware of this development before it responded to APR's letter of Sept. 8. If it did know that the Emergency Transportation Act did not cover porters, the response to APR takes on added significance. It would mean that the Pullman Company had reached the point of extending common courtesy and had not acted out of fear that its position had weakened.

CHAPTER VII

A Winner Never Quits

> Hundreds of men lost their jobs in the conflict. Leaders of the Movement, like Ashley L. Totten, Milton P. Webster, Bennie Smith, E. J. Bradley, and C. L. Dellums lost their homes and underwent severe privations to put the union over. Totten was nearly murdered by thugs in Kansas City and Smith was threatened with a lynching and driven out of Jacksonville, Florida. These men were former porters, all. None of them received any pay over half the life of the Brotherhood.
>
> — A. Philip Randolph, *Opportunity*, XV (Oct., 1937)

The spirit of hope that the Roosevelt Administration had brought to the country affected porters, too. In 1933-34, during what was one of the Brotherhood's darkest periods, the spirit of eventual success endured as always. Eastman's unfavorable ruling, indeed, caused the union's leadership to fight even harder for a successful completion of their dispute with Pullman and for establishment of the Brotherhood as a permanent part of the American labor movement. For their part, porters began to drift back into the union; their numbers increased from the low of 658 in 1933 to 2,627 by the end of 1934.[1]

It was in this spirit that BSCP leaders went to the AFL convention in 1933, determined to gain support from the House of Labor for its efforts to improve the transportation act by extending coverage to the Pullman Company and porters. They deemed such action essential because Eastman's ruling that the Emergency Transportation Act did not apply to porters had left the BSCP without federal protection. Pointing out that the National Industrial Recovery Act also excluded porters — because under terms of that legislation porters were defined as railroad workers — Randolph told the convention that the Brotherhood would not allow the company to escape supervision by both the ETA and NIRA codes. BSCP officials insisted that porters should be covered by the Emergency Transportation Act and not NIRA because, despite opinions to the

[1] Brailsford R. Brazeal, *The Brotherhood of Sleeping Car Porters* (New York: Harper and Brothers, 1946), 222.

contrary, porters were railroad workers and demanded to be treated as such. Randolph called on the AFL to request President Roosevelt to use his executive powers to bring porters under jurisdiction of the transportation act, and threatened that the porters were prepared to strike if necessary to rectify their situation.[2] Actually, porters were not the only class of railroad workers excluded from both emergency transportation and national recovery labor legislation: white sleeping car conductors and refrigerated car employees found themselves in the same situation. Thus, the BSCP undoubtedly received more support from the convention than it would have if porters had been the only employees left unprotected. Leaders of white railroad unions, working through the Railway Labor Executives Association (an all-white group that had consistently refused Randolph membership since 1926), were already busy preparing legislative proposals to improve their members' standing before federal bodies.[3] Given these circumstances, Randolph's powerful appeal had a telling effect on the delegates, and the convention unanimously endorsed his proposals.[4]

During late 1933 and early 1934, the BSCP and the AFL joined forces to secure federal recognition of the rights of porters as workers. Employing mass demonstration tactics, the Brotherhood carried on a publicity campaign to pressure Congress to include porters in future railroad legislation, and to inform the public that neither the ETA nor NIRA codes covered Pullman's relations with porters. The BSCP also appealed to the White House for help in overcoming its difficulties. Green added his voice to the request for an executive order that would help the porters, and he called on leaders of the Railway Labor Executives Association to include porters in whatever proposals they produced.[5]

Both the executive and legislative branches of government paid heed to those who called for a new look at railroad labor legislation. Green reported that the president instructed Commissioner Eastman to take

[2] AFL Convention, *Report of the Proceedings* (Oct., 1933), 522.

[3] Green to APR, Jan. 19, 1934, GCB No. 481, p. 99. Green makes clear in his letter that the RLEA was well underway in drafting its proposals. A major reason for refusing APR membership in the Railway Labor Executives Association was that to admit him would have been to grant the BSCP parity with the white railway brotherhoods.

[4] AFL Convention, *Report of the Proceedings* (Oct., 1933), 523.

[5] Green to APR, Nov. 8, 1933, GCB No. 474, p. 90; Green to APR, Feb. 2, 1934, GCB No. 482, p. 851; Green in St. Louis *Argus*, Jan. 26, 1934; Edward Berman, "Pullman Porters Win," *The Nation*, CXLI (Aug. 21, 1935), 217.

prompt action to satisfy the BSCP's complaint,[6] while Senator Clarence Dill introduced a bill that would do explicitly what the Brotherhood had requested. Eastman had determined that the Emergency Transportation Act was an inadequate method by which to govern railway labor problems. What the nation needed was permanent new legislation. Thus, with strong backing from the White House, Eastman drafted a proposal to amend the Watson-Parker Act of 1926 to include the pro-labor features of the Emergency Transportation Act. Showing an awareness of BSCP and AFL pressure, Eastman included a recommendation that any new law explicitly cover sleeping car companies.[7] Dill's bill was soon set aside in favor of Eastman's proposals, and during the spring both houses of Congress held extensive hearings on recommendations for the new amendments.

Efforts to pass a new railroad labor law moved more rapidly in the House of Representatives. The House passed a version of the bill and sent it on to the Senate; there the Committee on Interstate and Foreign Commerce, of which Dill was chairman, took up the bill, and numerous witnesses appeared to present their points of view. Eastman represented the administration; George Harrison of the Brotherhood of Railway Clerks spoke for the Railway Labor Executives Association; George A. Kelly came for the Pullman Company; Randolph appeared for the Brotherhood of Sleeping Car Porters.

In expressing the view of those unions that were affiliated through the Railway Labor Executives Association, Harrison emphasized their hope that resulting new legislation would outlaw company unions, and he proposed inclusion under the new law of some workers who previously had not been covered. Sleeping car conductors and refrigerated car employees, for example, needed such protection, Harrison insisted. But showing total disregard for porters, whose union had been deeply involved in opposition to company unionism for almost a decade, and ignoring Green's direct appeal that the RLEA support the BSCP, Harrison refused to mention porters among those workers who should be

[6] Green to APR, Jan. 12, 1934, GCB No. 480, p. 409.

[7] Green to APR, Nov. 24, 1933, GCB No. 476, p. 410, refers to letter from Eastman to Green in which the coordinator of transportation informed the AFL president of his intentions to include porters in his forthcoming recommendations to Congress. The debate on proposals for changing railway labor legislation took place during spring, 1934. They are best recorded in *Congressional Record*, 73rd Cong., 2nd sess. Berman, "Pullman Porters," 217, also discusses those aspects of Eastman's proposal that were favorable to the BSCP.

covered by federal railroad legislation.[8] The fact is that white railway unions had no intention of helping an embattled group of black co-workers even when their interests were identical: from 35 to 40 percent of railway workers belonged to company unions in 1934.[9]

In presenting the Brotherhood's case, Randolph benefited from his political activities of the previous summer, when he had endorsed Dill's proposal to outlaw Filipino attendants on sleeping cars. As chairman of the Senate committee, Dill granted Randolph extended time to present his views. Appealing to the committee to require explicit inclusion of porters in any bill reported to the full Senate, Randolph laid bare the BSCP's precarious condition. He told the committee that neither he nor the fifteen other BSCP organizers received any salary for their work for the Brotherhood. The union, he reported, was a voluntary organization which represented 6,000 of the company's 9,000 porters (the total number had declined by approximately 25 percent from the 12,000 figure of 1925). The Brotherhood had maintained itself for nine years despite Pullman's terrible threats of intimidation against its members. Without federal protection, porters would remain at the mercy of the company and would be unable to improve their working conditions. During the course of his testimony Randolph was forced to indulge Dill as the senator renewed the issue of Filipino exclusion. Dill again asked

[8] George M. Harrison, Testimony before the Senate Committee on Interstate and Foreign Commerce, *Hearings on S3266*, 73rd Cong., 2nd sess., Apr. 11, 1934, p. 36. Hereafter cited *Hearings on S3266*. General studies of labor in the United States usually have overlooked the contributions of the BSCP to efforts to outlaw company unionism, while labor leaders of the period also refused to grant the Brotherhood more than veiled credit in this field. But BSCP leaders were certain that theirs was a major part of the fight against company unionism, and their success in maintaining a core of porters in the face of a strong ERP demonstrates effective leadership. Though the Brotherhood's impact might have been far less than Randolph and his associates believed, several black and white contemporaries commented on the role of the BSCP as an anti-company union force. Robert W. Dunn, executive secretary of the Garland Fund, contributes a major portion of a chapter in his book, *Company Unions* (New York: Vanguard Press, 1927), to Pullman's ERP and to efforts of the BSCP, which had "featured so emphatically in its organization program the defeat of a company union." For other views, see Victor Weybright, "Pullman Porters on Parade," *Survey Graphic*, XXIV (Nov., 1935), 544; T. Arnold Hill, "The Pullman Porter," *Opportunity*, XIII (June, 1935), 186; Berman, "Pullman Porters," 217; Pittsburgh *Courier*, June 7, 1930; Chicago *Defender*, Aug. 30, 1930; Frank R. Crosswaith, "The Future Is Ours," Statement on the 11th Anniversary of BSCP (1936), NLCRG Pas.

[9] Harrison, *Hearings on S3266*, 36; Richard Bransten, *Men Who Lead Labor* (New York: Modern Age Books, 1937), 169, writes explicitly that white unionists made no effort to include porters under provisions of the new law.

Randolph if the company should be required to use only American citizens as porters, and the labor leader dutifully said yes.[10]

The Pullman Company did not allow such testimony to go unchallenged. It sent its general counsel, George A. Kelly, to tell the committee that there was no need to place porters under the provisions of the impending act because no dispute existed between them and the company that could not be handled through the ERP. To prove the point, Kelly cited the fact that the porters had never appealed to the Mediation Board a decision of the ERP's Board of Industrial Relations. Kelly received a cold reception from the committee, especially from Dill and Senator Robert F. Wagner, a leading New Deal Democrat from New York. When they pressed him on the ERP, Kelly admitted that the governing document of the organization could not be amended without the company's approval, but he emphasized that this had been "arranged through agreement." He discounted the BSCP as an "outside" organization of troublemakers and said that Pullman did not know of a single porter who held membership in that union. In answer to Dill's query about the Filipinos, Kelly minimized their impact and denied that they had been employed to thwart the BSCP or to encroach on the seniority rights of porters. He alleged that one or two hundred Filipinos were necessary to the company's operations because black porters did not want the runs they handled.[11]

When it became apparent that the committee would recommend that the new law include porters and outlaw company unions, the white unions rushed to support the BSCP's demands. They could not allow the black union to receive sole credit for legislation which represented a

[10] APR, *Hearings on S3266*, Apr. 11, 1934, pp. 50-53. There is a discrepancy between the 6,000 figure Randolph quoted for BSCP membership and the actual published figure for the union at the time. Official figures show that, when Randolph made the statement, the union could count fewer than 3,000 members. This apparent discrepancy raises an important question about how truthful the BSCP was about its membership. Absence of papers from the union's headquarters for the years before 1940 makes the problem almost insoluble, but a statement by Webster at the 1935 AFL convention suggests that the union purposely kept its public membership figures lower than they actually were in order to avoid paying per capita tax to the AFL. According to MPW, this was an astute political move on the part of BSCP leaders. Rather than report their full membership to the Federation and pay taxes on them, the Brotherhood reported the bare minimum needed to keep its locals in the AFL and kept the bulk of its meager funds to maintain a national organization. See AFL Convention, *Report of the Proceedings* (Oct., 1935), 815. In 1935 the National Mediation Board certified that Pullman had 8,316 porters and maids.

[11] G. A. Kelly, *Hearings on S3266*, Apr. 12, 1934, pp. 84-85, 94.

major advance in curbing company unionism.[12] When the Senate bill came to the floor, pro-labor forces found themselves engaged in a minor filibuster. April 18 was the last day of the session, and Congress was under pressure of a threatened strike by the AFL and the railway unions if it failed to produce a law in the current session. Senator Dill and his colleagues secured sufficient strength to pass a bill that was an exact duplicate of the House version.[13] President Roosevelt signed the amended railway labor proposals into law on June 21, 1934.

In addition to extending explicit coverage to porters and others previously unprotected by federal railroad labor legislation, the Amended Railway Labor Act of 1934 included significant changes which placed organized railroad laborers in a much more favored position than previously. While incorporating the machinery of Watson-Parker — collective bargaining, mediation, and arbitration — the new law was unequivocal in its ban on company unions and "yellow dog" contracts, features that first had been expressed in the Emergency Transportation Act. The Amended Railway Labor Act provided that any union which represented a majority of a class of workers had the right to bargain for all laborers employed in that line of work. In cases where two or more unions claimed to represent a group of workers, the law empowered the new National Mediation Board to employ various means, including secret elections among affected employees, to determine which organization would have jurisdiction. To give meaning to the verbiage about the right of laborers to organize and bargain collectively, the law also *required* corporations to negotiate with the unions to which a majority of their employees belonged. Arbitration of disputes, however, still depended upon the voluntary agreement of both parties.[14]

Despite its shortcomings, the Amended Railway Labor Act of 1934 placed BSCP-Pullman relations on a new level and left the company in a vulnerable position. Because the act outlawed the ERP, the Pullman Company could no longer claim that it had adequate procedures for

[12] Bransten, *Men Who Lead Labor*, 169.

[13] *Congressional Record* (1934), *passim*. The Senate substituted the House version of the bill verbatim in order to preclude the necessity of having a conference committee to clear up discrepancies. For the effect of the threatened strike on speeding the proceedings through the Senate, see New York *Times*, June 18, 1934. In truth, the AFL left most of the lobbying on Watson-Parker amendments to the railway unions and reserved its own resources to work for passage of the Wagner-Connery bill that was under consideration in the Congress at the same time.

[14] Amended Railway Labor Act of 1934 (48 Stat 1185).

handling problems with its porters. Moreover, the union now had at its disposal federal powers to compel the company to confer with it if the Brotherhood could prove that it represented a majority of porters. Though the conflict was by no means over, BSCP prospects with Pullman were brighter than at any point since 1925, and its leaders could now realistically dream of a successful end to their fight.

At the very time when national lawmakers struggled to improve conditions of workers by writing effective labor legislation, black spokesmen and organizations were reassessing their own activities and questioning whether their policies spoke to the needs of the black masses. By 1934, the sense of desperation that had existed in the BSCP before passage of the railway labor act was general among American blacks. Though a fundamental federal change in both philosophy and mode of operation had occurred with the election of President Franklin D. Roosevelt and a Democratic Congress, conditions remained bleak for Afro-Americans. Like the relationship between porters and the Emergency Transportation Act, some blacks came to believe that new federal legislation was intended to improve conditions for whites while, on occasion, actually working to the disadvantage of blacks. The Civilian Conservation Corps discriminated against blacks in recruitment, and when it accepted Afro-American youths the blacks found themselves set aside in segregated camps; agricultural relief funds helped landowners more than they did sharecroppers and tenants; and blacks continued to be last hired and first fired.[15]

A group of young black leaders including Abram L. Harris, Charles H. Houston, and Ralph J. Bunche of Howard University and E. Franklin Frazier of Fisk University pressed the leading black advancement organization, the NAACP, to pay more attention to the economic needs of the black masses. Others, notably John P. Davis and Robert Weaver, founded new organizations specifically designed to insure that Afro-

[15] Raymond Wolters, *Negroes and the Great Depression* (Westport, Conn.: Greenwood, 1970), 3-55, deals specifically with agricultural difficulties blacks faced under AAA. Nancy J. Weiss, *The National Urban League: 1910-1940* (New York: Oxford University Press, 1974), 237-40, discusses the dire conditions of blacks in urban regions as reflected in relief and unemployment figures. The issue of the *Journal of Negro Education* for Jan., 1936, is a special volume containing the litany of wrongs and proposals for improving conditions for Afro-Americans; it developed from papers read at a special conference on blacks and the New Deal sponsored by the Joint Committee on National Recovery and the political science department at Howard University in the summer of 1935.

Americans received an equitable share of funds administered by the multifarious New Deal agencies.[16] The main thrust of their demands was that black leaders should pay much more attention to the difficulties suffered by their brethren because of economic insecurity and exploitation. One way to solve this problem, some argued, was to educate black workers to think in terms of class consciousness and to foster close relations between Afro-Americans and organized labor. Long an advocate of such views, leaders of the Brotherhood of Sleeping Car Porters now found themselves in respectable company. Partly because of BSCP pressure, but also because of coercion from the Communists and certain elements of black leadership, some black advancement organizations gradually began to move in that direction.

The NAACP's change toward a stronger emphasis on economic issues had evolved over a long period and quickened in the early 1930s. From its earliest days, some NAACP leaders had made pronouncements on the values of organized labor, and in 1930 the Association had announced its intention to push for wider participation of blacks in the trade union movement. But this had not evolved into concrete action. Then in 1933, at the Second Amenia Confererence, a group of young black intellectuals convened under NAACP auspices to discuss the status of black people and to suggest methods by which the Association could better respond to the economic needs of Afro-Americans. Though the meetings revealed a wide range of views, most members urged the NAACP to move away from its long-time emphasis on seeking to secure for blacks their constitutional rights, instead paying more attention to economic problems.[17] Soon after that conference, as part of its growing

[16] Davis and Weaver founded the Joint Committee on National Recovery in 1933 to keep the special problems of blacks squarely before New Deal authorities and to serve as a clearing house for black groups on economic problems. Numerous black groups affiliated with the Joint Committee. Davis, who had strong leftist leanings, had moved close to the Communist party by the outbreak of World War II.

Robert Weaver, a young Harvard Ph.D. in economics, was to have a brilliant career in government service, as was Ralph J. Bunche, a Harvard Ph.D. in political science. Weaver served as special assistant to the secretary of the interior during FDR's administration, becoming a nationally recognized expert on problems of housing and eventually advancing to the position of secretary of housing and urban development during the administration of Lyndon B. Johnson. Weaver became the first black citizen to attain cabinet rank. Bunche was chairman of the political science department at Howard University during the Depression. He went on to a distinguished career with the United Nations after World War II, where his services earned him a Nobel Peace Prize.

[17] B. Joyce Ross, *J. E. Spingarn and the Rise of the NAACP, 1911-1939* (New

interest in economic matters, the NAACP board of directors named a special Committee on Future Plan and Program to study the organizational structure and goals of the NAACP and to make specific proposals for the Association's long-range development. Under the chairmanship of Dr. Abram L. Harris, a recent appointee to the board and an advocate of moving the NAACP toward economic radicalism, the committee made sweeping suggestions. Echoing many of the ideas that had been expressed at Amenia the year before, its report called on the NAACP to strengthen its relationship with the masses of blacks and to shift its emphasis from what they saw as the egalitarian search for civil rights toward a more mass-oriented concern for jobs and economic betterment.[18]

Debate over the Harris Report, as it was commonly called, occurred in late 1934 and early 1935. Recognizing considerable merit in the suggestions, the NAACP's leadership, particularly Walter White, Roy Wilkins, and Joel Spingarn, thought the NAACP might profitably move slightly in the direction Harris and others had suggested; however, they believed it would be unsound for the organization to give up the field of work at which it had been so successful for almost a quarter-century. Other board members expressed objections to Harris's economic views; opinions ranged from overt opposition to trade unionism to the fear that such policies as those Harris proposed were not suited for "a middle class organization like ours." One member even suggested that the NAACP could not undertake this program because it would thereby encroach on the work of the National Urban League. In the end the Association moved in the general direction indicated by the Harris Report, but it did not rush to implement the most radical findings on either economics or reorganization of the NAACP power structure.[19]

York: Atheneum, 1972), 169-85; Wolters, *Negroes*, 219-27. This conference of 1933 was called the Second Amenia Conference because in 1916 the NAACP had held a major meeting to map its future at the same site. See Ross, *Spingarn*, 47.

[18] Ross, *Spingarn*, 217-41, discusses in detail the internal struggle to make economic radicalism a central feature of the NAACP's work. Wolters covers the same ground from a different perspective in *Negroes*, 302-42.

[19] Ross, *Spingarn*, 217-41; Wolters, *Negroes*, 302-42. The NAACP's reluctance to change its emphasis was one aspect of the complex struggle that led to Du Bois's resignation from the association in 1934. See Ross, *Spingarn*, 211-16; Wolters, *Negroes*, 266-94; and Du Bois, *The Autobiography of W. E. B. Du Bois* (New York: International, 1968).

During the same years the National Urban League was undergoing a reassessment of its own. Weiss, *National Urban League*, 281-87, writes about the League's establish-

Undoubtedly aware of the new urgency among black leaders on economic questions, Randolph undertook in 1934 to use the prestige he had garnered by the congressional victory to channel the interest into effective action. During the summer he laid plans to challenge the American Federation of Labor on its racial policies. Intending to go beyond the perennial pleadings he had made since his first AFL convention in 1929, the BSCP leader planned to go to the San Francisco meeting in October armed with the backing of leading black organizations and an extensive body of facts to support his allegation of racial discrimination within the organized labor movement. Randolph turned to Walter White and the NAACP for help in collecting the evidence he needed.[20] Assistant Secretary Roy Wilkins advised his boss against becoming involved with the Randolph maneuver,[21] but White was feeling the pressure of Harris and others to participate in efforts to improve labor conditions for blacks. He agreed to cooperate, though he warned Randolph that he was not "optimistic about your getting too far with the AFL under the present leadership."[22]

When AFL delegates arrived in San Francisco to attend the 1934 convention, they witnessed an unfamiliar sight: a well-organized picket demonstration against them. The San Francisco–Alameda County branches of the NAACP, on orders from White and perhaps at Randolph's suggestion, came out in force to express the view that the AFL had not done enough to improve conditions for blacks and to force discriminating unions to remove their color bars.[23] Because the demonstration ran afoul of California laws governing picketing, and in the minds of many whites was taken to have Communist implications, it was

---

ment of workers' councils to inculcate a labor class consciousness among black workers, while Guichard Parris and Lester Brooks, *Blacks in the City: A History of the National Urban League* (Boston: Little, Brown, 1971), 227-39, discuss NUL attempts to encourage official Washington to pay more attention to the special needs of blacks. In pp. 248-60, Parris and Brooks discuss NUL attempts in encouraging blacks to join labor unions and emphasize the League's work with workers' councils. Harris's proposals to the NAACP Board included a recommendation that the Association set up workers' councils, too. The League's official organ, *Opportunity* (1934-35), *passim*, is a valuable source on NUL activities.

[20] White to APR, Aug. 31, 1934, NAACP Pas, C414, LC.

[21] Memorandum, Wilkins to White, Sept. 4, 1934, *ibid*.

[22] White to APR, Aug. 31, 1934, *ibid*.

[23] White to Leland Hawkins of San Francisco Branch NAACP, Sept. 25, 1934, *ibid*. Although it must remain in the realm of speculation, it seems quite possible that White might have ordered the demonstration at Randolph's suggestion.

not as effective as Walter White and others had hoped.[24] Moreover, William Green, undoubtedly aware of disquiet among blacks, had attempted to soothe them before the meeting even started. In an article in *Opportunity*, Green wrote that black workers had begun to show a new awareness of trade unionism and had turned to the labor movement with new conviction, a development which he and his associates welcomed.[25] Nonetheless, despite Green's efforts and the laws of California, the campaign did demonstrate a changed attitude among black leaders as to the importance of trade unionism for Afro-Americans.

Meanwhile, Randolph carried the fight to the convention floor. Renewing his long-standing charge that the AFL had not done all it could for blacks, he pointed to the NAACP demonstration as evidence that the masses of blacks were becoming increasingly discouraged and disgruntled. Previous AFL resolutions on racial discrimination were "splendid and of high moral value," he said, but they did not adequately solve the problem.[26] He then proceeded to introduce two resolutions that Webster thought likely to "split the convention wide open."[27] First, Randolph called on the convention to demand that member unions eliminate color clauses from their constitutions and expel those which failed to comply. Second, and less radically, he again demanded that the Federation hire black organizers to work among Afro-Americans, because white organizers did not understand blacks, and the latter did not trust the white organizers. In fact, Randolph wanted the convention to authorize Green to establish a special committee to study the problems of black workers and to propose methods of improving the Federation's efficiency in organizing Afro-Americans.[28]

The Brotherhood received support from two important sources on the hot issue of expelling overtly racist unions: John L. Lewis of the United Mine Workers and David Dubinsky of the International Ladies Garment Workers spoke in favor of the resolution.[29] Webster thought he detected support among other delegations as well, but it did not materialize.

[24] For problems the demonstrators encountered, see Telegrams, White to Leland Hawkins and Hawkins to White, Oct. 5-6, 1934, *ibid*.

[25] *Opportunity*, XII (Oct., 1934), 299.

[26] AFL Convention, *Report of the Proceedings* (Oct., 1934), 530.

[27] MPW to Emmett Smith, Oct. 12, 1934, BSCP ChiPa.

[28] AFL Convention, *Report of the Proceedings* (Oct., 1934), 230-31, 530.

[29] MPW to Smith, Oct. 15, 1934, BSCP ChiPa; Frank Crosswaith, "Sound Principles of Trade Unionism," *Opportunity*, XII (Nov., 1934), 341. Significantly, the support came from industrial unions.

When the resolutions committee issued its report, the delegates accepted its recommendation that the convention reject Randolph's proposal. The leadership explained that the AFL had no control over the constitutions of national and international unions, and even refused to allow adoption of a general statement opposing racial discrimination.[30]

Though it lost on the issue of expelling discriminatory unions, the BSCP registered a token victory when the convention overrode the resolutions committee and instructed Green to appoint a select committee to undertake the study Randolph had requested; the group was to report its findings to the convention the following year.[31] Walter White later claimed that the pressure of the NAACP demonstration had forced this small concession.[32] If so, there is little evidence to support the claim, and White and Randolph never discussed the effectiveness of the demonstration.

The BSCP's insistence that the AFL move rapidly to rid itself of discriminatory practices and extend membership to blacks on terms of full equality, piercing as it did the rhetorical facade that cloaked the Federation's racism, threatened to destroy the delicate relationship that Green and others had tried to fashion between blacks and organized labor. As one delegate pointed out from the convention floor, they believed Randolph's proposals were pushing the AFL much faster than it should go.[33] Thus, though the convention instructed Green to appoint a committee to conduct Randolph's study, Green had no intentions of seeing the committee undertake the exhaustive investigation demanded by BSCP officials.[34] Green waited until June, 1935, before appointing the committee and ordered it to hold its hearings and report to the Executive Council prior to the Federation's meeting in October.[35]

Green telegraphed Randolph on June 27 that the Committee of Five would hold hearings in Washington on July 9-10; he further advised

[30] AFL Convention, *Report of the Proceedings* (Oct., 1934), 331.

[31] *Ibid.*, 334.

[32] White to John L. Lewis, Nov. 27, 1935, NAACP Pas, C414, LC.

[33] AFL Convention, *Report of the Proceedings* (Oct., 1934), 332-34.

[34] White to Lewis, Nov. 27, 1935, NAACP Pas, C414, LC. White wrote that the committee's work was "promptly hamstrung."

[35] Green to John M. Garvey, June 10, 1935, GCB No. 533, p. 55. Along with Garvey, other members of the committee were John G. Rooney of the Operative Plasterers and Cement Finishers; Jerry Hanks, Journeyman Barbers; P. C. Carroll, Brotherhood of Maintenance of Way Employees; and chairman John Brophy, United Mine Workers. Garvey represented the United Hod Carriers. All members of the committee were white.

Randolph to appear before the committee to produce evidence to support the allegations he had made at San Francisco.[36] Randolph again turned to Walter White for help, and he also called on leaders of the National Urban League and other black groups.[37] White asked Charles H. Houston, an outstanding young black dean of the Howard University Law School and the Association's first full-time staff counsel, to represent the NAACP at the hearings and to secure witnesses to support the BSCP's position. Reginald A. Johnson, executive secretary of the Atlanta Urban League and the National Urban League's chief lobbyist in Washington, testified for his organization; in addition, John P. Davis, executive secretary of the Joint Committee on National Recovery, appeared to provide technical and statistical evidence on the difficulties experienced by blacks because of union discrimination. Other witnesses included Robert C. Weaver, who was presently working at the Department of the Interior.[38]

The 1935 hearings of the AFL Committee of Five on Negro Discrimination marked the public announcement of a significant shift that had come about within the NAACP on the question of trade unionism. They also demonstrated the Association's recognition that, as Houston put it, "it was necessary to lay a sound economic foundation in order for civil liberties to survive." Houston's statement to the committee, which he summarized in a memorandum to White, was a clear indication that NAACP leaders were trying to respond to the pressures imposed by Harris and other young radicals within the organization. Indeed, Houston's very presence as the Association's representative at these potentially important hearings underlines the view that the NAACP was moving toward a stronger economic interest. Though completely loyal to Walter White, Houston was nonetheless sympathetic with the views of Abram Harris, Ralph Bunche, and John Davis, and he urged White to lead the NAACP toward economic radicalism. As responsible as he was loyal, there was little likelihood that Houston would sit before the committee and utter views that were likely to embarrass White and other NAACP officials. He told the Committee of Five that the NAACP would in the future be keenly interested in the general economic status of

[36] Telegram, Green to APR, June 27, 1935, NAACP Pas, C414, LC.

[37] APR to White, July 3, 1935, *ibid*.

[38] Charles H. Houston, Memorandum to Walter White, July 11, 1935, *ibid*.; *Opportunity*, XIII (Aug., 1935), 247-49.

blacks, particularly in their relationship with trade unions.[39]

One of the major arguments of the witnesses was that depression conditions restricted testimony of black workers to those who lived in the Washington area. Moreover, the brief advance notice of the hearings had enabled them to do little more than introduce the range of discrimination in organized labor. They convinced the majority of the committee to recommend that the Executive Council authorize regional hearings in order to gather further data.[40] The committee's response raised the hopes of Randolph, White, and T. Arnold Hill, all of whom dispatched direct appeals to Green urging that regional investigations be started immediately.[41] Green agreed to lay the request before his colleagues on the Council, but he made clear his attitude on the question when he informed Randolph that he did not consider regional hearings to be part of the committee's mandate.[42] When the Council met, it upheld Green's views and refused to authorize further hearings, instead ordering the Committee of Five to submit its final report.[43] Green then explained to Walter White that the Executive Council had unanimously agreed that "there was no necessity for holding such hearings."[44] Infuriated, White retorted that such comments would serve only to heighten feelings already current among black workers that the AFL never intended to undertake a thorough job of investigation. He added that the Council's action would intensify black hostility and distrust of the Federation.[45]

When the Committee of Five reported, the majority not only pointed out the necessity of holding regional hearings, but also revealed widespread racial discrimination among AFL affiliates. They recommended that the Federation demand that such discrimination cease and expel

[39] Houston, Memorandum to Walter White, July 11, 1935, NAACP Pas, C414, LC. See also Wolters, *Negroes*, 179-80, and Weiss, *National Urban League*, 288-90. Houston explicitly assured the Urban League that the Association did not intend to intrude upon the League's field of work, and explained that this new emphasis on the part of his organization simply represented the increasing awareness of the importance of economics as the foundation for the enjoyment of a full life.

[40] Houston, Memorandum to Walter White, July 11, 1935, NAACP Pas, C414, LC. The Urban League printed Johnson's statement to the committee in *Opportunity*, XIII (Aug., 1935), 247-49. Houston summarized the testimony of other witnesses in his memorandum to White.

[41] APR to White, July 25, White to Green, Aug. 2, 1935; both in NAACP Pas, C414, LC; T. Arnold Hill to Green, July 23, 1935, NUL Pas, LC.

[42] Green to APR, July 29, 1935, GCB No. 537, p. 292.

[43] Green to John Brophy, Aug. 26, 1935, GCB No. 539, p. 778.

[44] Green to White, Aug. 29, 1935, NAACP Pas, C414, LC.

[45] White to Green, Sept. 3, 1935, *ibid.*

internationals which refused to do so. One committee member, Jerry Hanks of the barbers' union, was adamant in his opposition to the majority report and insisted that Green make his minority view known to the convention.[46]

The enabling resolution that established the Committee of Five at the AFL convention of 1934 had provided that the committee would report its findings directly to the convention the following year, but, undoubtedly fearful of the likely impact of the majority's original report, the Executive Council received the report itself and drafted a different version for the delegates' eyes. One Council member, George M. Harrison, president of the racist and discriminatory Brotherhood of Railway Clerks, was responsible for writing a revised version of the report.[47] Harrison's draft watered down the committee's findings of discrimination in AFL affiliates and completely eliminated the call for expulsion of unions that continued to discriminate. This emasculation of the original report was presented to the convention, and even then Green delayed discussion of the question until the late hours of the final day.

Randolph recognized the Council's clear intentions, but he was determined to press the issue. He termed the Executive Council's actions a "dignified, diplomatic camouflage" and demanded that the original report be presented for discussion.[48] Green permitted Randolph to have the floor, and, in a heated debate involving even the president of the Federation, the matter was thrashed out. AFL leaders proclaimed again that they were interested in organizing black workers but warned Randolph that he was going too fast. His demands, they said, would do more to harm relations between black and white workers than to improve them. In an attempt to justify his report, Harrison explained that the Council could not present the original statement of the Committee of Five because one member of the committee had submitted differing views. Harrison implied that, instead of raising objections, the convention owed him a vote of thanks for performing the difficult task of assembling all the findings.[49]

[46] AFL Convention, *Report of the Proceedings* (Oct., 1935), 808-19; W. C. Hushing to Hanks, Sept. 20, 1935, GCB No. 541, p. 36. Hushing was AFL national legislative representative and an assistant to Green.

[47] Harrison was the man who, as representative of the Railway Labor Executives Association, had refused to include porters among those to whom railway legislation should be extended when he testified before the Senate Committee on Interstate and Foreign Commerce during April, 1934. See discussion earlier in this chapter.

[48] AFL Convention, *Report of the Proceedings* (Oct., 1935), 809.

[49] *Ibid*.

Officials of international unions that maintained color restrictions leapt to Harrison's aid. Staunchly defending their position, they proudly informed Randolph that their organizations represented all workers in their crafts in wage and grievance negotiations, regardless of race. That black workers had no say in determining the union's demands struck them as a minor detail. Randolph refused to accept any of these arguments. He insisted that, whether organized in separate federal locals or denied membership in unions altogether, black workers had no control over their conditions of employment. The fault lay with discriminatory affiliates, and as long as they were allowed to maintain such policies and remain within the House of Labor, blacks would continue to distrust the Federation. But Randolph's arguments were in vain. The eloquent BSCP leader received little support, as the convention denied his motion to substitute the policies outlined in the committee's report for those of the Council.[50]

Randolph continued to carry the fight to future AFL conventions, even though the Federation's actions in the short run came as a setback to black leaders, many of whom had approached the convention with a sense of urgency. President Roosevelt had just signed the Wagner-Connery Act on July 5. The act guaranteed trade unions exclusive bargaining rights when they represented a majority of the employees in union shops, and resulted in consolidating union strength. Since the law did not provide protection against racial discrimination, however, blacks were now at the mercy of bodies which had consistently chosen to exclude them. In view of the opinions expressed at the convention of 1935, most AFL unions apparently intended to maintain their exclusionist policies, perpetuating a situation that blacks could no longer tolerate.[51] Randolph began openly to work with John L. Lewis and his newly formed Committee for Industrial Organizations, a group of industrial unions whose eventual expulsion from the AFL had been

[50] *Ibid.*, 808-19, covers discussion of Committee of Five Report.

[51] See, *e.g.*, T. Arnold Hill, "Minority Groups and American Labor," National Convention of Social Welfare *Proceedings of the Convention*, LXIV (1937), 402. Black leaders lobbied for amendments to the Wagner Act which would have given explicit protection to blacks against union discrimination, but Congress turned them down. Senator Wagner explained that he could not support such an amendment because it would risk losing the whole piece of legislation. See also St. Louis *Argus*, May 24, 1935, and Green to White, May 2, 1934, GCB No. 492, p. 557. Wolters, *Negroes*, 182-87, discusses in some detail NAACP and NUL attitudes toward the Wagner Act.

presaged at the very session in which the Federation refused to take action against racial discrimination in affiliated unions. Walter White indicated to Lewis that the future for black workers lay with the CIO, affirming that the AFL's hypocritical attitude at the convention had "destroyed the last vestige of confidence" black workers had in that organization.[52]

Beyond his deep concern for the masses of black workers, Randolph's activities before the AFL in 1934-35 were clearly part of his strategy of attaining recognition for the Brotherhood of Sleeping Car Porters. During the winter of 1934, a series of events had begun that seriously threatened the BSCP's continued existence as an independent union. The Order of Sleeping Car Conductors had applied to the Executive Council for jurisdiction over porters. In a case based on conditions imposed by the Great Depression, the conductors claimed that Pullman, in order to cut back on its wage bill, had expanded the practice of running porters "in charge," thus eliminating the conductors on many of its lines. Doing so represented a considerable saving for the company: instead of paying the conductor his minimum monthly wage of $150, in addition to the porter's minimum $72.50, Pullman could run a porter "in charge" and pay him only $10 above his regular monthly rate. Conductors wanted to represent porters and maids so they could write a contract with Pullman limiting the number of porters used "in charge." Moreover, the Order of Sleeping Car Conductors contended that two unions of service employees in one company caused undue duplication and did not work to the best advantage of the employees concerned.[53]

The Council acted favorably on the request. Green informed Randolph that the Executive Council had decided to grant the Order of Sleeping Car Conductors jurisdiction over porters. Green would arrange a conference between the BSCP chief and M. S. Warfield, president of

[52] White to Lewis, Nov. 27, 1935, NAACP Pas, C414, LC. The actual suspension and subsequent expulsion of industrial unions came through action of the Executive Council during 1936, but the issue had been well decided at the Atlantic City convention in 1935, when the industrial forces lost a major debate on the question of future organizational tactics which the Federation should employ in mass production industries. See Philip Taft, *The AF of L from the Death of Gompers to the Merger* (New York: Harper, 1959), 140-203. Records of debate over industrial unionism at 1935 convention appear in AFL Convention, *Report of the Proceedings* (Oct., 1935).

[53] AFL Convention, *Report of the Proceedings* (Oct., 1934), 707-9. Green's Copy Books do not contain incoming correspondence; thus the best source on the conductors' demands is the *Report of the Proceedings*.

the conductors' union, whereby the two men could work out the details of the proposed new arrangement.[54] Randolph refused even to discuss such a change in the BSCP's relationship with the AFL. He would prefer to have the Brotherhood go it alone, rather than submit to control of the Order of Sleeping Car Conductors.[55]

Later in 1934 Warfield renewed his request. Green, still convinced that the conductors' case was sound, arranged a meeting between Randolph and Warfield at the convention in San Francisco.[56] Sensing the difficulty he faced before the all-white Council, Randolph decided to carry the problem to the floor of the convention. He knew that full power to issue or change charters in the AFL lay with the Executive Council, and that the delegates in convention could do nothing more than offer moral pressure. Nonetheless, Randolph introduced a resolution calling on the delegates to endorse the BSCP's bid for an independent international charter. He astutely recognized that such a move, though having no legislative effect, would enable him to publicize the Council's attempt to take away the BSCP's independent status.[57]

During debate on his resolution, Randolph eloquently disputed the sleeping car conductors' claims to represent the porters and maids. He argued that where the BSCP had organized those employees only after years of extreme suffering and a huge outlay of money, Pullman conductors had done nothing to help the company's black service employees. He pointed out that the Order of Sleeping Car Conductors' constitutional ban against black membership — a clause the conductors defended on grounds that it was dictated by Pullman's requirement that conductors be white — would render the conductors' union utterly impotent to organize porters, even if that union were granted jurisdiction over them. Randolph reminded his colleagues that the BSCP had made significant gains in both membership and its legal position with Pullman since passage of the Amended Railway Labor Act of 1934, and that it would soon be able to write a contract. These developments, he believed, dictated that the AFL grant the BSCP an international charter and refuse further consideration of the conductors' claims.[58]

[54] Green to APR and Green to M. S. Warfield, both Feb. 15, 1934, GCB No. 484, pp. 75-76.

[55] APR's letter is unavailable, but Green summarized his attitude in Green to Warfield, Mar. 21, 1934, GCB No. 487, p. 877.

[56] Green to Warfield, Sept. 2, Green to APR, Sept. 3, 1934, GCB No. 506, pp. 44-45.

[57] See AFL Convention, *Report of the Proceedings* (Oct., 1934), 709.

[58] *Ibid.*, 707-9.

Randolph's eloquence and the justice of his appeal failed to sway the Council. The Brotherhood leader learned soon after the close of the convention that, as far as the American Federation of Labor was concerned, the BSCP no longer existed as a group of independent affiliated unions. Green advised Randolph that "after careful deliberation the Executive Council decided that the economic and industrial interests of Pullman porters and maids would be served through an extension of the jurisdiction of the Order of Sleeping Car Conductors over these groups of workers." Green cited the effects of the Great Depression on the conductors' status, and the Council's desire to limit the number of unions among Pullman's service employees, as the prime reasons for its decision. He assured Randolph that "the Executive Council was firmly convinced that the highest and best interest of all affected, particularly the Pullman porters and maids, would be served, protected and prompted through affiliation of the workers with the Order of Sleeping Car Conductors." Green expressed confidence that Randolph and other BSCP officials would grant the conductors' union "a full measure of cooperation and support" in its effort to organize the porters and maids.[59]

BSCP officials had no intention of complying with this decision, let alone offering the conductors "cooperation and support." Webster was furious when he learned of the Council's action, and he insisted to Randolph that the Brotherhood should not accede to the order in any way. The union had come too far by its own efforts to allow someone else to direct its affairs at this point. The Brotherhood would leave the AFL if such action was necessary to maintain its independence.[60] Seemingly unmindful that much of its legitimacy had been stripped away, the BSCP went about its business of trying to write a contract with the Pullman Company.

Pullman's activities between passage of the railway labor act in June, 1934, and the AFL convention in October necessitated that the BSCP take immediate and direct action, lest its position erode on that front just as it had in the AFL. Though Congress had passed the new law, the company did not accept recognition of the Brotherhood as inevitable. Technically it obeyed the law and ceased operation of the ERP, but by October another union had been created: the Pullman Porters and Maids

[59] Green to APR, Oct. 15, 1934, GCB No. 509, p. 909. See also Green to Warfield, Oct. 15, 1934, GCB No. 509, p. 911.

[60] Telegram, MPW to APR, Oct. 22, 1934, BSCP ChiPa.

Protective Association (PPMPA). Many of the people who had been officers and porter representatives under the ERP ran the new organization, a union Randolph claimed had been "practically gotten together overnight by Mr. F. L. Simmons."[61] From his point of view (with which many others agreed), the company had simply rearranged the earlier representation system under a new name to meet legal requirements.[62]

Both Pullman officials and leaders of the Protective Association denied that the company had initiated the new union, maintaining instead that the porters had founded the PPMPA out of a sense of helplessness after Congress legislated the ERP out of business. These men had floundered about for several months, meeting in homes of different associates to discuss their situation, and had decided finally that the BSCP was not representative of porters mainly because its leaders were not working porters themselves. The allegation that the BSCP was a group of outside agitators had been one major reason for the company's antagonism toward it. In order to make itself fully representative, the PPMPA restricted membership to current employees of the Pullman Company.[63]

Strictly speaking, the Protective Association was not a company union. Its members financed the union's activities out of their own resources, and the attorney who drew up its bylaws was not in the employ of Pullman. Nonetheless, the company still favored the new union over the Brotherhood because members of the Protective Association had remained loyal to Pullman throughout the long controversy. And although the company did not officially control the PPMPA, members of the new union spied on BSCP activities and reported their findings to company officials.[64]

Early in November, 1934, Randolph wrote to President D. A. Crawford requesting a conference between Pullman and the BSCP which, as it turned out, set in motion a series of events that led to the eventual settlement of the BSCP-Pullman representation dispute. The company's

[61] APR, "Pullman Porters Vote for Union They Want," *American Federationist*, XLII (1935), 727.

[62] Weybright, "Pullman Porters on Parade," 572; Berman, "Pullman Porters," 217.

[63] Memorandum, H. R. Lary to D. A. Crawford, Mar. 12, 1935, PC Pas.

[64] *Ibid.* APR scoffed at how much the union could do for the porters on the small income it received from twenty-five-cent monthly dues.

reaction to Randolph's letter was much the same as it had been the year before. Some officials, notably general counsel Kelly, still recommended that the company refuse to respond, and that if it had to answer it should address Randolph personally and continue to disregard his position as president of the BSCP.[65] Again it was President Crawford who insisted that under the terms of the new law the company had no choice but to respond. He warned his colleagues that it would be futile "and not in keeping with a common sense acceptance of the statutory position of claimants to representation of employee groups" for Pullman to continue to ignore Randolph's official position, especially since the BSCP was a publicly known member of the AFL.[66] Crawford's views prevailed. On November 27, 1934, F. L. Simmons again wrote Randolph — as BSCP president — to say that the company had received his communication. He informed the Brotherhood chief that the company did not think the Brotherhood represented the porters. Pullman still would not consent to a conference with the union.[67]

Upon receipt of Simmons's letter, BSCP officials appealed to the National Mediation Board for relief, claiming that the Pullman Company had refused to negotiate with the duly authorized representative as required by law. The board agreed to investigate the complaint and requested both the Brotherhood and the PPMPA to present evidence which would support their claims to represent porters and maids. In response, the BSCP presented the board with more than 5,000 signed affidavits in which porters named the Brotherhood their representative, while the Protective Association handed over 2,054 authorizations of its own. Upon examination of the documents, the board found that numerous porters, in an apparent attempt to protect themselves, had signed with both organizations; the papers contained a 20 percent duplication.[68] Horrified that the duplications might cause the board to authorize an election to determine the legitimate representative of porters and maids, Randolph and Webster went to Washington in early January to outline the history of the relationship between Pullman and the BSCP and to insist that the Mediation Board certify the Brotherhood on the

[65] Memorandum, G. A. Kelly to D. A. Crawford, Nov. 19, 1934, PC Pas.

[66] Memorandum, Crawford to Kelly, Nov. 19, 1934, *ibid.*

[67] *Ibid.*; Simmons to APR, Nov. 27, 1934, *ibid.*; *The Black Worker*, June 15, 1935.

[68] National Mediation Board Report, *BSCP* v. *PPMPA*, July 1, 1935, copy in BSCP ChiPa.

basis of its membership affidavits. The BSCP's long and bitter experience with Pullman's ability to influence porters made Randolph and his colleagues fearful of an election. Although the railway labor act of 1934 explicitly forbade Pullman from interfering in elections among its employees, BSCP leaders feared that, in the event of an election among porters and maids, the company would revert to its earlier methods to assure election of the Protective Association. Moreover, many of the Protective Association's authorizations were legitimate. Porters who had opposed the BSCP for ten years must have been reluctant to place their futures in that union's hands, and the affidavits presented to the Mediation Board suggest that a significant number of porters believed they should be represented by co-workers in the PPMPA, rather than by nonporters like Randolph, Webster, Dellums, and others.

The Mediation Board summoned BSCP officials to Washington for a second conference on March 29, 1935, and informed them that duplication in authorization cards was sufficiently high to necessitate that the board settle the issue of jurisdiction by secret ballot. The board then scheduled an election to run from May 27 through June 22. The BSCP thereby became the first union to invoke a nationwide jurisdictional election.[69] Mediation Board member H. H. Reed, with six assistants and a representative of each contesting organization (Webster represented the Brotherhood), administered the election and certified those porters eligible to participate. Election procedures provided sixty-six districts around the country in which the porters could vote and established a special mail process for those who did not have easy access to established polling places. The board made one important concession to the BSCP in forbidding polling to take place on Pullman property. Instead, the porters voted at black churches and YMCA buildings.[70]

Both the BSCP and the PPMPA carried on vigorous campaigns for the porters' support during the balloting. The PPMPA used as its slogan "representation from within the ranks of working Pullman employees," claiming that outsiders like Randolph could not really speak for the porters.[71] The BSCP, meanwhile, appealed to the men to repudiate Pullman's control which they had endured during the long existence of

[69] *The Black Worker*, Apr. 15, 1935. APR had publicly predicted as early as January that the board would order an election to settle the dispute. See St. Louis *Argus*, Jan. 18, 1935.

[70] *The Black Worker*, June 15, 1935.

[71] St. Louis *Argus*, Jan. 18, 1935.

the ERP. It warned the porters that the same people who had run the ERP were now in charge of the PPMPA and insisted that there was little difference between the two. Even now, the Brotherhood declared, the PPMPA was using company superintendents and other company officials to disseminate information among the porters.[72]

The BSCP accused the company of interfering with the election by trying to intimidate porters to vote for the PPMPA. The Brotherhood asked a group of supporters, organized as the Chicago Citizens Committee, to write to Pullman demanding that such practices cease, especially since no procedure existed for handling grievances while the election was in progress.[73] In replying to the committee Crawford denied that the company had in any way interfered in the election and insisted that, contrary to the committee's opinion, procedures did exist for handling grievances among porters. He personally would listen to any complaint from his employees at any time. Offering assurances that he had investigated and found groundless the charges which the committee had passed on to him, Crawford warned its members that their human sympathies had been stirred by "agitators willing to misinform them and seek personal advantage by creating friction between employer and employees, with advantage neither to the public service or to the employee incited to dissatisfaction and poor performance of his job."[74]

Meanwhile, BSCP officials attempted to take advantage of the considerable excitement which the election stirred among blacks. Still maintaining that the election was between the Brotherhood and the Pullman Company, and not between two independent unions, Randolph said that porters, "the vanguard of black workers in America," would feel greater security in the fight if they knew they had the support of their church, their press, and their educational leaders. He then turned to the NAACP and the National Urban League for assistance in securing support for the BSCP.[75] White offered his support and that of the

[72] BSCP Bulletin, n.d. [1935], BSCP Oakland Pas.

[73] Chicago Citizens Committee to Crawford, June 27, 1935, BSCP ChiPa. Among the members of the committee was Paul Douglas, professor of economics at the University of Chicago, who later became a senator from Illinois.

[74] Crawford to Chicago Citizens Committee, July 2, 1935, *ibid*. The BSCP had been asking groups of individuals and organizations — among them the NAACP and the NUL — to write the company on its behalf since 1926. This was the first time the company answered the correspondence. Significantly, the response came from the very highest level.

[75] APR to White, May 23, 1935, NAACP Pas, C414, LC.

NAACP, and T. Arnold Hill committed the Urban League. Hill called the election a "momentous decision of far-reaching importance" to black workers and added that it would decide whether "a company union or a labor union would be recognized." He called on all black professionals and other Afro-American leaders to support the Brotherhood's campaign in the interest of all black workers.[76]

It is difficult to determine how effective these expressions of support were to the Brotherhood's cause. At any rate, when the balloting ended on June 27, returns showed that the BSCP had won a smashing victory. The porters endorsed it as their bargaining agent by an overwhelming margin of more than four to one, with 5,931 BSCP votes to 1,422 for the PPMPA. The Brotherhood carried all but four cities, even winning the unanimous endorsement of the porters in Seattle. So widespread was the victory that few intricate patterns emerge from the vote. Perhaps the only noteworthy trend is that all BSCP losses occurred in the South — but even so the union received heavy votes in some southern cities, notably Jacksonville, where a Brotherhood operator had earlier experienced difficulties. The fact that the board's report listed the vote by city means that there is no way to determine the extent to which the PPMPA picked up support from outlying rural districts. Similarly, the tabulation fails to indicate the relative strength of the rival unions among older porters. Aside from the scope of the victory, no other judgments are possible.

On July 1, 1935, the board officially informed the BSCP, the PPMPA, and the Pullman Company that "on the basis of the investigation and report, the National Mediation Board hereby certifies that the Brotherhood of Sleeping Car Porters has been duly designated as the representative of the Pullman porters and maids."[77] Thus ended one of the longest continuous struggles for recognition in the annals of American trade unionism. After ten years the Brotherhood had achieved the position it had always envisioned for itself.

With a feeling of great joy and jubilation, the BSCP immediately dispatched a request that the Pullman Company meet with it to negotiate a contract for the porters. The company did not presume to protest the Mediation Board's decision. In a most cordial response, which seemed

[76] *Opportunity*, XIII (June, 1935), 186.

[77] National Mediation Board Report, *BSCP* v. *PPMPA*, July 1, 1935, BSCP ChiPa. An interesting question (and one which defies answer) is what attitude did AFL officials take on the election, since it no longer recognized the BSCP? Green congratulated APR on the victory in a telegram, June 28, 1935, GCB No. 534, p. 743.

TABLE I: VOTE OF PORTERS BY CITY*

City	BSCP	PPMPA	Eligible Voters	Void
Chicago	1,496	296	1,952	18
St. Paul	145	17	182	5
Omaha	35	7	43	1
Denver	82	12	95	1
Kansas City	90	37	129	0
New York City	1,208	158	1,496	12
Philadelphia	128	27	175	2
Washington	226	38	318	3
St. Louis	271	77	386	3
Indianapolis	36	8	47	1
Louisville†	23	57	88	1
Cincinnati	98	41	153	3
Cleveland	98	5	108	0
Detroit	72	11	91	1
Los Angeles	176	32	222	2
Oakland	125	7	152	1
Portland	43	2	48	0
Seattle	30	0	30	0
New Orleans	191	41	245	4
Houston†	29	37	75	4
San Antonio	48	34	87	0
Dallas-Fort Worth	83	46	136	0
Memphis†	24	48	73	0
Jacksonville	158	42	212	3
Atlanta†	19	83	110	3
Richmond	18	12	34	0
Pittsburgh	171	17	200	1
Buffalo	68	9	80	0
Boston	185	40	245	5
By Mail	555	181	1,106	17
Collectively	5,931	1,422	8,316	89

*National Mediation Board Report, *BSCP* v. *PPMPA* (July 1, 1935), in BSCP ChiPa.
†Cities the BSCP lost.

practically to ignore the ten years of bitter strife preceding, Pullman invited BSCP representatives to a conference at Pullman headquarters on July 29, 1935.[78] When Brotherhood representatives arrived at the Pullman Building on that date, they found a polite group of Pullman officials to welcome them. Yet they also found the company adamant on one point: though it would discuss the porters' wages and working

[78] Hungerford to APR, July 13, 1935, BSCP ChiPa. Hungerford was vice-president and general manager of the Pullman Company.

conditions on this one occasion, Pullman had no intention of recognizing the union as a full-time collective bargaining agent for its employees. Randolph recalled in later years that Champ Carry, the company's vice-president and negotiation representative, told BSCP officials at that first meeting that "we ain't recognizing no union."[79] The Brotherhood was as determined to win total recognition as Pullman was to deny it, and after preliminary discussions the union requested a break in negotiations in order to work out its case and to involve the Mediation Board in the proceedings. Pullman agreed to postpone further talks until the BSCP was ready.

While the BSCP's economic expert worked to prepare the union's demands, Brotherhood officials tried to solidify the union's position among the porters. Randolph and Webster wrote numerous letters and broadsides to potential members and traveled around the country to inform them of the union's new status. This campaign was necessary because, although the BSCP had secured the porters' support in the election, many of them did not belong to the organization or pay membership dues.[80] Part of the reason for some porters' reluctance to join the union officially was the continuing existence of the PPMPA as a potential challenger to the BSCP's right to represent the men. Although it had lost the initial certification election, the Protective Association had not retired from contention. It contained a closely knit core of leaders and members who continued to oppose the policies and activities of the Brotherhood on both philosophical and personal grounds. As late as May, 1937, PPMPA members and representatives still maintained their organizational structure, regularly reporting to Pullman officials on the movements and activities of BSCP leaders.[81]

The BSCP's showing in the certification election must have shocked AFL officials who had so recently decided to jettison the Brotherhood. They began to pay closer attention to the union; when Randolph renewed

[79] Interview with APR, Jan. 19, 1972.

[80] Brazeal, *The Brotherhood*, 222, lists the BSCP membership at 4,165 by the end of 1935, almost 2,000 fewer than had voted for the union in the May-June election. Recruitment activities thereafter narrowed the gap. By the end of 1936 the membership had reached 5,219, and in 1937 it approached the total number of those who had voted for the Brotherhood two years earlier.

[81] See, for example, several memoranda from PPMPA representatives to Pullman officials, PC Pas. Daniel Katz, "Social Psychology and Group Processes," in C. P. Stone and D. W. Taylor, eds., *Annual Reviews of Psychology*, II (1951), 137-72, argues that it is common for anti-union workers to be more outspoken in their opposition to unions than pro-union workers are about their employers. See esp. p. 156.

his application for an international charter, he received an immediate and positive response. In a letter to Green three days after the Brotherhood's initial meetings with the Pullman Company, Randolph pointed out the changed relationship between the union and the company. He maintained that the Brotherhood's victory in the election, and the fact that it was now actually involved in negotiations with Pullman, justified the charter demand.[82] The Executive Council, which was currently in session, agreed with Randolph's appraisal of the BSCP's status and granted the Brotherhood an international charter in early August, 1935, though Green advised the BSCP president that official word could not be given out until the Council could inform all unions that might make jurisdictional claims to the porters and maids. Such talks could be held in October at the upcoming AFL convention. Green and his colleagues succeeded in solving jurisdictional questions at the 1935 convention and notified BSCP officials of its permanent decision on October 10.[83] But since the BSCP became the first all-black union to receive an international charter from the AFL right after the turbulent summer when the Committee of Five report was so prominently before blacks, few Afro-Americans saw it as a remarkable accomplishment. For example, Walter White's letter to John L. Lewis decrying the Executive Council's handling of the committee's report makes no mention of the BSCP's charter, though he was undoubtedly aware of it. White recognized that the Federation had acted under pressure and deserved little credit. Indeed, he condemned the AFL out of hand and turned his attentions to the CIO.[84]

Meanwhile, after BSCP and Pullman representatives resumed their talks during August and September of 1935, the company's position became increasingly clear. Pullman intended to remain firm in its refusal to grant total recognition as bargaining agent in all aspects of working conditions among porters, nor would it acquiesce to the union's immediate demands for changes in wages and working conditions. Still hopeful that the porters would eventually turn to the PPMPA, Pullman undoubtedly wished to make a spectacle of the BSCP, presenting it to the porters as an inept organization unable to bargain effectively even

[82] APR to Green, Aug. 1, 1935, BSCP ChiPa.

[83] Telegram, Green to APR, Aug. 9, 1935, GCB No. 638, p. 300. See also Green to APR, Oct. 3, 1935, GCB No. 542, p. 405; MPW to Emmett Smith, Oct. 12, 1935, BSCP ChiPa.

[84] White to Lewis, Nov. 27, 1935, NAACP Pas, C414, LC.

when armed with federal recognition and support. Company officials probably believed that protracted negotiations would wear down the porters' resolve to support the Brotherhood. Fully aware too that provisions in the railway labor act outlawing company unions was being contested in the courts, the company wanted to await a decision, since a declaration of the act's unconstitutionality would remove the requirement that Pullman negotiate with the Brotherhood.

Recognizing its difficulties, the BSCP withdrew from direct negotiations in early December and appealed to the Mediation Board to mediate the dispute. The board accepted the case and named Robert F. Cole its representative. Cole ordered mediation procedures to begin on January 23, 1936.[85] Under the watchful eye of the mediator, the union now had an opportunity to make an exhaustive statement on working and living conditions among porters. To justify its demands for a wage increase and improved working conditions, it called upon Professor Edward Berman, chairman of the economics department at the University of Illinois, to prepare for the board a detailed brief describing the economic realities of the industry.[86] The Berman brief, an ingenious document, revealed more than the Pullman Company would have wished about what had happened to porters' real wages between 1926 and 1935, and about how their pay compared to that of others similarly employed. The brief placed the Brotherhood in the strongest possible position when presenting the porters' case to Cole.

On the matter of real wages, Berman's figures showed that though porters averaged $78.11 per month from the company in 1926, as compared to $87.58 in 1934-35, overall porters had received more money in the former period than in the latter. This was so, he argued, despite the fact that porters' job-related expenses had declined from $33.82 per month in 1926 to $21.47 in 1934-35, after Pullman took on more responsibility for providing required materials. Berman pointed out that this apparent improvement was more than outweighed by a drop in tips from an average of $58.19 per month in 1926 to only $21.88 in 1934-35. On balance, the decrease in earnings between 1926 and 1935 came to $14.49 per month.[87] When hours of work were calculated into

[85] *The Black Worker*, Feb.-Mar., 1936.

[86] Berman brief (1935), copy available among BSCP ChiPa. The exact date for the Berman brief is difficult to determine. It carried its survey of porters' conditions through Feb., 1935, and at one point refers to an even later date.

[87] *Ibid.*, 3. Part of the intent of this discussion was to show the problems inherent in depending on tips for a living.

porters' earnings, the extent of their exploitation compared to workers in other industries became clearer still. The Berman brief showed that porters earned 27.8 cents per hour in 1934. The average hourly wage paid in manufacturing throughout the country, including both skilled and unskilled workers and those situated in large cities as well as small towns, was 54.8 cents. During the same year the government paid workers on federal projects at the average rate of 57.8 cents per hour.[88]

Berman then took the analysis one step further by surveying the budget estimates prepared by various official and private sources to determine how porters' wages compared with the minimum living requirements established in those studies. In each case porters earned considerably less than the amounts specified, with the discrepancies ranging from $193 between porters' pay and the lowest budget estimate to $755 between their pay and the highest figure.[89]

TABLE II: PORTERS' ANNUAL INCOME AND STANDARD BUDGETS, 1926

Regular porters' annual income	$1,230
Budget A	2,101
Budget B	2,009
Budget C	1,948
Budget D	1,669
Budget E	1,528
Budget F	1,461
Budget G	1,450
Budget H	1,379

To meet the company's contention that such budgets should not apply to porters, whether because of their function or because of their place of

[88] *Ibid.*, 11.

[89] *Ibid.*, 6. The budget estimates which Berman used for his comparisons were: (A) the minimum health and decency budget for a family of five by the New York Bureau of Municipal Research; (B) the minimum health and decency budget for a family of three calculated for laborers by the California Civil Service Commission; (C) the minimum comfort budget for a family of five calculated by the National War Board in 1918 and revised to comport with changes in cost of living; (D) the minimum American Standard budget for a family of four living in New York City, calculated by the National Industrial Conference Board, an employers' research group; (E) the minimum health and decency budget for a family of five calculated by the Bureau of Labor Statistics; (F) the minimum subsistence budget for a family of five, headed by a laborer in New York City, calculated by the New York City Board of Estimate; (G) the minimum subsistence budget for a family of five living in a small city (Marion, Ohio), calculated by the National Industrial Conference Board; (H) the minimum subsistence budget for a family of five living in Chicago or New York City calculated by Professor W. F. Ogburn.

residence, the Brotherhood pointed out that the men represented by the BSCP were not unskilled workers, and that the majority of them did live in large cities. Maintaining that technical requirements were not the only measurement of skilled labor, the BSCP argued that the wide range of activities required of porters, and the multitude of responsibilities assigned to them, set them apart from common laborers. As to whether the budget comparisons made sense in terms of place of residence, it was only necessary to examine Pullman payrolls and the Mediation Board's own figures from the recent representation election to establish that

TABLE III: PORTERS' ANNUAL INCOME AND STANDARD BUDGETS, 1934[90]

Regular porters' annual income	$1,058
All porters' annual income	880
Budget A	1,635
Budget B	1,564
Budget C	1,516
Budget D	1,299
Budget E	1,189
Budget F	1,144
Budget G	1,129
Budget H	1,073

porters were overwhelmingly city dwellers. On both counts they were clearly underpaid.[91]

On the basis of this information the BSCP asked the Mediation Board to support it on several new demands covering wages, seniority rights, and adequate employment opportunity. To diminish the disparity between porters' earnings and those of other workers, the union demanded that the company pay porters on an hourly/mileage rate, rather than on a strictly mileage scale. Eight thousand miles, rather than the current 11,000, would constitute a month's work. Porters would not be expected to work more than 340 hours in a month. The union demanded that Pullman compensate porters for work in excess of either limit (whichever occurred first) at the rate of time-and-a-half, and that porters be paid for all services performed for the company, especially terminal and preparatory functions. In addition to important changes in computing pay, the Brotherhood added the demand that porters' wages be raised by 20 percent down the line, as follows:[92]

[90] The figures for "all porters" are determined when the average income of a large group of extra porters is calculated into the total amount Pullman paid porters.

[91] Berman brief, 7. See chapter 4 for discussion of porters' responsibilities.

[92] *Ibid.*, 24-25. These changes in wages and working conditions amounted to a 44.3 percent wage increase. See *ibid.*, 28.

TABLE IV: BSCP 1935 WAGE DEMANDS

Time in service	1935 monthly wages	BSCP demands
1 to 5 years	$77.50	$ 93.00
5 to 10 years	81.00	97.20
10 to 15 years	85.00	102.00
15 or more years	88.50	106.20

The BSCP sought to protect the seniority rights of its members by demanding that all porters be assigned runs in accordance with their place on the district seniority roster; this move was calculated to remove Pullman's alleged use of run assignment to show favoritism among porters. It also demanded that all persons who performed services usually considered porter services, whether the company called them attendants or by some other name, must be covered by the BSCP agreement — a crucial stipulation, because the company had begun during 1936-37 to reclassify some of its porters, though the employees under the new names continued to perform the same services as before.

To insure that its members received regular work, the union demanded that the company pay extra porters at the rate of at least 75 percent of the regular porters' monthly wage, whether it had work for them or not. The BSCP hoped thereby to force Pullman to lay off some of the extras and provide regular employment for all men who remained. Nor would this work a hardship on the extras since, as the Brotherhood believed, Pullman would place more men in the regular service rather than pay porters at the higher rate for overtime.[93]

The Pullman Company would not accept the demands set forth in the union's brief. The major points of difficulty centered on the issues of the wage increase, the hourly/mileage basis for wages, non-deductible sleep time for porters, and the right of the BSCP to jurisdiction over attendants.[94] Even at the urging of the Mediation Board the company did not progress toward an agreement. Apparently Pullman still hoped the Supreme Court would invalidate the Amended Railway Labor Act of 1934.

The BSCP again appealed to the porters for support. It circulated a ballot asserting that the company did not intend to negotiate in good faith and urged the porters to authorize a strike. It is not clear to what extent the porters supported the idea of a strike, but it is certain that BSCP

[93] *Ibid.*, 19.

[94] BSCP Strike Ballot, 1937, BSCP ChiPa.

leaders made definite plans for a confrontation with Pullman. Randolph went so far as to request porters in the New York area to collect information on the schedule and direction of trains carrying Pullman cars so the union could decide which lines could be hit most effectively and could assign porters to do the required tasks.[95] Furthermore, although the BSCP was affiliated with the AFL, its leaders negotiated with the more militant CIO for support in the impending strike. When the BSCP had threatened to strike in 1928, Pullman maintained a nonchalant and daring attitude; however, its officials were quite concerned about the union's activities in 1937.[96]

If Pullman had been basing its plans on the hope that the courts would strike down the Amended Railway Labor Act of 1934, its position was effectively undermined on March 29, 1937, when the Supreme Court upheld the act on all counts.[97] The ruling, coupled with the BSCP's threatened strike, caused the company to reevaluate its situation. On April 19, finally convinced that there was no way to avoid "the Randolph matter," Pullman agreed to settle the dispute with the BSCP.[98]

Though ostensibly renewed in earnest, negotiations progressed slowly, lasting three months more. On July 13 Cole presented both sides with what he considered his final compromise proposal. Supporting the

[95] Statement of APR to New York porters, reported to Champ Carry by the Pullman Superintendent at New York City in Memoranda, Mar. 27 and 30, 1937, PC Pas.

[96] *Ibid*.; Memorandum, New York office of Pullman Company to Headquarters, Apr. 30, 1937, *ibid*.

[97] *Virginian Railway Company* v. *System Federation No. 40 et al*. (300 U. S. 515). Ironically, Judge John J. Parker, whom organized labor had opposed for a seat on the Supreme Court because of his anti-labor views, wrote the circuit court opinion which the Supreme Court upheld.

The Court's decision in *Virginian Railway Company* was merely representative of the new status which organized labor would attain during the New Deal, and of the shift that came over the Court under pressure from the White House and public opinion. Soon after the elections of 1936, President Roosevelt announced plans for a reorganization of the Supreme Court to prevent it from further dismantling New Deal legislation. Largely to preserve the Court's credibility and prestige, Chief Justice Charles Evans Hughes and Associate Justice Owen J. Roberts changed their opinions on the commerce powers of the federal government. Their switch was sufficient to form the majority necessary to uphold the Wagner Labor Act. Just two weeks after the *Virginian Railway* decision, the Court voted 5-4 in favor of the government in *NLRB* v. *Jones and Laughlin Steel Corporation*. This decision guaranteed for all workers the right to bargain collectively. For discussions of the politics involved in the shifts of Hughes and Roberts, see Alpheus Mason, *The Supreme Court from Taft to Warren*, rev. ed. (Baton Rouge: Louisiana State University Press, 1968), 97-128; and James MacGregor Burns, *Roosevelt: The Lion and the Fox* (New York: Harcourt, 1956), 303-4.

[98] Brazeal, *The Brotherhood*, 113.

BSCP's demands on all major points, the mediator's proposals even granted the Brotherhood jurisdiction over attendants, or any other employees who performed porters' duties. Although Cole's recommended rates of pay for beginning porters varied depending upon the class of Pullman car involved, the average was $93 per month, the exact figure the BSCP had demanded in its brief. The mediator further recommended that porters' pay be computed on an hourly/mileage basis as the Brotherhood desired; he set the maximum mileage at 10,800, instead of the 8,000 the union demanded, with proper pay for overtime.[99] Even though the company found itself in an increasingly untenable position, it did not rush to settle with the BSCP; rather, it procrastinated for another month and a half, bickering with the mediator and the union on every minor point. Then, unexpectedly, on the morning of August 25, 1937, exactly twelve years after the founding of the BSCP, Champ Carry entered the negotiating session and announced "Gentlemen, the Pullman Company is ready to sign."[100] With this laconic statement the company finally recognized the BSCP as the representative of porters and maids.

The signing on this date does not mean that the BSCP had attained sufficient power to force the company to back down at this dramatic moment. The fact is that Pullman reached its decision because of events only remotely connected with the porters. On the day that Carry made his statement, the major railway unions had announced that they intended to pose a nationwide strike because of their own contract disputes.[101] Understandably, Pullman officials did not want their porters, who had already threatened to strike, to involve the company in a nationwide conflict.

Partly because of the larger issue of an impending rail strike, the BSCP's victory received scant notice in the daily press. Even black newspapers did not comment on the event until two weeks later, and their announcements then appeared on back pages. Both the Chicago *Defender* and the Pittsburgh *Courier* considered Joe Louis's successful defense of his heavyweight title much more important, emblazoning accounts of this event on their front pages.[102] Neither paper commented

[99] Mediator Cole's Final Compromise Proposal, July 13, 1937, BSCP ChiPa.

[100] Interview with APR, Jan. 19, 1972.

[101] G. James Fleming, "Pullman Porters Win," *American Federationist*, XLIV (Nov., 1937), 332.

[102] Pittsburgh *Courier* and Chicago *Defender*, both Sept. 4, 1937. Andrew Buni,

editorially on the porters' contract, although the *Defender* did run a favorable cartoon showing that the BSCP had won.[103] The most generous tribute came from Elmer Carter, editor of *Opportunity*, who praised the porters for the job they had done and acclaimed Randolph as among the top ten, "and if one wanted to be absolutely impartial, among the top five," labor leaders in the United States.[104]

Although little publicity accompanied the BSCP's contract, August 25, 1937, was a happy day for Brotherhood leaders. Randolph considered the signing of the agreement to be one of the most significant events in his life.[105] Webster, Smith, Totten, Bradley, Dellums, and others must certainly have seen the occasion as a dream come true. They watched the signing ceremony with pride and a feeling of deep relief. For twelve years they had fought against overwhelming odds and had weathered the worst depression in the nation's history, and they had won.

Though they had not received the $150 they had demanded in 1926, BSCP officials were pleased with the terms of the agreement they had negotiated. The union published for its members a pamphlet listing the agreement's most favorable features, pointing out, for example, that the union had forced the company to grant porters a wage increase which amounted to approximately $1.25 million per annum. The Brotherhood rejoiced that Pullman had been forced to grant the union jurisdiction over attendants, favorably comparing the porters' contract with that of Pullman conductors and other railroad employees. Brotherhood officials believed that they had "brought Pullman to its knees," as they had vowed to do in 1925. They had justified their faith in Randolph's constant reminder that "a winner never quits." Now they could hold their heads high in the knowledge of a struggle heroically waged and won.

Robert Lee Vann of the Pittsburgh Courier: Politics and Black Journalism (Pittsburgh: University of Pittsburgh Press, 1974), 254-56, points out that Vann made a near fetish of his coverage of Louis in the *Courier*, and that the editor had his staff cover the young fighter's every move.

[103] Chicago *Defender*, Sept. 4, 1937.

[104] *Opportunity*, XV (Oct., 1937), 294.

[105] Interview with APR, Jan. 19, 1972. APR explained that he considered the BSCP the movement upon which he based his later success. The men who sat on the negotiating committee were APR, MPW, Ashley L. Totten, C. L. Dellums, Bennie Smith, E. J. Bradley, vice-president T. T. Patterson of New York, and vice-president L. O. Manson of Chicago.

Conclusion

Armed with the agreement between the Pullman Company and the Brotherhood of Sleeping Car Porters, A. Philip Randolph made a triumphal return to Harlem in August, 1937. Porters turned out in force to welcome their chief and to proclaim that he had kept his promise to "bring the company to its knees." But Randolph could not but reflect on how different the New York of 1937 was from the one in which he had functioned as a publisher and street-corner orator before 1925. Indeed, all of American society had been affected radically by the economic debacle of the 1930s. The Great Depression had left no stratum untouched, but as always black people suffered more than others. Their privations, and the pressing need for jobs, forced black leaders to emphasize the importance of economics for advancement of Afro-Americans; that priority, in view of New Deal labor legislation, necessarily focused in large part on trade unionism. Though numerous groups and individuals contributed to this new attitude, the BSCP played a major role, and in the process enhanced its own image as well. Randolph and his colleagues saw the BSCP as both a black-advancement group and a labor union. They spoke of the Brotherhood interchangeably as "the union" and "the movement," and insisted that their efforts against both the Pullman Company and the racial policies of the American Federation of Labor were intended to improve conditions for all black workers. BSCP leaders kept before black people the importance of labor organizations — and solidarity in general — for advancement of Afro-Americans. The perseverance of the "pillow punchers" through hard times, and their resilience in the face of many obstacles, seemed proof that the porters were right. By 1937 the Brotherhood had attained a position of prominence that marked it as a leader among black organizations.

When the small group met in August, 1925, to found the BSCP, they encountered considerable opposition, both among blacks and from the Pullman Company. Large portions of the black press opposed the idea of unionism among blacks and encouraged the porters to remain loyal to their employer. Moreover, most porters supported the concept of company benevolence and were reluctant to jeopardize what seemed to be prized positions. The Pullman Company endeavored to exploit both the fear and the gratitude of its employees, while at the same time capitalizing on black leaders' general hostility toward the organized labor movement. The company stepped up the activities of the ERP to show porters that it worked, fired known union porters and used intimidation and coercion to keep others in line, and used its bountiful treasury to encourage numerous black individuals and newspapers to work against the Brotherhood. The union's leaders publicly challenged black opposition, but maintained the tightest secrecy over its membership rolls in order to protect porters from Pullman. And even then few porters signed up. Indeed, throughout the twelve years of conflict the BSCP was largely a paper organization, never enrolling a majority of the porters. Through effective use of propaganda and mass appeal, the small cell of leaders maintained among blacks a degree of support that virtually obscured their lack of a firm membership among porters.

Under Randolph's leadership, BSCP officials saw the Brotherhood as a pioneering wedge that would open the doors of the general American labor movement for Afro-Americans. Randolph recognized the hostility that had existed between blacks and white organized labor since the Civil War, but he believed that sensible men on both sides would recognize their community of interest and take steps to convince their followers to break down senseless racial barriers. The BSCP originated during the period when organized labor throughout the country struggled against the menace of company unionism. Randolph believed that the Brotherhood's opposition to the ERP at Pullman placed the union in the forefront of the anti–company union fight. Its efforts would demonstrate to blacks and whites alike the importance of legitimate unionism for Afro-American workers. Through its publicity, the BSCP incessantly pointed out how workers could not depend upon the good will of their employers. White labor leaders generally refused to admit that the BSCP played a major role in the eventual overthrow of company unionism, but some of them, notably President William Green of the AFL, recognized the Brotherhood's contribution to the struggle and provided reluctant and limited support for Randolph and his activities.

More than achieving an end to company unions, Randolph wanted to legitimize his union through an international charter in the AFL. The question of a charter for the BSCP remained before the Executive Council of the Federation for almost a decade, with the Council acting on several occasions to deny Randolph's request. The Brotherhood faced opposition from white unions desiring jurisdiction over porters for various reasons; it was this opposition which caused the Council to admit the BSCP through federal locals and delay for years a final decision on an international charter. But opposition from other unions was only part of the reason why the BSCP failed to attain its own charter. Unlike the general public, Green and his colleagues on the Council were hardened political operators who understood the risks involved in chartering a union as weak and ephemeral as the BSCP; they undoubtedly feared that the BSCP might fail and thus reflect adversely upon their own judgment. It was one thing for a local to go out of business, but the failure of an international affected the whole labor movement.

Pragmatic considerations alone, however, do not explain the AFL's policy toward the BSCP and black workers generally, for the old question of racism remains as part of the problem. Randolph and other blacks perennially appealed to AFL leaders to take overt actions to end discrimination and to organize black workers in all trades in which they were employed. Federation officials met each request with high-sounding rhetoric about the non-discriminatory stance of the American Federation of Labor, and refused to change the racism they in fact countenanced. It was not until 1934 that Randolph, with support from powerful leaders of white industrial unions, could even convince the AFL to investigate charges of racial discrimination within its affiliates. And when Green's own select committee reported that international unions did indeed discriminate against black workers, the Federation killed the report at the convention of 1935. Randolph raised questions concerning participation of blacks in the general labor movement, but he failed to effect changes during the 1930s.

Through the 1920s and into the Great Depression, the Brotherhood operated in a generally hostile official climate. The United States Mediation Board, established in 1926, failed to bring about mediation or arbitration in 1927; the Interstate Commerce Commission refused to order an end to tipping in 1928; the Mediation Board would not support the BSCP's plea for an emergency board during the strike fiasco of 1928. Moreover, between 1930 and 1933 the Brotherhood met repeated setbacks in its litigation before federal courts, and the Hoover Administration would not countenance a federal investigation of Pullman's hiring and wages policies even after Green joined Randolph in requesting such a study.

One cannot overemphasize the importance of changes wrought by the Great Depression, particularly the New Deal, to the success of the Brotherhood. The economic sufferings of that era caused widespread reevaluation of goals and tactics among Americans of various persuasions, not least blacks. The NAACP and the National Urban League, partly under their own impetus and partly under pressure from the masses, demonstrated increased interest in economics and the problems of workers. Randolph effectively channeled this interest to the aid of the BSCP. More important, the Brotherhood of Sleeping Car Porters profited from the Roosevelt Administration's insistence on protecting the rights of organized labor, a shift from the policy of previous administrations. Passage of the Amended Railway Labor Act of 1934 explicitly forbade company unions in the railroad industry and required railroads to negotiate with unions that represented a majority of their employees. An "act with teeth in it," as Randolph called the new law, the 1934 measure also empowered the newly created National Mediation Board to determine which union should have the right to represent employees in times of dispute. Pullman could no longer simply ignore the BSCP. In retrospect, given the numerical weakness of the porters' union, it is hardly surprising that Randolph placed great emphasis upon attaining the union's goals through the intercession of government agencies and federal courts.

Officials of the Brotherhood of Sleeping Car Porters deserve great credit for having maintained the machinery of their union so that they could benefit from the new legislation. They persisted to the end, even having to appeal directly to Congress to insure that new railroad labor laws applied to them and their employer. But it is still somewhat ironic that the BSCP's chance for success came in 1934, just when the union's fortunes were at their lowest ebb. In the end, the Brotherhood succeeded partly because of improved conditions for all of organized labor.

Analysis of BSCP leadership provides the best method for understanding why the Brotherhood stood ready to profit from the legislative developments of the 1930s and eventually gained recognition from Pullman. Study of the union's leadership also underlines the importance of the symbiotic relationship that existed between Randolph and his lieutenants. Officials of the BSCP evidenced two types of leadership: the public and wide appeal of the charismatic A. Philip Randolph, and the activities of those whom Milton Webster epitomized through his efforts to sign up porters and operate the union on a daily basis.

Charisma is a difficult concept to define, though social psychologists, sociologists, historians, and political scientists have expended much scholarly energy explaining how certain individuals exercise wide influence, and sometimes even power, over people by force of personality. Such individuals usually manifest certain common characteristics. According to the pioneer sociologist Max Weber, and scholars who have followed him, charismatic personalities usually originate under conditions of stress, show an absence of formal rules of routine administrations, reject rational economic conduct, and prevail for short or intermittent periods. Moreover, charismatic leaders have the ability to issue statements clearly at odds with facts and have their words accepted as truth, and they demonstrate at all times an air of personal incorruptibility. But Weber and other warn that leadership is a relationship between followers and leader. A charismatic leader can function in that manner only as long as his followers believe in his charisma.[1]

Randolph possessed most of the personal characteristics of charismatic leaders. Handsome and almost exquisite in bearing, a master of rhetoric and oratory, he spoke in a musical baritone voice that had a hypnotic effect upon his audience. He carried himself with an air that exuded confidence — so much so that opponents found it almost impossible to deny the wisdom of his arguments, and supporters were loyal almost to his every word. Yet Randolph's ability to inspire people did not transfer into the routine skills required to run an organization on a daily basis. Rather, he moved in the public realm, stimulating debate on the question of whether blacks should join trade unions and generating propaganda to publicize his views and the goals of the BSCP. Functioning as he did on the broadest possible plane, he left the daily operations

[1] Literature on charisma and leadership characteristics is rich and voluminous. For extended discussion of the concept, see particularly Max Weber, "The Sociology of Charismatic Authority," in H. H. Gerth and C. Wright Mills, eds., *From Max Weber: Essays in Sociology* (New York: Oxford University Press, 1958), 245-51; Max Weber, *The Theory of Social and Economic Organization* (New York: Oxford University Press, 1947); Arthur Schweitzer, "Theory and Political Charisma," *Comparative Studies in Society and History*, XVI, 2 (Mar., 1974), 150-81; Ann Ruth Willner, *Charismatic Political Leadership: A Theory* (Princeton: Princeton University Press, 1968); K. J. Ratnam, "Charisma and Political Leadership," *Political Studies*, XII, 3 (1964), 341-54; and various studies in Dankwart A. Rustow, ed., *Philosophers and Kings: Studies in Leadership* (New York: Braziller, 1970). The articles by Rustow, "The Study of Leadership," 1-32; and Robert C. Tucker, "The Theory of Charismatic Leadership," 69-94, are especially useful studies in that volume.

of the union to trusted lieutenants who were loyal to him personally and to his ideas.

As president and general organizer of the Brotherhood, Randolph was the union's dominant public figure; it was largely because of his activities that the Brotherhood became a common name among both blacks and whites, and he himself attained national reknown. A sensitive man who exhibited great faith in the virtues of truth and justice, Randolph functioned as if he never doubted that his cause was right and that the union would succeed. It is clear that Randolph's faith and determination affected porters and maids, and that they continued to recognize in him important qualities of leadership. Little other than the intangible powers of charisma can explain why service employees of the Pullman Company, when given a chance to choose a bargaining agent under federal protection in 1935, chose the BSCP, whose tangible successes in the past had been negligible. In a real sense, they placed their faith not in the organization but in Randolph, who stood before them as a symbol of perseverance and courage.

Though clearly charismatic in manner and in the responses which he generated among people, Randolph never lost touch with reality. He recognized the weaknesses of his union and made effective use of mass appeal and propaganda to bring outside forces to his aid. His strength lay partly in his realization that the BSCP could not defeat the Pullman Company solely over the issue of who would represent the porters and maids, though he would never admit that fact in public. Indeed, part of his genius was his capacity to operate from a position of weakness while convincing influential individuals and organizations to support his cause. (He would use this same tactic on the national level in the March on Washington Movement in 1941.) Moreover, Randolph was an individual who fixed on a goal and held to it with dogged determination. He wavered on matters of immediate tactics and from time to time showed an inclination toward compromise and indecision. But in the end his hallmark was perseverance. His rise to prominence through his work with the porters' union, and the wide attention he attracted through his techniques and philosophy, established Randolph as a new black leader who at least talked about organizing the masses for political action.

It is hardly original to point out that Randolph was the dominant figure in the BSCP, but even the most charismatic individuals require a base from which to operate in order to legitimize their activities. Randolph was able to function as he did because of a network of loyal and competent associates who carried out the day-to-day work of running the BSCP and signing up porters while Randolph spent much of his time lining up support among influential blacks and liberal whites. Previously seen as fringe individuals, these men — Milton P. Webster, C. L. Dellums, Ashley L. Totten, Benjamin Smith, E. J. Bradley, and others — emerge as leaders indispensable to the BSCP's success. Though dedicated to the union and loyal to Randolph, they believed that they too should have a voice in important decisions. Thus Randolph did not wield absolute power in shaping the Brotherhood's policies, particularly after 1928. Webster, head of the BSCP's strongest local, exercised especially wide influence in developing union policy. After the strike fiasco of 1928, and largely at Webster's insistence, power to direct the Brotherhood passed from Randolph's hands into those of the Policy Committee, which Webster chaired. Numerous fights over policy and personality developed within the union both before and after the expanded leadership roles of Webster and others. Indeed, Randolph and Webster argued heatedly on several occasions about union matters, but each man recognized in the other qualities that complemented his own. Randolph succeeded with the porters' union precisely because he had strong and loyal associates; the very absence of such associates explains his failure as president of the National Negro Congress, a position he assumed in 1936. There Randolph functioned largely as a symbolic figure, but the men who ran the Congress, notably John P. Davis, did not share his goals. In the end Randolph had no choice but to resign. In the BSCP, on the other hand, when private arguments between Randolph and Webster ended, the two men stood shoulder to shoulder in struggling for a common goal.

If one were to distinguish between Randolph and Webster (and between Randolph and other BSCP leaders whom sources do not illuminate as clearly as they do Webster), it could be argued that one was a national black leader and the other a union organizer. Randolph thought in wider terms; he saw the problems of blacks in the totality of American society, whereas Webster thought mainly of the porters and of finding ways to improve their conditions at Pullman.Because of their different perspectives, they complemented each other. Randolph, who took the wider view, was prone to compromise and to believe that people finally would treat him fairly. Thus he could employ indirect means to attain the union's goals and could even find value in moral victories. Webster lacked such illusions, insisting that the union must be militant and unyielding if it was to prevail. Likewise, Webster convinced Randolph that porters (and by extension other blacks) must finance their own organizations and not depend on outsiders for support. By 1937, after twelve years of close association and interaction, Randolph had overcome much of his earlier faith that justice would inevitably prevail, and Webster had acquired some of Randolph's wider vision.

BSCP leaders claimed that they represented the "New Negro" in leadership circles, but in truth they functioned much in the tradition of other black leaders. Randolph and Webster insisted that Brotherhood leadership remain black, especially when it appeared that the BSCP might fall under the dominance of a white union. However, neither man had compunctions about using white expertise or collecting money from white liberal sources. Just as the NAACP retained white attorneys and actively sought financial support from foundations like the Garland Fund, the BSCP relied heavily upon well-trained and highly placed whites to provide technical expertise and money. Henry T. Hunt, Fiorello La Guardia, and Donald Richberg served as attorneys; Labor Bureau, Inc., and Stuart Chase Associates provided financial consultation; and Edward Berman prepared economic justifications for the BSCP's demands during the negotiations of 1935-37. Moreover, Randolph placed a great premium upon having respectable white professionals write letters to Pullman and government agencies on the union's behalf, either as individuals or through citizens' committees. The BSCP wished to attain the best help available, and it made effective use of prestigious individuals to extract favorable decisions from judges and government agencies. Their efforts often failed, but association of such people's names with the BSCP was valuable propaganda to the union. Far from representing accommodation, the Brotherhood's actions show that black organizations enlisted the aid of white professionals because blacks recognized the racial realities of that benighted age.

Twelve years of effort brought success for the BSCP and made its leaders, particularly Randolph, nationally known figures. Though before 1925 Randolph was already quite prominent in New York through the *Messenger*, that magazine was in trouble when he joined efforts to found the Brotherhood. Without his union, he might easily have fallen into the relative oblivion that engulfed his friend and associate Chandler Owen. But despite the BSCP's weaknesses, occupation of its presidency provided Randolph with the forum he needed to speak with authority on a wide range of issues, a license his own special abilities equipped him to exploit. Randolph led the March on Washington Movement which forced creation of the Fair Employment Practices Committee in 1941; Webster served as a presidential appointee on this committee from 1941 until Congress allowed it to pass out of existence in 1946. Later, after the AFL-CIO merger in 1955, Randolph gained a seat on the powerful Executive Council.

Ironically, the Brotherhood of Sleeping Car Porters triumphed while the industry which employed its members was falling into sharp decline. Randolph and other BSCP leaders had complained as early as 1931 about the damage which air travel and improved highways and automobiles would do to the railroad industry and to porters. By 1937 they must certainly have wondered if the twelve years of struggle had been worth the suffering. All BSCP organizers went without pay during much of the 1930s; some even faced threats of jail and physical violence if they did not quit the union. Worse still, others lost their families and homes because of their commitment to the BSCP. Their consolation was that they had contributed to a new understanding between black and white workers and had through their efforts raised the level of participation for black people within American society. Today Pullman sleeping car service is but a ghost of what it was in 1925, and the BSCP is itself only a relic. Nonetheless, the changes it inspired among black people, and the moral support it offered to other blacks during its twelve years of struggle, mark the Brotherhood of Sleeping Car Porters even in ruins as a lasting and important monument to the progress of Afro-Americans.

Appendix

BROTHERHOOD OF SLEEPING CAR PORTERS' MEMBERSHIP FIGURES, 1925-38

Eastern Zone	1925	1926	1927	1928	1929	1930	1931	1932	1933	1934	1935	1936	1937	1938
New York, N.Y.	400	1,000	1,150	1,100	800	300	200	100	40	500	900	1,000	1,000	1,200
Boston, Mass.	40	210	200	220	70	20	9	3	3	75	137	140	170	170
Albany, N.Y.	2	—	—	—	—	—	—	—	—	—	15	21	23	25
Buffalo, N.Y.	7	—	—	—	—	—	—	—	—	40	55	60	70	85
Jersey City, N.J.	—	—	—	—	—	—	—	—	—	—	35	150	200	215
Philadelphia, Pa.	5	—	—	—	—	—	—	—	20	45	75	135	155	160
Baltimore, Md.	—	—	—	—	—	—	—	—	—	—	—	2	8	10
Washington, D.C.	100	175	175	175	50	5	5	5	5	50	100	140	153	175
Richmond, Va.	20	15	25	25	—	—	—	—	—	15	28	28	33	40
Norfolk, Va.	25	30	40	40	—	—	—	—	—	12	20	25	28	31
Asheville, N.C.	2	2	2	2	2	2	2	2	2	11	9	15	20	22
Wilmington, N.C.	—	—	—	—	—	—	—	—	—	—	—	1	10	9
Charleston, S.C.	—	—	—	—	—	—	—	—	—	—	3	5	5	7
Augusta, Ga.	—	—	—	—	—	—	—	—	—	—	—	3	5	18
Atlanta, Ga.	—	—	—	—	—	—	—	—	—	—	2	20	45	50
Birmingham, Ala.	—	—	—	—	—	—	—	—	—	—	—	—	—	10
Savannah, Ga.	—	—	—	—	—	—	—	—	—	—	—	—	7	10
Jacksonville, Fla.	45	50	100	200	65	30	21	11	10	110	125	150	175	185
Tampa, Fla.	—	—	—	—	—	—	—	—	—	10	30	30	34	34

Brotherhood of Sleeping Car Porters' Membership Figures, 1925-38 (Cont.)

Detroit Zone	1925	1926	1927	1928	1929	1930	1931	1932	1933	1934	1935	1936	1937	1938
Detroit, Mich.	60	65	80	88	65	20	15	15	15	15	50	70	77	80
Toronto, Ont.	—	—	—	—	—	—	—	—	—	—	10	10	15	20
Montreal, Que.	—	—	—	—	—	—	—	—	—	—	—	10	15	20
Cleveland, Ohio	25	75	100	100	10	10	10	10	10	9	38	79	100	110
Columbus, Ohio	20	20	25	25	—	—	—	—	—	10	12	14	18	25
Pittsburgh, Pa.	50	75	100	100	10	—	—	—	—	—	142	150	153	160
Indianapolis, Ind.	3	6	11	12	—	—	—	—	—	—	5	9	10	12
Louisville, Ky.	2	15	20	20	15	—	—	—	—	8	8	8	9	11
Nashville, Tenn.	—	—	—	—	—	—	—	—	—	—	—	15	10	12
Chattanooga, Tenn.	—	—	—	—	—	—	—	—	—	12	8	8	11	15
Cincinnati, Ohio	8	10	12	25	11	—	—	—	—	10	25	30	35	50
Midwestern Zone														
Chicago, Ill.	600	700	1,100	1,150	700	600	500	300	250	900	1,100	1,400	1,500	1,650
Kansas City, Kans.	100	127	160	175	50	40	10	10	8	55	100	150	165	165
Omaha, Nebr.	10	25	40	40	—	—	—	—	—	47	50	60	66	70
Minneapolis–St. Paul, Minn.	55	75	175	225	100	75	50	50	40	100	175	175	200	235
Denver, Colo.	10	25	37	37	20	9	—	—	—	18	45	75	116	120

Brotherhood of Sleeping Car Porters' Membership Figures, 1925-38 (Cont.)

Southwestern Zone	1925	1926	1927	1928	1929	1930	1931	1932	1933	1934	1935	1936	1937	1938
St. Louis, Mo.	75	100	175	200	60	60	60	60	50	100	160	175	275	320
Memphis, Tenn.	—	—	—	—	—	—	—	—	—	10	20	30	35	45
Little Rock, Ark.	—	—	—	—	—	—	—	—	—	5	15	20	21	30
Shreveport, La.	—	—	—	—	—	—	—	—	—	11	11	15	20	25
New Orleans, La.	45	75	10	163	25	20	10	10	10	20	100	150	150	167
Dallas, Tex.	—	—	—	—	—	—	—	—	—	5	15	25	35	41
Fort Worth, Tex.	—	—	—	—	—	—	—	—	—	10	15	25	30	32
Houston, Tex.	—	—	—	—	—	—	—	—	—	—	10	10	20	22
San Antonio, Tex.	—	—	—	—	—	—	—	—	—	22	40	50	60	66
Pacific Coast Zone														
San Francisco, Calif.	40	100	150	200	150	100	97	90	80	100	150	160	179	195
Los Angeles, Calif.	75	100	150	200	70	50	75	75	75	295	200	214	214	217
Portland, Ore.	20	22	25	25	25	20	10	8	8	18	25	50	57	65
Seattle, Wash.	40	45	50	60	60	30	15	20	30	50	55	55	55	65
Spokane, Wash.	20	25	25	25	10	2	2	2	2	2	15	16	20	20
Salt Lake City, Utah	—	—	—	—	—	—	—	—	—	10	12	16	30	35
El Paso, Tex.	—	—	—	—	—	—	—	—	—	11	20	20	25	25
Total	1,904	3,167	4,227	4,632	2,368	1,403	1,091	771	658	2,627	4,165	5,219	5,938	6,581

Source: Brazeal, *The Brotherhood*, 221-22.

Note on Sources

MANUSCRIPT COLLECTIONS

A study of the Brotherhood of Sleeping Car Porters must begin with the Brotherhood of Sleeping Car Porters Chicago Division Papers (Manuscripts Division, Chicago Historical Society). These records are particularly important for the years before 1940, because the papers of the union's national headquarters are not available among the Records of the Brotherhood of Sleeping Car Porters (Manuscripts Division, Library of Congress). The Chicago Papers contain numerous letters between Randolph and Webster, along with a few items of correspondence between the Chicago office and other regional officials. The Randolph-Webster letters cover a wide range of subjects, both about the union and about personal matters. The records are weakest in shedding light on the union's numerical and financial strength; the Chicago Division did not keep complete listings of its local membership and had nothing on the general condition of the organization. The Chicago Papers also contain numerous press releases and broadsides which help to tell the public story of the union. The value of the papers decreases for periods when Randolph and Webster were together. During the Depression years, when Randolph spent much of his time in Chicago to help prosecute the union's court cases, we learn little from the Chicago collection because the two men did not correspond.

The Chicago Papers are supplemented by Brotherhood of Sleeping Car Porters Pacific Coast Division Papers (C-A 393, Manuscripts Division, Bancroft Library, Berkeley). This small portfolio contains useful material on the aftermath of the abortive strike of 1928. It also helps to convey a clearer picture of union operations outside the New York-Chicago hub.

The Papers of the American Fund for Public Service (Manuscripts and Archives Division, New York Public Library) contain items that describe the important relationship between the Fund and the Brotherhood during the crucial years before 1928, as well as the Fund's other labor-related activities. In addition, the papers contain useful information on economic aims of the NAACP and the National Urban League; they provide helpful insights into the manner in which James Weldon Johnson functioned on behalf of blacks generally, but particularly in the interest of the NAACP.

The Pullman Company's story is not so easy to compile from primary sources. A few helpful Pullman papers are available. The Pullman Company in Chicago has a small number of papers from the period before 1940, but the personal and official papers of the company's major figures involved with the BSCP are not among them. We cannot learn from Pullman sources what positions were taken concerning the BSCP, except from a sprinkling of items from the very early years, and a few pieces from the period just before the two parties settled the dispute. The Pullman Company's vast archives, recently made available to scholars at the Newberry Library in Chicago, are still in disarray; additional information might be forthcoming when the papers are organized.

Board of Mediation Case C-107, *Brotherhood of Sleeping Car Porters* v. *Pullman Company* (Record Group 13, Records of the National Mediation Board, National Archives and Records Service), and ICC Case #20,007, *Brotherhood of Sleeping Car Porters* v. *Pullman Company* (Interstate Commerce Commission Files, Washington), contain official records of the BSCP's appeal to these two federal agencies during 1926-28. Neither the National Archives nor the National Mediation Board has files on the final BSCP-Pullman controversy during 1934-37.

The papers of both the National Association for the Advancement of Colored People and the National Urban League (Manuscripts Division, Library of Congress) are indispensable for tracing the ramifications in official black circles of the efforts to organize the Pullman porters. Among the NAACP Papers, files C413 and C414 contain much information about the Walter White–Randolph relationship and about the development of an official economic policy in that organization. In addition to NAACP Papers, the Association's *Annual Reports* (New York, 1910-35) contain invaluable material on the NAACP's public policy.

For a survey of pre-1925 trade unionism among blacks in New York, one might profitably see the Negro Labor Committee Record Group Papers (Manuscripts Division, Schomburg Branch, New York Public Library). Mainly the papers of the Trade Union Committee for Organizing Negro Workers and of its executive secretary, Frank Crosswaith, they contain valuable information about the Socialists' interest in organizing black workers. After Crosswaith left the TUC to join the BSCP, the value of the papers diminishes until he was forced out of the union in 1928 and again pursued his independent trade union work.

Two other small collections were also helpful. One is the Department of Justice Mail and Files Division #9-12-725 (National Archives). This small portfolio contains the letters that circulated in the Department of Justice and among several congressmen in the attempt to find ways to silence the *Messenger*. The story of the Communists' interest in black workers and their attempt to use blacks and black organizations is available in the other file, a collection of selected papers entitled Workers' Party of America (Microforms Division, Indiana University Library, Bloomington).

The best record of the official relationship between the American Federation of Labor and the BSCP is contained in correspondence of William Green. Housed in the headquarters of the AFL-CIO, Green's Copy Books include numerous letters from Green to Randolph, and a few from Green to other labor leaders on BSCP matters. The major disappointment in using Green's Copy Books is that they do not include incoming correspondence.

Secondary Sources

The relationship between black workers and organized labor has received considerable scholarly attention. The most recent general account of the subject is Philip S. Foner, *Organized Labor and the Black Worker, 1619-1973* (New York: Praeger, 1974). Two older books, Charles H. Wesley, *Negro Labor in the United States, 1850-1925* (New York: Vanguard, 1927), and Sterling D. Spero and Abram L. Harris, *The Black Worker: The Negro and the Labor Movement* (New York: Columbia University Press, 1931), provide excellent treatments of organized labor and black workers through the 1920s. Herbert Northrup, *Organized Labor and the Negro* (New York: Harper and Brothers, 1944), carries the story somewhat forward, but presents no new insights into the problems facing black workers. In an early study of racism in American industry and its effect upon employment opportunities for Afro-Americans, Herman Feldman, *Racial Factors in American Industry* (New York: Harper and Brothers, 1931), discusses the restrictions on blacks entering skilled employment and the enmity that existed between black and white workers.

Though providing little insight into the relations between organized labor and black workers, several volumes on the general labor movement are indispensable for understanding the atmosphere within which the BSCP operated during the 1920s and 1930s. Among those are Joseph G. Rayback, *A History of American Labor*, rev. ed. (New York: Free Press, 1966); Irving Bernstein, *A History of the American Worker, 1920-1933: The Lean Years* (Boston: Houghton-Mifflin, 1960); and Philip Taft, *The AF of L from the Death of Gompers to the Merger* (New York: Harper, 1959). The development of federal policy toward labor disputes in the railway industry is best described in Gerald E. Eggert, *Railroad Labor Disputes: The Beginnings of Federal Strike Policy* (Ann Arbor: University of Michigan Press, 1967).

The best source on racial policies in admissions to unions early in the twentieth century is F. E. Wolfe, *Admission to American Trade Unions* (Baltimore: Johns Hopkins University Press, 1912). W. E. B. Du Bois, ed., *The Negro Artisan* (Atlanta: Atlanta University Publications, 1902), is a penetrating account of the effect of union racism and discrimination on the economic development of black workers. Ira DeA. Reid and Charles S. Johnson undertook a similar survey for the National Urban League during the 1920s. Their findings, published as Reid, *Negro Membership in American Labor Unions* (New York: Alexander Press, 1930), show that conditions for blacks had improved little since Wolfe's and Du Bois's earlier accounts.

Some of the most important literature on black workers and the early trade unions, and on the racial views of unions, has appeared in articles. Bernard Mandel's study of the dominant figure in organized labor during the late nineteenth and early twentieth centuries, "Samuel Gompers and the Negro Workers, 1886-1914," *Journal of Negro History*, XL (Jan., 1955), 34-60, is a classic. Another fine study of the late nineteenth century is Sidney H. Kessler, "The Organization of Negroes in the Knights of Labor," *Journal of Negro History*, XXXVII (July, 1952), 248-76. Julius Jacobson, ed., *The Negro and the American Labor Movement* (Garden City, N.Y.: Anchor Books, 1968), contains several useful analyses of the involvement of blacks in the trade union movement from the Civil War to the present. Several contributions to that volume, particularly August Meier and Elliott Rudwick, "Attitudes of Negro Leaders toward the American Labor Movement"; Herbert G. Gutman, "The Negro and the United Mine Workers of America"; and Marc Karson and Ronald Rodash, "The American Federation of Labor and the Negro Worker," present significant insights on those subjects.

A good study of George Pullman's obsession with order and of the origins of the Pullman Company and the town of Pullman, Illinois, is Stanley Buder, *Pullman: An Experiment in Industrial Order and Social Planning, 1880-1930* (New York: Oxford University Press, 1967). Almont Lindsey, *The Pullman Strike: The Story of a Unique Experiment and of a Great Labor Upheaval* (Chicago: University of Chicago Press, 1942), is a vivid account of Pullman's labor policy and of the bitter strike of 1894. Lindsey analyzes the federal report on the strike and discusses the reasons for unrest in Pullman plants. An unusually informative account of developments among blacks during the same years (mainly in the South, where many of the porters came from) which briefly comments on working conditions among porters and on the company's attitude toward labor organization is the brilliant autobiography of Benjamin E. Mays, *Born to Rebel: An Autobiography by Benjamin E. Mays* (New York: Scribners, 1971).

The backgrounds of the men who made the BSCP are difficult to discover because of the sparse literature on them. Jervis Anderson's recent biography of Randolph, *A. Philip Randolph: A Biographical Portrait* (New York: Harcourt Brace Jovanovich, 1972), is a highly favorable account of the union leader's career. Two older assessments of Randolph's work give limited insights into how the man functioned. Julius Adams, *The Challenge: A Study in Negro Leadership* (New York: W. Malliet, 1949), and Edwin R. Embree, *13 Against the Odds* (New York: Viking Press, 1944), devote a chapter each to Randolph. Webster is still sorely deserving of scholarly attention.

There is at present one other book on the BSCP. Brailsford R. Brazeal, *The Brotherhood of Sleeping Car Porters: Its Origin and Development* (New York: Harper and Brothers, 1946), is a solid treatment of the organization of the union. An economist, Professor Brazeal was more interested in the economic development of the union that in its wider influences. His book is particularly useful for BSCP membership, since the papers from which his figures are derived subsequently have been destroyed. Spero and Harris devote a chapter of their monumental *Black Worker* to the Brotherhood. Unfortunately, the book appeared at a time when the union was at its lowest ebb; believing that it had failed, the authors treat it unfavorably. Murray Kempton, *Part of Our Time: Some Ruins and Monuments of the Thirties* (New York: Simon and Schuster, 1955), presents a more sympathetic view in an analysis that focuses on Thomas T. Patterson, vice-president of the New York local. Another positive account appears in Robert W. Dunn, *Company Unions* (New York: Vanguard Press, 1927). Though Dunn's book appeared shortly after the BSCP was organized, it nonetheless credited the Brotherhood with being the only union ever founded in direct opposition to a company union.

The recent appearance of Andrew Buni's fine study, *Robert L. Vann of the Pittsburgh Courier: Politics and Black Journalism* (Pittsburgh: University of Pittsburgh Press, 1974), fills some of the need for a first-rate scholarly interpretation of the black press. Though only a history of the *Courier* and heavily concentrated on Vann, Buni's book gives helpful insights into the development of the black press generally during the crucial years of the 1920s and 1930s; in addition, it illuminates the relationship between Vann and Randolph. Roi Ottley, *The Lonely Warrior: The Life and Times of Robert S. Abbott* (Chicago: Regnery Press, 1955), covers the Chicago *Defender*, another major black paper. Ottley presents an overly laudatory account of the career of Robert Abbott, the *Defender*'s owner-editor. He has, in fact, written a commissioned biography of the important publisher. One might also see Theodore Kornweibel, "The *Messenger* Magazine, 1917-1928" (Ph.D. dissertation, Yale University, 1971), for a discussion of that journal.

For the general conditions among blacks during the Great Depression and the responses of black leadership, two important sources are Raymond Wolters, *Negroes and the Great Depression: The Problem of Economic Recovery* (Westport, Conn.: Greenwood, 1970), and B. Joyce Ross, *J. E. Spingarn and the Rise of the NAACP, 1911-1939* (New York: Atheneum, 1972), complementary volumes that help to explain the internal factors contributing to the Association's shift on economic policy during the 1930s. For the Urban League, see Nancy J. Weiss, *The National Urban League, 1910-1940* (New York: Oxford University Press, 1974). Walter White, *A Man Called White: The Autobiography of Walter White* (Bloomington: Indiana University Press, 1970), is an excellent expression of the personal views of the Association's leader on the changes that were occurring in his organization during the 1930s. John Finney, Jr., "Negro Labor during and after World War I" (Ph.D. dissertation, Georgetown University, 1967), is a good discussion of various attempts by blacks to improve their economic condition during those years.

NEWSPAPERS AND JOURNALS

The *Messenger* is almost as important for a study of the Brotherhood of Sleeping Car Porters as are the Chicago Papers for the years 1925-28; during those years the magazine served as the union's official publication. It provides a month-by-month account of union activities and enables one to follow the development of the union's publicity in a clear and orderly fashion. An important part of American literary history vanished from the scene when the *Messenger* ceased publication in the summer of 1928. From its quiet beginning in 1917, the magazine had developed into one of the most important black publications in the country by the time Randolph began to work with the porters in 1925; it is an indispensable source for the development of Randolph's thought up to that date. When the *Messenger* failed, the BSCP founded the *Black Worker* to publicize its views. This journal, more a newspaper than a magazine, failed before 1937 to attain the importance and circulation that the *Messenger* had enjoyed. Nonetheless, it is a helpful guide to BSCP views and activities.

The official magazines of the NAACP and the National Urban League, the *Crisis* and *Opportunity*, respectively, are useful gauges of the changing attitudes of the two organizations between 1925 and 1937. Both magazines carried numerous articles and editorials on the BSCP and on black labor and trade unionism generally. W. E. B. Du Bois at the *Crisis* was particularly helpful in supporting the Brotherhood in its early days, and the union received the same support from Elmer Carter at *Opportunity* as the BSCP neared the culmination of its struggle.

The official organ of the American Federation of Labor, *The American Federationist*, was also helpful. It occasionally carried articles by Randolph and other Brotherhood leaders, but, more important, it provided information on the official views of the Federation regarding black unionism. The AFL's convention *Proceedings* were indispensable for following the participation of BSCP officials in the conventions as they pressed the case of black workers.

Two criteria were used in choosing black newspapers for systematic study. One was circulation, and presumably influence, which led to the Chicago *Defender* and the Pittsburgh *Courier*. The second was that opinion for and against the Brotherhood had to be represented. The St. Louis *Argus* was outstanding for its opposition almost throughout the struggle, although it was known in the St. Louis area as a "strong *race* paper." The New York *Age* was milder in its opposition. As it turned out, most significant were the two giants of black journalism, the *Defender* and the *Courier*, each of which took turns trying to destroy the union. In a less systematic manner, I used the major daily press, particularly the New York *Times* and the Chicago *Tribune*, to gauge wider reactions to specific BSCP activities.

Government Documents and Publications

Among the more important government publications are the *Reports* of the United States Mediation Board (1925-34) and its successor, the National Mediation Board (1935-39). In addition, the *Reports* of the Interstate Commerce Commission (1928) cover that body's decision on the BSCP's request that it outlaw tipping. The hearings that led to the Amended Railway Labor Act of 1934 are covered in 73rd Cong., 2nd sess., Senate Committee on Interstate and Foreign Commerce, *Bill to Amend the 1926 Railway Labor Act, Hearings* (April, 1934). Congressional debates appear in *Congressional Record*, 73rd Cong., 2nd sess., *passim*. Finally, in 1920 the New York State Joint Legislative Committee on Seditious Activities (the Lusk Committee) published a massive account of radicalism. Forty-four pages of the report (pp. 1476-1520) deal with radicalism among blacks. The *Messenger* was the major magazine covered.

Selected Additional Bibliography

Books

Bransten, Richard. *Men Who Lead Labor*. New York: Modern Age Books, 1937.

Cayton, Horace R., and Mitchell, George S. *Black Workers and the New Unions*. Chapel Hill: University of North Carolina Press, 1939.

Cottrell, W. Fred. *The Railroader*. Stanford: Stanford University Press, 1940.

Davie, Maurice R. *Negroes in American Society*. New York: McGraw-Hill, 1949.

Davis, Jerome, ed. *Labor Speaks for Itself on Religion*. New York: Macmillan, 1929.

Dunlop, John. *Industrial Relations System*. New York: Holt, Rinehart, 1958.

Foner, Philip S. *History of the Labor Movement in the United States*. New York: International, 1965.

Harris, Herbert. *American Labor*. New Haven: Yale University Press, 1938.

———. *Labor's Civil War*. New York: Alfred A. Knopf, 1940.

Jones, Harry E. *Railroad Wages and Labor Relations*. New York: Bureau of Information of the Eastern Railroads, 1953.

Meier, August. *Negro Thought in America, 1880-1915*. Ann Arbor: University of Michigan Press, 1963.

Parmelee, Julius H. *The Modern Railway*. New York: Longmans, 1940.

Perlman, Selig. *A History of Trade Unionism in the United States*. New York: Macmillan, 1929.

Rudwick, Elliott. *Race Riot at East St. Louis, Illinois, July 2, 1917*. Carbondale: Southern Illinois University Press, 1964.

Uhl, Alexander. *Trains and the Men Who Run Them*. Washington: Public Affairs Institute, 1954.

Wolfe, Harry D. *The Railroad Labor Board*. Chicago: University of Chicago Press, 1927.

Articles

"A. Philip Randolph." *Opportunity*, XV (Oct., 1937), 294.

"The AFL and the Negro." *Opportunity*, VII (Nov., 1929), 335-36.

"AFL Moves South." *Time*, XXXV (Jan. 20, 1930), 16.

Alexander, William W. "A Strategy for Negro Labor." *Opportunity*, XII (Apr., 1934), 102-3.

Allen, A. J. "Selling Out the Workers." *Crisis*, XLV (Mar., 1938), 80.

"The American Federation of Labor and the Negro." *Crisis*, XXXVI (July, 1929), 241.

"At the Listening Post: Labor's Attempt to Organize in a New Field." *Literary Digest*, CXVII (Mar. 31, 1934), 12.

Baldwin, Roger N. "Negro Rights and Class Struggle." *Opportunity*, XII (Sept., 1934), 264-66.

Bent, S. "On Riding in a Pullman." *Outlook*, CXLIII (June 27, 1928), 343.

Berman, Edward. "Pullman Porters Win." *Nation*, CXLI (Aug. 21, 1935), 217-18.

"Black and White Workers." *Crisis*, XXXV (Mar., 1928), 98.

"Black Brotherhood." *Time*, XXX (Sept. 20, 1937), 10.

"The Black Man in Labor." *Crisis*, XXXI (Dec., 1925), 60.

Brewer, James H. "Robert Lee Vann, Democrat or Republican: An Exponent of Loose-Leaf Politics." *Negro History Bulletin*, XXI (Feb., 1958), 100-103.

Carter, Jessie. "Deadhead: A Pullman Porter Steps out of Character." *Opportunity*, XIII (Aug., 1935), 243-44, 251.

Covington, Floyd C. "Union Styles." *Social Science Abstracts*, III (Oct., 1931), 1453.

Crosswaith, Frank R. "Porters Smash a Company Union: Showdown Approaches." *Labor Age* (Jan., 1928), 15-16.

———. "A Relic of Slavery or the Tragedy of Segregation." *Messenger*, VIII (Feb., 1926), 42-43.

———. "Sound Principle and Unsound Policy." *Opportunity*, XII (Feb., 1934), 340-42.

———. "Toward the Home Stretch." *Messenger*, VIII (July, 1926), 196.
———. "The Trade Union Committee for Organizing Negro Workers." *Messenger*, VII (Aug., 1925), 296-97.
———. "A Year of History Making." *Messenger*, VIII (Sept., 1926), 281.
Davis, John P. "What Price National Recovery?" *Crisis*, XL (Dec., 1933), 271.
Du Bois, William E. B. "The Negro Citizen." *Crisis*, XXXVI (May, 1929), 154-56.
Dunne, William F. "Negroes in American Industry." *Workers' Monthly*, IV (Mar.-Apr., 1925), 206-8.
"Equality by Law." *Time*, XXXV (Feb. 5, 1940), 21.
"Exploitation or Cooperation." *Crisis*, XXXVI (Dec., 1929), 405-6.
Fleming, G. James. "Pullman Porters Win Pot of Gold." *Crisis*, XLIV (Nov., 1937), 332ff.
Francis, Robert C. "The Negro and Industrial Unionism." *Social Forces*, XV (Dec., 1936), 272-75.
Frazier, E. Franklin. "Occupational Classes among Negroes in Cities." *American Journal of Sociology*, XXXV (Mar., 1930), 718-38.
Frey, John P. "Attempts to Organize Negro Workers." *American Federationist*, XXXVI (Mar., 1929), 296-305.
Gannett, Lewis. "Negroes and Jobs." *Survey Graphic*, XXVIII (Feb., 1939), 10.
"George Sees a Yellow Peril." *Business Week*, (Mar. 29, 1933), 20.
Granger, Lester B. "The Negro — Friend or Foe of Organized Labor?" *Opportunity*, XIII (May, 1935), 142-44.
———. "Stepchildren of the Depression." *Opportunity*, XII (July, 1934), 218-19.
Green, William. "Letter to the Editor." *Opporutnity*, VII (Dec., 1929), 381-82.
———. "National Negro Labor Conference." *American Federationist*, XXXVII (Jan. 30, 1930), 21.
———. "Negro Wage Earners and Trade Unions." *Opportunity*, XII (Oct., 1934), 299.
———. "Our Negro Worker." *Messenger*, VII (Sept., 1925), 332.
———. "Warning." *Time*, VI (Aug. 17, 1925), 4.
———. "Why Belong to the Union?" *Opportunity*, IV (Feb., 1926), 61-62.
Hall, H. N. "The Art of the Pullman Porter." *American Mercury*, XXIII (July, 1931), 329-35.
Harrington, M. "Carry Your Bags, Sir?" *American Magazine*, CVI (July, 1928), 32-33.
Harris, Abram L. "Negro Labor's Quarrel with White Workingmen." *Current History*, XXIV (Sept., 1926), 903-8.
———. "The Negro Worker." *Labor Age*, XIX (Feb., 1930), 5-8.

Harshberger, B. "Don't Call the Porter George." *American Magazine*, CXIII (Mar., 1932), 70.
Hazell, C. "End of a Red Cap." *Nation*, CXLV (Nov. 6, 1937), 499-500.
Hill, T. Arnold. "The AFL and the Negro Worker." *Tuskegee Messenger*, V (Jan. 25, 1930), 3.
———. "The Dilemma of Negro Workers." *Opportunity*, IV (Feb., 1926), 39-41.
———. "Labor." *Opportunity*, VIII (Mar., 1930), 92.
———. "Labor Marches On." *Opportunity*, XII (Apr., 1934), 120-21.
———. "Let Us Have a Plan." *Opportunity*, X (June, 1932), 185-87.
———. "The Negro and the CIO." *Opportunity*, XV (Aug., 1937), 243.
———. "Open Letter to William Green." *Opportunity*, VIII (Feb., 1930), 56-57.
———. "A Plea for Organized Action." *Opportunity*, XII (Aug., 1934), 250.
———. "The Pullman Porter." *Opportunity*, XIII (June, 1935), 186.
———. "Recent Developments in the Problem of Negro Labor." National Conference on Social Welfare *Proceedings*, XLVIII (1921), 321-25.
———. "Social Significance to Minority Groups of Recent Labor Developments." National Conference on Social Welfare *Proceedings*, LXIV (1937), 399-408.
———. "When Better Times Come." *Opportunity*, X (Sept., 1932), 285-86.
Holden, Arthur C. "Pullman Porters and Race Progress." *Messenger*, VIII (Mar., 1926), 88, 91-92.
Houchins, Joseph R. "Racial Minorities and Organized Labor." *Opportunity*, XIII (Apr., 1935), 109.
Johnson, Charles S. "Changing Economic Status of the Negro." American Academy of Political and Social Sciences *Annals*, CXL (Nov., 1928), 128-37.
———. "Negro Workers and the Unions." *Survey*, XL (Apr. 15, 1928), 113-15.
———. "The New Frontiers of Negro Labor." *Opportunity*, X (June, 1932), 168-73.
Johnson, Reginald A. "The Urban League and the AFL." *Opportunity*, XIII (Aug., 1935), 347-49.
"Labor and Race Relations." *Opportunity*, IV (Jan., 1926), 4-5.
"Labor and the NRA." *New Republic*, LXXVII (Jan. 17, 1934), 282.
Lasker, B. "Race and the Job." *Survey*, LV (Oct. 15, 1925), 77-79.
Leary, J. J. "The Porter Wants More Than a Tip." *Today* (Mar. 24, 1934), 7.
Lore, Karl. "Labor Faces the Company Union." *Nation*, CXXXVIII (Apr., 1934), 406-8.
McFeely, Otto. "Pullman Porters." *Survey*, XXXIV (May 8, 1915), 132-33.
McFeeters, A. "Contented Red Cap." *Nation*, CXLV (Dec. 4, 1937), 628.

McKay, Claude. "Harlem Runs Wild." *Nation*, CXL (Apr. 3, 1935), 382-83.

Mann, Arthur. "Gompers and the Irony of Racism." *Antioch Review*, XIII (Summer, 1953), 203-14.

Manning, Seaton W. "Negro Trade Unionists in Boston." *Social Forces*, XVII (Dec., 1938), 256.

Miller, Kelly. "The Negro as a Working Man." *American Mercury*, VI (Nov., 1925), 310ff.

Miller, Leon P. "The Negro and the Closed Shop." *Opportunity*, XIII (June, 1935), 168-70, 189.

Mufson, I. "Organizing the Unorganized." *Survey*, LIX (Mar. 15, 1928), 657-58.

Murchison, John P. "Some Major Aspects of the Economic Status of the Negro." *Social Forces*, XIV (Oct., 1939), 114.

"Negro in Industry." *American Federationist*, XXXII (Oct., 1925), 915-20.

"Negro Membership in American Trade Unions." *Opportunity*, VIII (July, 1930), 200.

"Negro Workers and the Unions." *Survey*, LXXI (Aug., 1935), 243.

"Our Economic Future." *Crisis*, XXXV (May, 1928), 169-70.

Owen, Chandler. "The Negro Press in the Hands of White Folks Niggers." *Messenger*, VIII (Mar., 1926), 83-85.

Oxley, Lawrence A. "Occupations, Negroes and Labor Organizations." *Occupations*, XIV (Mar., 1936), 520-25.

"President of the AFL Replies." *Opportunity*, VII (Dec., 1929), 367.

"Pullman Ouster." *Time*, X (Jan. 3, 1927), 10.

"Pullman Porter, His Duties and Labor History." *Fortune*, XVII (Feb., 1938), 101-2.

"Pullman Porters." *Crisis*, VII (Feb., 1914), 165.

"Pullman Porters." *Crisis*, XXXI (Jan., 1926), 113.

"Pullman Porters." *Crisis*, XXXIV (Dec., 1927), 348.

"Pullman Porters." *Nation*, CXXII (June 9, 1926), 625-26.

"Pullman Porters Benefit Association." *Crisis*, XIII (Dec., 1916), 91.

"The Pullman Porters' Victory." *Opportunity*, XIII (Aug., 1935), 230-31.

Randolph, A. Philip. "The Case of the Pullman Porters." *American Federationist*, XXXIII (Nov., 1926), 1334-39.

———. "The Economic Crisis of the Negro." *Opportunity*, IX (May, 1931), 145-49.

———. "The Negro and Economic Radicalism." *Opportunity*, IV (Feb., 1926), 62-64.

———. "The Plight of the Pullman Porter." *American Federationist*, XL (July, 1933), 704-10.

———. "Porters Fight Paternalism." *American Federationist*, XXXVII (Dec., 1930), 666-73.

———. "Porters Seek Injunction." *American Federationist*, XXXVIII (June, 1931), 681-92.

———. "Pullman Porters Have Grievances." *Nation*, CXXI (Sept., 1925), 357.

———. "Pullman Porters Vote for the Union They Want." *American Federationist*, XLII (July, 1935), 727-29.

———. "The Pullman Porters Win." *Opportunity*, XV (Oct., 1937), 299ff.

———. "Sixth Annual Statement of Achievements and Hopes of the Porters' Union." *American Federationist*, XXXIX (Mar., 1932), 300-303.

———. "Too Many Toms." *Time*, VI (Aug. 31, 1925), 4-5.

———. "Trade Union Movement and the Negro." *Journal of Negro Education*, V (Jan., 1936), 54-58.

———. "Why a Trade Union?" *American Federationist*, XXXVII (Dec., 1930), 1470-82.

Reid, Ira DeA. "Lilly White Labor." *Opportunity*, VIII (June, 1930), 170-73ff.

———. "Negro Membership in American Labor Unions." *American Journal of Sociology*, XXXVII (Sept., 1931), 309-10.

Richberg, Donald. "How Railway Labor Act Will Work." *Messenger*, VIII (Aug., 1926), 228ff.

Rischin, Moses. "From Gompers to Hillman: Labor Goes Middle Class." *Antioch Review*, XIII (Summer, 1953), 191-201.

Ruttenberg, Harold J. "Negroes in the Labor Movement." *Survey Graphic*, XXVIII (Sept., 1939), 550-51.

Sagittarius, A. "A Dip into Speculative Philosophy." *Messenger*, VIII (Apr., 1926), 120.

Senior, Clarence O. "The Negro Labor Conference." *American Federationist*, XXXVI (July, 1929), 800-802.

Stevens, J. "Conservatives in Overalls." *Saturday Evening Post*, CCI (Sept. 22, 1928), 49.

Stolberg, Ben. "Pullman Peon." *Nation*, CXXII (Apr. 7, 1926), 265-67.

Thomas, Jesse O. "Negro Workers and Organized Labor." *Opportunity*, XII (Sept., 1934), 277-78.

"Tips or Wages, Which?" *Outlook*, CXLVII (Oct. 5, 1927), 134.

"The Unionizing of Black Labor." *Crisis*, XXXIII (Jan., 1927), 130.

"Unions." *Crisis*, XXXIII (Jan., 1927), 131.

Wesley, Charles H. "Organized Labor's Divided Front." *Crisis*, XLV (July, 1938), 223.

Weybright, Victor. "Pullman Porters on Parade." *Survey Graphic*, XXIV (Nov., 1935), 540-44ff.

Woofter, T. J. "Economic Status of the Negro." *Monthly Labor Review*, XXXII (Apr., 1931), 847-51.

Young, M. H. "Will You Abolish Tips?" *American Restaurant* (Jan., 1925), 40-41.

Miscellaneous Documents

Agreement between the Pullman Company and the Brotherhood of Sleeping Car Porters and Maids (Aug. 25, 1937), BSCP ChiPa.

Edward Berman for Brotherhood of Sleeping Car Porters. "Brief on Wages and Working Conditions of Porters" (1935), BSCP ChiPa.

Boston Citizens Committee. "The Pullman Porters' Struggle" (1926).

Brotherhood of Sleeping Car Porters. "Petitioner's Brief on Defendant's Motion to Dismiss," *BSCP* v. *Pullman Company*, Interstate Commission Case No. 20,007 (1927), NA.

———. "The Pullman Porter" (1926), BSCP ChiPa.

Federal Council of Churches. "Pullman Porters Attempt to Organize," *Information Service* (Feb. 9, 1929), 1-4. The journal is a publication of the Federal Council of Churches' Department of Research and Education.

Index